D1167599

THE EMERGENCE OF LATIN AMERICA
IN THE NINETEENTH CENTURY

11.95

The Emergence
of Latin America
in the Nineteenth Century

DAVID BUSHNELL
University of Florida

NEILL MACAULAY
University of Florida

New York   Oxford
OXFORD UNIVERSITY PRESS
1988

Oxford University Press

Oxford   New York   Toronto
Delhi   Bombay   Calcutta   Madras   Karachi
Petaling Jaya   Singapore   Hong Kong   Tokyo
Nairobi   Dar es Salaam   Cape Town
Melbourne   Auckland

and associated companies in
Beirut   Berlin   Ibadan   Nicosia

Copyright © 1988 by Oxford University Press, Inc.

Published by Oxford University Press, Inc.,
200 Madison Avenue, New York, New York 10016

Oxford is a registered trademark of Oxford University Press

All rights reserved. No part of this publication may be reproduced,
stored in a retrieval system, or transmitted, in any form or by any means,
electronic, mechanical, photocopying, recording, or otherwise,
without the prior permission of Oxford University Press.

Library of Congress Cataloging-in-Publication Data
Bushnell, David, 1923-
The emergence of Latin America in the nineteenth
century.

Bibliography: p.   Includes index.
1. Latin America—History—1830–1898.   2. Latin
America—History—Wars of Independence, 1806–1830.
3. Liberalism—Latin America—19th century.
I. Macaulay, Neill.   II. Title.
F1413.B88   1988   980'.031   87-25323
ISBN 0-19-504463-0
ISBN 0-19-504464-9 (pbk.)

10 9 8 7 6 5 4 3 2 1

Printed in the United States of America

To Ginnie and Nancy, our spouses, who are always de facto coauthors; to our students, on whom many of these ideas were first tried out; and to the people of Latin America, who have made the study of their history a pleasure as well as a challenge.

LATIN AMERICA

ABOUT THE MIDDLE
OF THE
NINETEENTH CENTURY

(Most South American Boundaries
Approximate and In Dispute)

Contents

THE EMERGENCE OF LATIN AMERICA
IN THE NINETEENTH CENTURY

1

Introduction

The term *Latin America* means different things to different people. For an economist or a geographer, it might well encompass all lands lying to the south of the continental United States. A linguist, however, would presumably exclude the English-speaking Caribbean islands and ought to exclude as well the sometimes large enclaves within Spanish-speaking countries in which American Indian languages predominate. For the historian, the term normally refers to those independent New World nations that were at some point colonized by the "Latin" nations of Europe or, even more specifically, Spain and Portugal. "Hispanic" or "Ibero-" America would really be more suitable: the generic designation "Latin" America, though apparently first used by the Colombian publicist José María Torres Caicedo in 1856, was quickly taken up and promoted by French ideologues in an effort to stake out for France a partial claim to what Spain and Portugal had founded.[1] The one republic that is in fact an offshoot of the French empire, Haiti, stands apart from the mainstream of Latin America not just in language but in the unusually heavy African contribution to its ethnic stock and popular culture. Though Haiti cannot be disregarded entirely, it will be mentioned in this book only in passing.

To be sure, the Latin America that is a product of Spanish and Portuguese colonization was inhabited long before the first Europeans arrived and in such cases as Aztec Mexico and Incan Peru had achieved a high level of civilization. Legacies of that civiliza-

3

tion are strongly evident today. Nevertheless, what gives Latin America its unique flavor is the combination of a dominant culture ultimately derived from the Iberian variant of Western, with a historical condition that by conventional Western standards is "underdeveloped."

The Colonial Heritage

The society that Iberian colonizers implanted upon preexisting Indian society, in some cases virtually obliterating the latter in the process, inevitably reflected the values and institutions that characterized the mother countries in the Age of Conquest. It was, first and foremost, a highly stratified society, not just in the obvious sense of a large gap between those at the top and those at the bottom—a gap in material comfort, social prestige, pretty much everything—but also in the further sense that society consisted of a complex layering of strata and substrata, of layers within layers. The historian can, though, distinguish separate categories of social differences, which overlapped to some extent but not completely. One such category concerned economic condition purely and simply. There were the few rich, the great many poor, and scattered groups in between, including petty bureaucrats, independent craftsmen, and in some places middling landowners. There were also those who owned property and those who did not, broadly the same as the rich and poor but with some important nuances and exceptions. The owner of a large hacienda in a region little touched by commercial agriculture might not have much cash income, but the size of his estate and his control over the workers on it would give him superior social standing and, at local level anyway, political power. Likewise, the Indian peasant who retained membership in a communal landholding village, as had been the pattern among all the settled agricultural peoples before the Conquest, had greater (though still not unlimited) control of his own destiny and a slightly higher social position than the rural hired worker or tenant, even in those cases where their material conditions of life were closely similar.

Among the noneconomic factors that affected social position, the most obvious as well as the most complicated was race. In general, whiteness was accepted as a mark of superiority, and there was a rough correlation between the amount of wealth and property one had and the whiteness of one's face. Yet ethnic considerations involved more than color. In the Spanish and Portuguese colonies one's skin could be whiter than white, but if a single grandparent was Jewish one had to watch out. Not many people with Jewish grandparents got to the colonies, since Roman Catholic orthodoxy was a legal requirement for admission, but some slipped through the net, to Brazil more often than to Spanish America. When caught, such people meant extra work for the Inquisition, the special tribunal set up to protect the purity of the faith. However, even if one's forebears had been practicing Catholics for centuries, it still made a difference whether one happened to have been born in the mother country or in the colonies. Spanish-born whites, or *peninsulares* as they were known (and *reinóis*, the Portuguese equivalent in Brazil), considered themselves superior to native-born whites or creoles and did not mind showing it. They also tended to monopolize the highest positions in church and state. On the other hand, the owners of the means of production, the very group that Karl Marx, for one, assumed to have the controlling hand in any social formation, were mostly native-born—the *hacendados* (*fazendeiros* in Brazil), or large landowners, as well as the mine owners, who inherited their wealth from the original settlers or from later waves of Iberian immigrants who came out to make a fortune and did.

A wealthy creole landowner might well affect to look with disdain on new arrivals fresh off the boat from Spain as mere pen-pushing bureaucrats or money-grubbing small tradesmen who had not yet scaled the social heights. Even so, the creole hacendado probably would not disdain to marry his daughter to the new arrival, for, if nothing else, the fact of being born in the Old World was reasonably good proof of being pure white. That could not quite be taken for granted even among the wealthiest members of the colonial aristocracy, whose ancestors had been living for years alongside not just the Indians but also the blacks brought originally as slaves from Africa and an infinite number of racial combinations. Indian genes were seen as less undesirable than African, so that just beneath the creoles in racial ranking came the mestizos, of mixed European and Indian descent. The *pardo*, or mulatto, ranked lower still, though above the pure black, to say nothing of the *zambo*, or mixture of African and Indian whom bigoted whites believed to inherit the worst traits of both ancestors. It is harder to say where ethnic Indians fit into the picture. Within the Indian population itself, there had existed from pre-Conquest times an Indian nobility whose members tended to receive the treatment of honorary whites. Then there is the practice of the Spanish regime—and to a lesser extent the Portuguese, though Indians were fewer in Brazil, and Indian policy there was never as systematic—of keeping Indians as far apart as possible from the rest of the population, living in their separate villages under a distinct set of laws and institutions. This was ostensibly for their own protection, and they were not immune to Spanish forced-labor systems even in their own villages. Still, the result was that Indians did not so much occupy a particular rung on the same social-racial ladder as creoles, mestizos, and the rest as take their places on a separate ladder of their own, slightly off to one side.

A final complication, as far as ethnic stratification is concerned, was the general Latin American pattern, still perfectly evident today, of looking at race not in terms of a few highly simplified classifications like white or black but in terms of a color spectrum made up of an almost infinite number of shades. Moreover, all sorts of trade-offs were allowed between degrees of skin color and economic or cultural characteristics, so that a wealthy black was likely to be perceived more as a mulatto, an educated mestizo essentially as a creole, and so forth. Hence, racial differences never exactly coincided with socioeconomic ones, even though they did, on the whole, reinforce the latter— and vice versa.

Racial differences similarly reinforced and were reinforced by a final category of distinctions having to do with legal privileges and disabilities. Of course, the special status of the Indians, already noted, was itself mandated by law, and the inferiority of even free subjects of African or part-African descent was reflected in legal provisions that in theory barred them from specific occupations and regulated their dress and conduct in often

humiliating ways. Still more fundamental was the legal distinction between slave and free, with the slave population—largely
black or mulatto, at least after the early years of colonization in
which Indian enslavement was widely practiced—concentrated
in Brazil and in the Caribbean and circum-Carribbean lowlands.
There were, in addition, the special privileges that accrued to
different elements of the population by reason of either birth or
royal grant (as in the case of nobility) or by membership in some
occupational group, such as the clergy, the military, or the craft
guilds. Both clergy and armed forces had a *fuero*, or code of
privileges, whose centerpiece was exemption from the jurisdiction of the ordinary courts. Even for the colonial equivalent
of mail fraud or traffic violations, their members had to be tried
by their own ecclesiastical or military courts. Guild members
had no similar sweeping exemption, but guilds might receive
some judicial authority in cases relating to their own trade, and
they also had numerous prerogatives in the regulation of that
trade.

   Obviously, an individual's place in colonial Latin America depended more on the accidents of birth and on belonging to
particular functional or other categories than on personal merit
and achievement. Society was seen as properly consisting not of
individual citizens actively pursuing their separate interests but
of legally recognized groups of individuals pursuing their corporate interests (and discharging their corporate responsibilities)
under the ultimate guidance of the state. In this sense, the structure of colonial society is often described as "corporatist" in
nature. Such a social structure easily lent itself to the perpetuation
of profound inequalities. It had the compensating virtue of let-
ting people know at all times where they stood and giving them a
certain feeling of security in that social niche, but the fact remains that a relatively small number of individuals accumulated
a disproportionate share of honor, goods, and power. More often
than not, that fortunate minority was notable above all for its
ownership of land, agriculture being far and away the leading
industry; but the occupation of landowner was not incompatible
with that of miner or merchant or with the liberal professions.
It was incompatible with that of manufacturer only insofar as

manufacturing in the Spanish and Portuguese colonies was primarily of the artisan-handcraft variety.

There was a divorce, however, between socioeconomic power and political power, at least at the upper levels. In principle, the Spanish empire was a highly centralized and rigidly controlled structure in which the last word on everything was reserved for the king. In practice, needless to say, that word was often spoken for him by the Council of the Indies or other members of the royal bureaucracy. At the American end, the top officials—viceroys, judges, provincial governors, and so forth—were appointed from Spain and were most often peninsulares. Except at the level of the *cabildos*, or municipal councils, which were often (not invariably) elective in origin, there was no element of formal popular representation whatsoever; least of all was there anything corresponding to the elected assemblies of the English colonies that both served as lawmaking bodies and, through their control of colonial taxation, had considerable leverage even over officials sent out directly from London.

Nevertheless, in the Spanish colonies, too, appointed royal officials had to live and work with the colonial population itself, and inevitably they found that a good relationship with prominent local residents made their jobs easier. They formed friendships on the spot, sometimes married into creole families even though the practice was technically frowned on, and often consented to supplement their salaries by accepting bribes from the people they were supposed to regulate. Thus, while the government of the Spanish colonies was a theoretical royal absolutism, it was an absolutism tempered by a great deal of informal bargaining, compromising, and outright corruption in everyday life. And much the same can be said about Portuguese government in Brazil, although even on paper the Portuguese system was less tightly structured than the Spanish.

A similar tempering of imperial principles by everyday realities could be seen in economic matters. As in other colonial empires of the period, the intent of official rules and regulations in the Spanish and Portuguese colonies was to maximize the benefit of the mother country. In the Spanish case, direct trade between the colonies and non-Spanish ports was illegal under normal circumstances, and, the better to maintain strict control, the number of ports open even to legal trade between Spain and America was carefully limited. Certain kinds of industries—such as wine making or textile manufacturing—were restricted, lest they compete with the products of the mother country, and taxes were levied on colonial trade and everything else colonial, with the frank hope of shipping as much of the proceeds as possible back to Spain. A typical feature of the revenue system was the series of government fiscal monopolies that held exclusive right to sell articles such as tobacco, playing cards, and even snow— the latter packed hard like ice and brought down from mountain-tops to Mexico City and certain other population centers—with the profits going to the royal treasury. And yet the rather substan-tial part of the population that was subsisting on the margin of the money economy, growing its own food and making its own clothing and utensils, was not much affected by Spanish eco-nomic and fiscal legislation. Moreover, the fact that Spain itself was a not very dynamic economy operated in some respects in the colonies' favor. Spain was quite incapable of supplying all their needs for manufactured goods, while at the same time Spanish regulations made the goods of other European countries both scarce and expensive when legally imported through Span-ish ports. When illegally imported, as often happened, their price to the public was less, but it would still include enough of a markup to cover the smuggler's own risk and any unavoidable bribes to coast guards and customs officials. Hence, the colonies developed their own small handcraft industries, which could not have survived on anything like the same scale if the colonies had been open on a regular basis to legal British or Dutch trade. These were far from constituting a factory system and generally used quite primitive methods to turn out coarse end products. However, they satisfied most of the colonies' needs for nonluxury manufactured goods.

From Colonies to Nationhood

Colonial society was not, of course, a static affair, and in several key respects the pace of change accelerated from about the middle of the eighteenth century. Some forces for change were internal to Latin America, such as an increasing population that resulted in part from the mere fact that the Indians had become at last more or less accustomed to European diseases, putting an end to the disastrous decline of Indian numbers that began with the first exploration and settlement of America. The recovery of the Indian population was less dramatic, though, and less indicative of the shape of the future than was the increase in the number of mestizos, in both absolute and relative terms. The cumulative increase in size and wealth of the creole aristocracy and its ever weaker attachment to the land of its ancestors—with corresponding increase in its sense of American identity—were also important developments.

Other forces were of external origin, notably the imperial reforms of the Bourbon monarchs in Spain and of the marquis of Pombal as chief minister in Portugal. These reforms sought to make colonial administration more efficient, for the benefit not just of the crown's American subjects but also of the crown's control over them. A conventional example is the introduction of the intendant system at the level of provincial or regional government in Spanish America, replacing the preexisting governors with a smaller number of highly qualified and well-paid "intendants," whose duties were carefully standardized by imperial reformers. The heightened vigor of administration was accompanied by both a decrease in the rate of appointment of creoles to high office and an increase in tax collections. It further entailed a more vigorous assertion of royal prerogatives at the expense of the church, as exemplified in the summary expulsion of the Jesuits from the Portuguese empire in 1759 and from the Spanish in 1767. At the same time, there was increased freedom of trade *within* the Spanish empire, with the opening of additional ports on both sides of the Atlantic, though not between Spanish American and non-Spanish ports; and in both the Spanish colonies and Brazil there was much official encouragement of the natural sciences and useful arts, as the royal governments actively promoted the spread of those aspects of the European Enlightenment that did not directly undermine their own position. But subversive political ideas (not to mention news of the English colonies' subversive example) also did seep in, while the beginnings of the Industrial Revolution in northern Europe subjected the closed colonial commercial system to increasing pressure, by contraband and other means.

Many if not most of the sometimes contradictory changes taking place in the final years of the colonial period were helping to prepare the way for eventual independence. On the one hand, there was the gradual maturing of a colonial society whose more self-conscious members felt increasing confidence that they could go it alone. On the other hand, there was the ill-advised attempt of the mother countries—Spain and, to a lesser extent, Portugal the same as Great Britain—in the second half of the eighteenth century to tighten their control over the American population. For Spanish America, British historian John Lynch has aptly compared the process to a "second conquest."[2] The leaders of colonial society necessarily disliked this turn of events, and not merely because some of them had meanwhile been imbibing the fashionable new notions of popular sovereignty and natural rights associated with the American and French revolutions; after all, they had seen their own ability to shape or circumvent governmental policy appreciably lessened. And all this was in addition to any concrete grievances they had over taxation, government services, or the commercial regulations that, despite all loopholes and exceptions, still normally prohibited direct trading with foreign ports.

But colonial discontent in and of itself did not set off the movement for independence. Though it is hard to imagine the Spanish flag still flying in Tegucigalpa or the Portuguese flag in Rio de Janeiro under any circumstances, the break came when it did because of an external crisis that brought matters to a head, concretely the invasion of the Iberian peninsula by the French forces of Napoleon in 1807–8. This set in motion a sequence of events that culminated in total independence of continental Spanish America and Brazil, the attempt to fasten imperial rule more firmly on the colonies having proved thoroughly counterproductive. Some of the other innovations of Bourbon and Pombaline reformism would be continued or even extended, however, under the auspices of the revolutionary leaders and the new governments they set up. The position of the church was thus further weakened, the liberalization of trade within the empire was taken one step further with the removal of previous barriers to trade with foreign powers, and the latest political ideas now received the same welcome that imperial reformers had accorded to apolitical advances in science and technology. Moreover, if there was a common denominator to all these developments, including political independence itself, it was the progressive opening of Latin America to influences from northern Europe and the United States—influences which prior to independence had been transmitted through Spain and Portugal or clandestinely but henceforth entered directly and openly.

Another way of saying much the same thing is that Latin America in the course of gaining independence opted for an essentially liberal model of development, in principle not unlike that adhered to by Great Britain, the United States, and, most of the time, also France. This meant a project of representative constitutional government politically and in its socioeconomic and cultural dimensions a lowering of artificial barriers to individual initiative and expression. Latin Americans embraced the model in question selectively, for they did not find all "liberal" precepts equally adaptable to their needs. Neither were they always consistent in the way they applied the precepts they did profess, and needless to say the nature and extent of Latin America's commitment to liberalism was continually changing. Nevertheless, in the period from independence to the late nineteenth century, it did come as close as anything to serving as a dominant ideology; and it will provide one more common thread among the following chapters as they examine specific aspects of Latin America's postindependence experience.

2

The Founding of
a New Political System

For many years the attainment of political independence was looked upon in most Latin American countries as the all-important turning point in their histories. Everything before, a Venezuelan historian observed, was reduced to the status of prologue to independence, and everything since appeared as nothing but an epilogue to that glorious event.[1] More recently, the cult of independence and its heroes has come under attack. One approach has been that of socioeconomic historians intent on minimizing the importance of mere political changes: as social and economic topics have increasingly attracted the best historical scholars working in Latin America, the production of works dealing with independence has noticeably declined. Another approach has been that of Latin Americans disillusioned with the balance sheet of their countries' postindependence experience, who have decided either that separation from the mother country was somehow premature—a thesis put forward by quite a few conservative revisionists—or that dark intrigues, foreign and domestic, prevented the independence movement from realizing the total "national liberation" it aimed at. The latter thesis is currently popular among leftist writers, who like to argue that the "social revolutionary" aims of a few such leaders as Simón Bolívar in Venezuela and Colombia or Mariano Moreno, the chief civilian ideologue of the revolution in Argentina, were

13

betrayed and undermined by selfish oligarchs acting in collusion with Great Britain or the United States. Reasonable people may disagree about where the truth lies in these matters, but any serious answer must first take account of the nature of the struggle itself and of the specific changes that it wrought.

A Protracted Conflict

The first act of Latin American independence was actually played out in the French colony of Haiti, where a slave uprising that began in 1791 developed by stages into a movement for national independence as well as personal liberty. Independence was formally declared in 1804, by which time it was already an accomplished fact. Haiti thus became the second American nation to break loose from its mother country, and it was the one where the experience was most traumatic, leading to the transformation of a wealthy sugar colony into a nation of impoverished small farmers, with the white planter class obliterated in the process. Because the revolution was as much a social as a political movement, it differed from the struggle in Latin America as a whole; and because of the fate of the French planters, Spanish American creoles—uneasy about the intentions of their own blacks—regarded it as an example of something to be avoided. The main story of independence concerns instead the liberation of the Spanish and Portuguese colonies, where the underlying causes, briefly noted in chapter 1, bore at least a superficial resemblance to those that produced the revolution of the thirteen British colonies. As also mentioned, the triggering mechanism was an external event, the French invasion of the Iberian peninsula in 1807–8.

In Portugal, the royal family decided to get out of the way of the French and sailed out of Lisbon for Brazil with the first favorable winds after French troops entered Portuguese territory. They set up shop in Rio de Janeiro for the duration, and over the next few years any part of Portugal not under French occupation plus Portuguese colonies of Africa and Asia were taking orders from Rio, not Lisbon. Brazilian ports were thrown wide open to neutral and friendly (mainly British) shipping, and Brazil had most prerequisites of independence without firing a shot. The main exception was that Portuguese officials held the top positions exactly as when the court was in Lisbon. Only after the court returned to Europe did a serious move for separation from Portugal arise and result in a brief though fairly intense armed conflict. Its upshot was that the older son of Portugal's King John VI, purposely left behind when his father went home, became Emperor Pedro I of an independent Brazilian monarchy.

The Spanish royal family did not get away but was lured by Napoleon to France and sequestered there while he proceeded to establish his own brother, Joseph Bonaparte, as king of Spain. Since the American colonies refused to accept Joseph as ruler, the result from their standpoint was to create a temporary vacancy on the throne, to which most of them responded by organizing juntas of their own to rule on a provisional basis. These claimed at first to be acting in the name of the legitimate monarch, Ferdinand VII, until such time as he could get loose from French captivity and resume the job of running the Spanish empire. In practice, the American juntas were autonomous governments, and eventually the colonies declared themselves independent in name as well as in fact. Venezuela led the way on July 5, 1811. The Spanish Americans still did not have an easy time, since the highest royal officials in the colonies preferred to give allegiance to whatever anti-French rump government was hanging on precariously in some corner of Spain itself and did all in their power to make life difficult for the new governments. Usually they found enough collaborators even among the American population to put up a long, hard fight. But it was not equally long and hard in all places, so that the military history of independence broke down into a number of quite distinct regional theaters.

One theater was Mexico, where the movement began in 1810 with a string of smashing patriot successes under the leadership of the radical priest Miguel Hidalgo but failed to get control of the capital, Mexico City, and bogged down for roughly ten years in some nasty guerrilla warfare until Mexico finally did become independent in 1821. The nastiness was magnified by the fact that in Mexico the struggle took on many of the characteristics of a class war. Father Hidalgo proved so successful in exciting the masses of central Mexico to join the fight against peninsular oppression that they committed assorted outrages, which he seemed little concerned to prevent, against resident Spaniards; and though the creole upper class had its own complaints against Spanish rule, in its fear of becoming the next target of popular mob action it generally threw its support to the loyalists. Hidalgo was captured and executed, but José María Morelos, a mestizo priest of rather humble origin who became his successor as head of the patriot movement, did not inspire much more confidence among the Mexican aristocracy. The struggle was ended only in 1821, when a member of that same aristocracy, Agustín de Iturbide, changed sides, forged an alliance between the heirs of Hidalgo and Morelos (who meanwhile had also been caught and executed) and those like himself who had supported Spain, and quickly took control of the situation. Iturbide initially proposed a compromise settlement with Spain on the basis of crowning a Spanish prince as constitutional monarch of Mexico—which would have meant for Mexico to adopt the Brazilian solution—but when Spain proved uncooperative he allowed himself to become Emperor Agustín I.

Mexico was separated by a string of safely loyalist colonies that included Cuba, Puerto Rico, and Central America from the next main theater, which was northern South America. Here Venezuela, in particular, became the most fought-over of all Spanish colonies. It established a first ruling junta in 1810 and was reconquered by loyalists in 1812, reliberated in 1813, re-reconquered in 1814, and re-reliberated, for the last time, in 1821. Somewhat as in Mexico, the war in Venezuela for a time took on the appearance of racial and class conflict, although here the alignments were reversed: it was the Spanish who stirred up the nonwhite masses, including many slaves, to go on a rampage against the native creole aristocracy which from the outset held leadership on the revolutionary side.

One of the Venezuelan creole leaders, Simón Bolívar, was to become the preeminent figure of Latin American independence. A wealthy cacao planter whose personal background vaguely recalls that of George Washington, Bolívar is today the object of a cult in his own Venezuela and other countries that features even a Bolivarian version of the Apostles' Creed, composed in his honor by the Guatemalan Nobel Prize–winning novelist Miguel Angel Asturias:

> I believe in Liberty, Mother of America, creator of sweet seas upon earth, and in Bolívar, her son, Our Lord, who was born in Venezuela, suffered under Spanish power, was fought against, felt death on Mount Chimborazo, and with the rainbow descended into hell, rose again at the voice of Colombia, touched the Eternal with his hands and is standing next to God! . . .[2]

It is Bolívar who deserves much of the credit for finally detaching the masses from the loyalist cause in Venezuela. As a military man, he was largely self-taught, and he lost many battles on the way, but he won the last ones, which count most, as he carried the war back and forth between his native Venezuela and neighboring Colombia and ultimately on to Ecuador and Peru. He likewise drafted laws and constitutions, issued statements of revolutionary ideology, and was quite as important a political figure as he was in military exploits.

Northern South America was separated by another loyalist-held strip, mainly consisting of Peru, from the third main theater of patriot activity in the far south of the continent. Here the focal point of revolution was Buenos Aires, whose immediate hinterland, today Argentina, saw relatively little fighting on its own soil but carried on a continual struggle with loyalist forces based in neighboring colonies. In the process Argentina produced the second-ranking continental hero of independence in José de San Martín, who, unlike Bolívar, was a professional military officer and was fighting with the Spanish resistance against Napoleon in Europe when the conflict in America began. Argentine-born, he eventually returned to the homeland, and in 1817 he led the army that crossed the Andes to Chile and there revived a local movement for independence that had been all but stamped out. In 1820 he moved on to Peru, where he liberated Lima the following year but grew discouraged over the continued opposition of loyalists entrenched in the highlands and the seemingly fickle behavior of the Peruvian population, not to mention his own ulcer. In 1822 he resigned his command and departed on a course that finally took him to voluntary exile in Europe.

Peru, which all along had been the prime stronghold of Spanish power on the American continent, should perhaps be accounted a fourth great theater of the struggle, even though the main fighting there occurred after the war was virtually finished elsewhere. Thanks in part to latent distrust between whites and Indians intensified by memories of the massive Indian rebellion of 1780–81 under Túpac Amaru, Spanish forces kept a firm grip, only sporadically threatened by creole conspiracies and largely unfocused Indian uprisings. Their hold was broken only in 1820–25, by a combination of local guerrillas and invading armies that came in from the south under San Martín and from the north led by Bolívar, who took up where his Argentine counterpart left off. The battle of Ayacucho, won in the Peruvian highlands in December 1824 by Bolívar's right-hand man, Antonio José de Sucre, was the last major engagement of the war and among other things led to the collapse of the loyalists in Upper Peru or modern Bolivia. Even then, Cuba and Puerto Rico remained in Spanish hands, but that is another story. The islands just did not play a part in the independence movement of Spanish America as a whole, save as an offshore base for the loyalists and a place of refuge for loyalist fugitives, from Venezuela especially, once their side lost. Central America, for its part, had climbed bloodlessly onto the patriot bandwagon as soon as Spanish rule in Mexico was overthrown by Iturbide.

For Latin America in general, as compared with the experience of the thirteen British colonies, one thing that stands out is the sheer length of the independence struggle. The first, unsuccessful efforts to set up ruling juntas in America in response to the crisis of the Spanish throne occurred in 1808; the first successful revolutionary governments appeared in 1810; the last Spanish soldier on the mainland surrendered, in Peru to be exact, in January 1826. All this comes to eighteen years, as against eight from the battle of Lexington and Concord to the actual British recognition of United States independence. And if recognition is taken as the terminal date, then the war in Latin America lasted at least until 1836, when Spain recognized the very first of its ex-colonies, Mexico.

One reason for the length of the conflict is that Latin Americans received nothing like the foreign aid received by their British American neighbors. They obtained some moral support and even free-lance volunteers, many of them unemployed veterans of the Napoleonic wars in Europe. They also received military supplies and equipment, from uniforms to warships, but these did not come under any program of "military assistance." The Latin Americans were supposed to pay for everything that reached them, and the fact that in practice they could not was one of the sources of the foreign-debt problem that plagued the new nations almost from their creation. No foreign power declared war on Spain and put its regular forces in the field on the same side as the revolutionists, as both France and Spain did in the war against Great Britain. When the conflict was already mostly over, both Great Britain and the United States, the latter in the Monroe Doctrine of 1823, issued warnings to other powers not to try to intervene in Latin America to help Spain regain the ground lost, but the danger of such intervention was really somewhat insubstantial, and as between the colonies and their mother country the United States and British governments had followed an official policy of neutrality.

Latin Americans thus won independence largely on their own, and so another reason for the length of the struggle was the fact that the colonial population itself (as in British America, for that matter) was divided on the issue. Some native loyalists were diehard conservatives who opposed change on principle, or frightened members of the creole upper class who feared to rock the boat lest they inadvertently get the masses stirred up and set off either a slave uprising, Haitian-style, or a repetition of Túpac Amaru's rebellion in Peru. Such fears seemed vindicated by the mob disorders that characterized the revolution in Mexico in its earliest phase under Hidalgo. Yet in a climate of widespread social and racial tensions, it was also possible to stir up the masses in *defense* of the established order, as happened in Venezuela. Peruvian Indians likewise fought predominantly on the side of the king, less from conscious choice than because most of Peru for most of the time was under the loyalists' control, so that the latter were in the best position to draft Indians as soldiers. Or, again, some regions were loyalist out of local rivalry with another place that was patriot. Santa Marta on the Colombian coast was loyalist, while Cartagena, which had eclipsed it as a Caribbean port, was patriot; but it is hard to escape the conviction that if Cartagena had for any reason chosen to support the king, Santa

Marta, to be different, would as surely have been a bulwark of the republic.

Social Costs and Consequences

The admixture of regional, racial, and social rivalries magnified the bitterness of the conflict and thus too the casualties and destruction. But the impact was uneven. Venezuela, almost continually fought over, was the colony that suffered most; its population may well have suffered a net decline. At the other extreme Central America emerged almost unscathed. Economic losses ranged from the disruption of productive activities as a result of the drafting of men and animals, or the loss of liquid capital by both forced levies and capital flight, to the outright destruction of property by military action or sabotage. Recovery naturally took longer in some cases than in others. It was easier to get abandoned fields back in production than to repair and replace mining equipment, and it was the damage done to its critically important silver mines that made Mexico in the long run the one colony that suffered the greatest economic setback in winning independence.

Quite apart from the losses suffered, the independence struggle in and of itself had the further effect of accelerating various kinds of social and cultural change. It opened possibilities of upward mobility for military leaders of undistinguished social background, of whom various examples will appear elsewhere in this book. It caused downward mobility for still others whose assets were destroyed in the fighting or confiscated because they backed the wrong side; and since many regions changed hands more than once, almost anyone could suffer reprisals at some point. There was spatial mobility, too, as young creoles who had never been outside their own colony or field hands who had seldom left their hacienda were suddenly wandering up and down the continent, fighting for or against the king. When they came home, they brought new habits and interests with them; and, of course, sometimes they did not come home but put down roots in whatever ex-colony or new republic their service carried them to. A classic example of the latter sort is found in Ecuador, whose first president, Juan José Flores, was a Venezuelan general.

It was not only Latin Americans who were traveling around; during the independence period there was a sharp increase in the number of outsiders visiting the area. These included foreign merchants eager to take advantage of the elimination of colonial trade barriers, the soldiers of fortune who came to serve in patriot armies and navies, and even a few official agents; and, in addition to performing whatever mission had brought them to Latin America, these foreigners by their mere presence had a significant demonstration effect, since all who came in contact with them became more aware of the fads and fancies, life-styles and ideologies of the North Atlantic world. Because the English drank beer, a number of highly placed Colombians began to cultivate the same taste, which cost them dearly, since initially all beer was imported. On the other hand, the English notoriously disapproved of bullfights, and it was in large part to make a favorable impression on them that Buenos Aires first outlawed bullfighting as early as 1819. That prohibition did not stick, but neither was it the last. Meanwhile, Buenos Aires had even acquired a cricket club, as good an indicator of the English cultural presence as one could ask for.

Decrees against bullfighting were minor instances of a larger reforming impulse that was one more feature of the struggle for Latin American independence. Another example was the move by one revolutionary government after another to dismantle the terrible Inquisition. Its bonfires having ceased quite some time before the struggle began, it was no longer as fearsome as it once was, but its abolition had considerable symbolic importance nonetheless. Then, too, the upward mobility of nonwhite military leaders was aided or at any rate ratified ex post facto by the widespread abrogation of colonial restrictions that had discriminated against free persons on grounds of race. In some places a start was made toward abolishing slavery itself by a process of gradual emancipation. These and similar measures adopted during the very heat of conflict did not aim at a general transformation of social and economic structures, and the degree of reform activism among revolutionary leaders varied widely. Yet it would be an even more obvious characteristic of the immediate aftermath of independence and, after undergoing a relative eclipse in most countries during the 1830s and 1840s, would reassert itself with new vigor at midcentury.

The Fragmentation of Latin America

For many Latin Americans, not only were the miscellaneous reform measures adopted during the independence struggle of little immediate importance, but the transformation of the former colonial empires into a host of new sovereign nations was equally superficial. If one had asked an Indian of southern Mexico or the eastern plains of Colombia what "nation" he lived in, the answer—once the question was explained in terms meaningful to him—would no doubt have been Zapotec, Guahibo, or another Indian ethnic division, not some such abstract entity as Mexico or Colombia. Nevertheless, those political entities became the framework for the subsequent evolution of the area, and they would eventually be so taken for granted that few scholars, Latin American or otherwise, have bothered to analyze the process whereby the map of Latin America was originally carved up.

As compared to the older nations of western Europe, those of Latin America must appear slightly artificial by virtue of the fact that they are not clearly separated from one another by differences of language, historical tradition, and sometimes religion. Brazil and Haiti, as former colonies of Portugal and France, quite logically do stand apart. However, the main source of the proliferation of new nationalities was the disruption of the Spanish empire, each of whose offshoots began its national life with a similar set of laws and institutions, inherited from the same colonial past, with the same language (referring to that spoken by the dominant minorities who decided to establish the new nations), and naturally with the same religion. There were often much greater cultural and socioeconomic contrasts between different regions of a single nation than between that nation as a whole and its immediate neighbors. Thus, the reasons for the fragmentation of Latin, or at least Spanish, America are not quite self-evident.

To be sure, a single Spanish American nation-state stretching from Utah (Mexico's original far north) to Tierra del Fuego would have been totally unwieldy, especially with the transportation and communication existing at the time, and no one seriously proposed it. But a few attempts were made to at least combine into one nation several adjoining Spanish colonies that in the end went their separate ways. The best-known cases are Iturbide's Mexican Empire of 1821–23, which took in Central America as well as Mexico, and Gran Colombia, which was the creation of Bolívar and comprised all the former viceroyalty of New Granada, that is, Venezuela, Colombia, Panama, and Ecuador. The first of these two was no doubt doomed from the start not just by any latent incompatibilities among its constituent parts but by its association with an upstart monarch who could never truly please either dynastic legitimists or convinced republicans. And in the confusion that attended Iturbide's overthrow, Central America almost without opposition seceded to become a separate federal republic that remained more or less united (at least on paper) for about twenty years before disintegrating further into today's five minirepublics. Gran Colombia did better, lasting from 1819 to 1830 and briefly assuming a role of Latin American leadership. Yet, in the end, Gran Colombian leaders concluded that any possible advantages of keeping the union together just were not worth the human effort and material resources that would have been required. (See chapter 5.)

Indeed, the desirability of larger unions for purposes of national defense was questionable when the danger of Spanish reconquest was not really very great and when the combination of Monroe Doctrine and British Navy was enough to ward off threats from other foreign powers—except, of course, threats from the United States and Great Britain. But apart from the Falkland Islands, which they seized in 1833, the British were not interested in conquering territory; they aimed at peaceful economic penetration, which Latin American leaders from Bolívar down were initially disposed to welcome. The United States ultimately had more serious designs, but it is hard to see that maintaining Mexico's union with Central America would have changed the outcome of the U.S.-Mexican War. Nor is it easy to see the advantage of setting up national governments over larger expanses of territory for the purpose of regulating interstate commerce—another of the reasons given for creation of a federal union in the former British colonies—when almost all commerce in Latin America was strictly local or foreign. The fact that Latin Americans spontaneously looked overseas, especially to Great Britain, for trade and capital rather than looking to each other not only diminished the interest in larger unions but also, once the independence movement itself was over, decreased their opportunities for mutual contact, of which there had not been many even under the externally imposed unity of the Spanish colonial regime. At the same time, for providing such standard services as carrying the mail and adjudicating legal disputes, there was little that a Mexican Empire or a Gran Colombia could do that the units into which they broke up could not do about as well separately. Some things they could do better separately because of the smaller scale of operations.

If the practical advantages to be gained from union in those two instances were not compelling, it can be understood why in most other cases no attempt at union was even made. What came about was the breakup of the mainland Spanish empire initially along the lines of its major administrative subdivisions. These were not actually the viceroyalties, although viceroys were the officials who ranked highest in prestige, but rather, with a few exceptions, were those territories that in the colonial system had their own separate high courts, or *audiencias*, even if nominally subject to a viceroy. The colonial captaincy-general of Venezuela and presidency of Quito had both enjoyed such status within the viceroyalty of New Granada, as had the captaincy-general of Guatemala (i.e., Central America) in the viceroyalty of New Spain (i.e., Mexico). So had the captaincy-general of Chile within the viceroyalty of Peru and the presidency of Charcas (i.e., Bolivia) in the viceroyalty first of Peru and subsequently of the Río de la Plata.[3]

Even so, technically sovereign nation-states do maintain formal relations with one another, and one thing on which both Bolívar and his Argentine counterpart, José de San Martín, felt strongly was the need to create a lasting league or alliance of the new Spanish American nations. In this respect, the Panama Congress of 1826—the first inter-American conference of any kind—

was both a symbolic high point of cooperation and, in its outcome, a sign that the conditions for permanent alliance were not yet present. Bolívar, who was the prime mover behind the Congress, had not wished to invite the non-Spanish American states, because he wanted an association firmly grounded in common interests and historical antecedents, and he felt these were lacking in the case of the other American nations. Brazil had seemingly condemned itself to isolation by opting for monarchy as a political system, the United States was culturally distinct and not entirely to be trusted either, while Haiti was not merely different but dreaded by creoles of nearby countries for its example of slave rebellion. In the end, the United States and Brazil were invited anyway, contrary to Bolívar's original intention; and it made very little practical difference. Brazil did not accept, and though the United States did, one of its delegates died on the way, and the other arrived after the meeting was over. Nor did the gathering of Spanish American states, a majority of which did attend, produce substantial results; only Bolívar's Gran Colombia ratified a single one of the agreements drawn up. Already the new nations, not least Gran Colombia itself, were becoming too embroiled in internal troubles to think seriously about an American international system.

While Bolívar had not wanted to invite the United States to Panama, he wanted Great Britain to send a representative, and it did. Bolívar was in reality an admirer of both Anglo-Saxon powers, although his high praise for U.S. institutions was invariably coupled with the warning that they were not applicable to Latin America. He would rather see his fellow Spanish Americans adopt the Koran, he once said, than the government of the United States, even though it was "the best on earth."[4] Neither did his often-expressed regard for the civic virtues of the North American people offset his deep misgivings over the threat posed to their southern neighbors by their growing wealth and power. The United States, he observed on another occasion, appeared "destined by Providence to plague America with torments in the name of freedom."[5] The latter comment, which today is almost always quoted out of context, is contained in a letter to the British minister to Gran Colombia, whom Bolívar at the time was trying to interest in some sort of protectorate over the New World nation. The cultivation of close relations with Great Britain, as the dominant political and military power of the Western world and also chief rival of the United States for trade and influence in Latin America, was in fact a constant in Bolívar's policy. Britain, though, was interested in commercial, not political, understandings, and the United States, even as it accepted the invitation to Panama, made clear that it did not want entangling alliances with its immediate neighbors any more than with Europe. After all, the Monroe Doctrine itself had been a unilateral statement of policy, and for many years any overtures for its conversion into a multilateral instrument were brusquely rejected by Washington. Since the Latin American nations also proved unable to cement a lasting alliance among themselves, each was left to fend strictly for itself—for better or for worse.

How Latin America Was Ruled:
What Changed and What Did Not

Though privileged segments of the Latin American population had never lacked influence on the colonial administration and its policies, the final authority had always been external to Latin America itself. With independence, the ultimate power of decision making moved across the Atlantic, from Madrid or Lisbon to the new American nations, and the decision makers were no longer constrained by imperial considerations. In each capital they acted in the light of interests which might not be those of the population as a whole but were still those of locally dominant groups. No longer would trade with Spain or Portugal be legally favored, and much less would the treasury in Mexico City ship subsidies to that in Madrid. Neither would it continue subsidizing other parts of Spanish America, as it had often done before. (As a matter of fact, there was no money in it to pay subsidies with.) And the peninsular bureaucrats who, for reasons of paternalism or higher imperial interest, had occasionally intervened, say, to curb creole despoiling of Indian communal lands would no longer be able to do so.

The Indians themselves would have little more say in the new government than in the old, even though all or most countries adopted an outwardly representative, constitutional frame of government. The main exception was Paraguay, which somehow survived until the 1840s without anything that could seriously be called a written constitution. Even Mexico and Brazil, which started out as monarchies—Mexico for about two years, Brazil for most of the century—were constitutional monarchies, in which the crowned ruler shared power with an elected parliament and other institutions. In all cases, the first Latin American constitutions incorporated some kind of separation of powers and something ostensibly comparable to the U.S. Bill of Rights or (more likely) the French Revolutionary Declaration of the Rights of Man.

The new governments did not constitute full-fledged democracies, however, even on paper, despite the fact that most of their leaders spoke loosely of the institutions adopted as "democratic." With rare exceptions, the right to vote was limited to free men (obviously never the unfree or women) who enjoyed a minimum amount of income or property or occupational status, in terms that normally excluded all but five to ten percent or some other quite limited number of male adults. (Admittedly, this was more than voted at the time in such an enlightened nation as France or in Great Britain before the passage of the Reform Bill of 1832.) In certain cases, illiterates—perhaps amounting to ninety percent of the Latin American population, a majority overlapping with but not exactly the same as those excluded from suffrage on socioeconomic grounds—were also denied the vote, though often as not the enforcement of the literacy test was held in abeyance. In the Gran Colombian constitution of 1821, for example, the literacy test was set to go into effect only twenty years later. The reason for this curious suspended sentence against illiterates was that it seemed unfair to deny the vote to anyone who was unable to read merely because the wicked Spanish oppressors had failed to provide sufficient schools; but after twenty years of freedom, presumably, anyone who truly made the effort would know how to read. In such expectations, the Colombian founding fathers were wildly overoptimistic.

The new nations placed still more stringent limits on who might be elected, and it need hardly be added that these restrictions as well as those on suffrage did nothing but give legal sanction to a pattern of limited participation in the political process that was largely preordained by the sharp cultural and socioeconomic differences existing among elements of the population. Nevertheless, to have any representative institutions at all was an abrupt change from the previous regime, where only municipal governments (and not all of them) were of elective origin. Now at least a select minority would be voting in elections—and voting was a form of political participation even in those instances when the elections served only to ratify some fait accompli—while the number of those being elected was not inconsiderable. Quite apart from the popular election of republican chief executives, a single royal legislator had given way since independence to collective bodies of national congressmen who themselves were liable to be replaced by newly elected members every few years. In countries that opted for a federal type of internal organization, there were additional elections held for state or provincial governors and assemblies.

Increased opportunities for government service were not limited to elective positions but existed elsewhere, perhaps most obviously in the military. Although armed forces had not usually been large even in the wars of independence (Bolívar never took even as many as ten thousand men into battle with him), the military still could not wither away when peace returned, and they were at least more numerous than those stationed in Latin America in the colonial era. Quite apart from the hypothetical danger of Spanish reconquest or other threats from overseas, there were often boundary or similar disputes with neighboring countries, not to mention the need for military forces in the lack of a professional police to help maintain internal order. Order could no longer be maintained through the instinctive obedience automatically inspired by a legitimate monarch of the traditional house. Moreover, the military institution even more than civil government branches offered avenues of upward advancement for the less privileged social strata. Here perhaps the classic example is Venezuela's José Antonio Páez. A functionally illiterate ranch hand in trouble with the law when the independence movement began, Páez proved to be a gifted leader of the *llaneros*, cowboys of the Orinoco River plains, and played a critical role in winning them over to the patriot side. By the time the struggle ended, he held the highest military rank, had acquired vast landholdings (of originally loyalist ownership for the most part), and was also acquiring the rudiments of an education. Politically, even before Bolívar's death in 1830, Páez had become the dominant figure of independent Venezuela.

The pattern that Páez epitomized was often repeated in the postindependence years. Members of the traditional upper class generally held the top positions in the armed forces as elsewhere, but not enough of them felt called to a military vocation to fill all those available. Particularly in times of civil warfare, when forces expanded rapidly, there was room for tough, able, and often unscrupulous fighters to rise up through the ranks, and like Páez they might then parlay military success into political power and economic wealth. What usually came last, if at all, was acceptance as social equals by those who had been born into the upper strata—but their children would gain acceptance in any case. The fact remains that the armed forces were a shade more democratic in social makeup than other key institutions, and in this respect they clearly illustrate the increase of opportunities in public life that came about with independence.

The opportunities for upward mobility through the military were enhanced by the mere fact that political conditions in early independent Latin America were notoriously unstable. Social and economic conditions, it can be argued, were probably too stable, and the numerous "revolutions" for which Latin America became famous seldom involved many combatants; sometimes they did not even involve combat but rather shows of force and behind-the-scenes intrigue. Yet in Mexico, for example, during a period of almost thirty years only one president succeeded in serving out his entire term. As Argentine historian Tulio Halperín-Donghi has aptly put it, in nineteenth-century Latin America to lose an election was not the most common way for a party in power to go out of power.[6] It was even somewhat exceptional. And, if casualties were generally few—all nineteenth-century Latin American revolutions together came nowhere near to equaling the death toll of the one U.S. Civil War— they did represent a net loss of human resources. Economic costs were appreciable too, including not just the expenses incurred in waging or defending against insurrections but also the reduced growth resulting from even temporary interruption of productive activities and from the climate of uncertainty that inhibited investment and innovation.

One other thing that changed with the coming of independence, then, was the state of public order, which for Latin America as a whole visibly deteriorated, although there were wide differences in this matter among countries. Moreover, when political disturbances were brought under control or simply avoided, sometimes the successful formula involved blatant violation of constitutional procedures. One quite prevalent phenomenon was that of *caudillismo*, whereby a strongman, or *caudillo*, most often of military origin, came to exercise power regionally or nationally through his ascendancy over a band of personal followers, the use of various kinds of patronage to forge ties of clientelism with the surrounding population, and, where necessary, the use of brute force as well. The caudillo, if in command of the national government, might or might not be a full-fledged "dictator," but one can at least be sure that he did not feel strictly bound to observe all legal technicalities. In the political life of the new nations one could easily find still other unseemly practices, such as rigged elections and the casual usurpation of prerogatives of one branch of government by another, most often by the executive at the expense of congress or the courts. None of these practices was uniquely Latin American, none was universal, but they did seem all too characteristic of Latin American political behavior following independence.

The explanation most frequently encountered for the apparent gap between constitutional theory and practice (or, as some would have it, between the written and the unwritten constitutions of Latin America) is a supposed lack of prior experience in self-government. The Spanish and Portuguese colonies, unlike the English, had no trace of legal autonomy. They had no representative institutions except at the municipal level, and their higher officials were mostly sent from Europe rather than being natives of the colonies. As a result, so goes the argument, Latin Americans were quite unprepared to take over the management of their own affairs. It must be noted, however, that the great majority of public servants before independence *were* recruited locally. The very same postal clerks and corrupt customs officials were on hand (still with their hands out for bribes) to serve the new republics as had served the colonial masters. Hence, only at the top levels was experience in governmental operations literally lacking, and even there it is likely that a greater problem was the general unfamiliarity of the *type* of institutions adopted, ostensibly popular in origin and subject to constitutional limitations as distinct from the patriarchal absolutism of the old regime.

In effect, the highest authority in the land was no longer that benevolent father figure, the king, his rule hallowed by religious teachings and civil tradition, but a written document that was hard for either governors or governed to take as seriously as the king's command was taken in the days of old. The importance of this factor becomes evident when one stops to consider that Spain and Portugal, the former mother countries, in the nineteenth century went through exactly the same kind of political upheavals as their ex-colonies—coups and civil wars, caudillos and dictatorships. In their case, it was hardly for lack of prior experience in governing themselves, but having lost their American empires they were now engaged in an effort to substitute a new form of constitutional monarchy for the previous absolute version. This was less drastic than the introduction of republican government but produced many of the same contradictions between the institutions adopted and habits of behavior built up over past centuries, or between those institutions and the cultural idiosyncrasy of the Iberian peoples. In the latter connection, an influential school of opinion maintains that such traits as an exaggerated sense of personal honor and the Catholic tendency to see truth as one and indivisible were incompatible with the values of a liberal political system, which required thoroughgoing respect for individual rights and sociocultural pluralism.

Any contradiction between political habits and cultural traditions on one hand and liberal institutions on the other was compounded in the mother countries by the fact that both Spain and Portugal had active minorities that still upheld absolute monarchy and did not accept constitutional government even in theory, much less in practice. This was not so in Latin America, where military dictators either denied that they were dictators or insisted, sincerely or not, that their dictatorship was a temporary expedient to deal with a national emergency after which normal political processes would be restored. At some times and in some places, though, it seemed that dictatorship was really more "normal" than its opposite. And if doctrinaire absolutists were lacking, there was no lack of other issues on which peaceful compromise was either difficult or impossible to effect.

The Questions to Fight Over

One such issue was the status of the Roman Catholic church, which in the colonial period had a religious monopoly through the formal exclusion of other sects, a close alliance with the state, a fuero that exempted the clergy from the jurisdiction of the ordinary courts, and a vast amount of property and other wealth. The position of the church had already been adversely affected by some of the imperial reforms of the late colonial period, and it was further weakened by the wars of independence, in which it lost property as well as suffering some decline in numbers of clergy, most critically at the higher levels where Spanish-born priests had been disproportionately represented and often ended up in voluntary or involuntary exile. Even worse for the church, however, was the spread of anticlericalism, which did not challenge fundamental Catholic beliefs but did seek to diminish the role in society of the institutional church and of the clergy who administered it.

Anticlericalism resulted in part from secularizing tendencies in thought and culture that had been making headway since the eighteenth century as a reflection of the European Enlightenment and increased rapidly in scope once independence removed most of the previous legal barriers to their penetration from abroad. To some extent it resulted also from the desire of new creole and mestizo ruling groups to enlarge their own intellectual and socioeconomic spheres of activity at the church's expense. Abolishing the Inquisition had meant only that the holding of religiously heretical ideas was no longer in itself a punishable offense; to spread them by word of mouth or printing press or to hold worship services in accordance with them were different matters. After independence, however, the demand for full religious toleration was heard with increasing frequency. So were demands to end the fuero as contrary to the notion of equal rights before the law, proposals for confiscation and sale of church property, and much more along the same line.

A related issue concerned the *patronato*, or system of civil patronage over the church, whereby traditionally the state in Spanish (as also in Portuguese) America, in return for promoting the spread of Roman Catholicism, had received from the papacy itself the right to control ecclesiastical appointments and in general the purely administrative aspects of the church. With the monarchs to whom this privilege had been given now out of the picture, the patronato should logically have ended, but the new governments insisted on retaining it as an essential attribute of sovereignty, and initially they found the warmest support for this claim among anticlerical spokesmen, whose hope was to use the patronato to dampen the inevitable clerical opposition to the reforms they had in mind. Both over the patronato as such and over those other reform proposals, controversy arose in one country after another. The fact that it reflected opposing attitudes toward religious faith and practice, than which no one force in Latin American society was more pervasive and deeply felt, ensured that there would be no easy solutions.

The religious question was also destined to become the primary litmus test for differentiating "liberals" from "conservatives" in nineteenth-century Latin America's political conflicts. These conflicts often revolved around rivalries of personalistic caudillos, but in Latin America, as elsewhere, personal and factional squabbles could exist perfectly well alongside or in combination with real differences of policy and program. At times, opposing viewpoints on national issues might then be expressed through formal Liberal and Conservative parties. But even where that was not the case, it was often possible to distinguish contrasting approaches or states of mind to which the same terms could be loosely applied, without the initial capital letters.

It is true that in political matters the differences between liberals and conservatives (with or without capital letters) were mainly of tactics and degree. Not only did absolutism no longer have defenders, but monarchy was an issue only in Brazil or, intermittently, in a few places like Mexico. And virtually everyone who took active part in the political process gave at least lip service to the goal of representative, constitutional government, which was an essentially liberal objective. Hence, political conservatives were little more than moderate liberals, men who might be more inclined that their mainstream liberal counterparts to filter the expression of popular will through a system of indirect elections or to enlarge executive prerogatives. They were also less disposed than most liberals to look to the United States as model and more inclined, if borrowing laws and institutions, to adapt them from European constitutional monarchies. But there was also an evident tension within liberalism itself between the drive to expand individual liberty and a desire to use the power of the state to root out traditional abuses and humble any corporate groups that threatened individual liberty. (Liberal support for maintaining the patronato was just one example of the resulting inconsistencies.) In any case, political differences were by and large more of detail than of substance. The same was true in economic questions, where free-enterprise capitalism was generally accepted as the ideal, and disagreements concerned the relative haste with which colonial survivals that conflicted with the economic freedom of the individual—from human slavery to the official limitation of interest rates—ought to be liquidated. On economic issues, moreover, considerations of sheer personal and group interest almost always took precedence over ideological consistency.

This left the church question as the one issue on which the distinction between liberals and conservatives was most clearcut. Conservatives did not oppose all change in this area; neither did most of the clergy themselves. However, they valued the church not only for its spiritual consolations but also as a critically important underpinning of the social order. As the Mexican Conservative Lucas Alamán expressed it, "The first thing is to conserve the Catholic religion, because we believe in it, and because *even if we did not consider it divine*, we consider it to be the only common bond which unites all Mexicans, when all the rest [such as the monarchy] have been broken."[7] Alamán and those of like mind in other countries shed no tears for the Inquisition, but they were otherwise inclined to move slowly and cautiously in trimming away the power and privileges of the church, lest they diminish its usefulness for purposes of social control. They also quickly discovered that religion was the most effective single cause with which to stir the popular masses into action on their side, with the parish priest often serving as conservative ward boss in elections and even as recruiting officer in times of revolution. Although there was a liberal minority within the clergy itself, the clergy as a whole was overwhelmingly conservative, if only for reasons of self-defense. For the rest, while it may be possible to say that merchants or landowners or professional men were predominantly either liberal or conservative in a given country at a given time, it is not possible to generalize about the political alignment of groups other than the clergy in Latin America as a whole. The exceptions are just too numerous. Moreover, outside the middle and upper sectors of the population, most Latin Americans were simply indifferent to the political struggles taking place—if they were even aware that they were happening. Only in a few countries, of which Colombia and Uruguay are the best examples, did permanent political parties succeed in getting the masses to identify emotionally and instinctively with one or another of them; and even in such cases, when civil war broke out the average countryman was less interested in who won than in avoiding military service himself and keeping his domestic animals and valuables (if any) well hidden from either progovernment or revolutionary foragers. Neither was it a common occurrence, though it did happen, for political leaders to appeal for popular support by espousing policies geared to the specific interests of rural or urban working-class groups. More often those leaders, generally representing rival portions of the same dominant class, were content to enlist the followers they needed by personal patronage or some form of compulsion.

A problem that cut across both political and class lines was that of regional or sectional rivalries. These had their roots in social, cultural, and ethnic differences and differences of economic interest from one place to another that were aggravated by the broken topography of much of Latin America. They antedated independence but had for the most part been kept just beneath the surface during the colonial regime. With the greater fragility of postindependence public order, these rivalries now welled to the surface with frequent destabilizing effect. In the large countries, which had more and larger distinct regions, sectionalism often found expression in demands for federalism as a type of constitutional organization. The latter entailed something like the U.S. model in which states or provinces that retained effective control over local affairs jointly established certain "federal" authorities to treat matters of general interest. Those who called instead for concentration of power in the hands of the central or national government viewed federalism as a dangerous source of governmental weakness and attributed the widespread infatuation with it to slavish imitation of an inappropriate foreign model. In reality, though, while federalists might copy some of the outward forms of the U.S. Constitution, they were not federalists for having read Hamilton and Madison. They embraced federalism because they felt their own needs were different from those of the people in the next mountain valley and were sure they could handle them better than a congress or bureaucracy in the remote national capital.

Statistically speaking, there was a slightly greater probability that federalists would be liberals and centralists would be conservatives, but, as will be seen, this was no hard and fast rule. At most, there was an inherent logical compatibility between federalism and the liberal concept of limiting government lest it trample on individual rights. Indeed, the only rule that admits no exception is that federalists, whenever they actually got the national government in their hands, were inclined to interpret its proper sphere of action a little more broadly than while they were languishing in opposition. For that matter, regionalism did not have to express itself in federalist guise; it could also take the form of mere refusal to heed the demands of central authority or of support for a regional caudillo as he climbed to national supremacy.

Regional rivalries, like religion, generated strong feelings and thus contributed to the intensity of political conflict. They generated especially strong feelings when the regions of a country were separated not just by distance and life-style but by clearly perceived differences of economic interest. But that is only one of the ways in which the economic and social structure contributed to the weakness of the political. A general state of economic underdevelopment limited the resources at the disposition of the state for either good or ill, and the colonial legacy of pronounced social stratification, only partly offset by such phenomena as the upward mobility of plebeian military leaders, did not help the consolidation of anything remotely resembling democratic pluralism. Before examining some national case studies, therefore, it is time to look at the economic and social scene of newly independent Latin America in its own right.

3

The Economic and Social Dimensions

Some twenty million people lived in Latin America at the end of the wars for independence. They grew crops for food and fiber; tended cattle, sheep, llamas, pigs, poultry, and bees; hunted and fished; gathered wild nuts, spices, and tea leaves; collected bugs for making dye; dug silver, gold, and copper out of the earth; wove cloth; tanned leather; forged ironware; built canoes, boats, and ships; and engaged in countless other economic activities. Most of what they produced they consumed themselves; relatively little was shipped beyond the communities that produced it, and much less was exported to other countries. The silver of Peru and Mexico, the coffee and sugar of Brazil and Cuba, and the dyes of Central America were famous on world markets, but, except for Cuba—which remained a Spanish possession—only a small fraction of the population of these countries was directly engaged in export production. Independence brought some notable changes, and life became more uncertain for some Latin Americans, but for most the conditions of everyday existence remained much as they had been under colonial rule. Three more decades would pass before fundamental economic and social change got underway. Internal factors, not external ones, were largely responsible for this stability—or stagnation.

Latin America in the World Economy: Foreign Trade and "Dependency"

Before 1808, when the Latin American independence movement began, the external commerce of the Iberian colonies was legally channeled—with only a few exceptions, the most important of them involving the slave trade—through Spain or Portugal. By 1825 this system had been totally eradicated everywhere except in Cuba and Puerto Rico, where it had been substantially modified. Although the original sources of Latin America's imports and the ultimate destination of the region's exports were scarcely changed by the elimination of the Iberian transfer requirement, and while pervasive smuggling during the colonial period attested to the ineffectiveness of much mercantilist legislation, the legalization of direct trade with the nations of the world had real significance for the newly independent states of Latin America.

One of the most noticeable consequences of the shift to freer trade was the sudden appearance of non-Iberian foreigners in the ports and major cities of the region. Before 1808, for example, non-Portuguese merchant ships were barred from Rio de Janeiro, and practically no foreigners lived there; by 1820 more than three hundred foreign vessels a year were calling at Rio, and more than three thousand aliens were residing in the city, which had a total population of about a hundred thousand. In Buenos Aires the number of foreign-born surpassed thirty-seven hundred by 1822, accounting for nearly seven percent of the city's total population. As Spain's other colonies secured their independence and opened their doors to international trade—simultaneously throwing out resident Spanish merchants, or at least making them feel unwelcome, and suppressing their monopolistic export-import guilds, the *consulados*—foreign commercial communities materialized in these countries as well. Most of the new residents were from Great Britain, the country with the most goods to sell in Latin America.

The British trade offensive in Latin America was launched in response to the effective establishment of Napoleon's Continental System in Europe. When Portugal was forced into the French system in 1807, Britain was deprived of the last of its European trading partners. The Portuguese regent, Prince John, was aware that Britain was intent "on repairing in the New World the losses which her commerce had sustained in the Old" when he enlisted British help in transferring his court to Brazil. What the British had in mind was the opening of Brazilian markets not to all the nations of the world but only to Britain; they would make Brazil a British dependency, establishing between Britain and Brazil "the Relation of Sovereign and Subject," as the British minister in Lisbon boasted in a report to London.[1] But once the wily Prince John was in Brazil, he took advantage of the temporary absence of the British minister to declare the ports of Brazil open to the commerce of all friendly nations.

It was not until the 1840s that the government in London adopted the free-trade prescriptions of the Scottish economist Adam Smith. In the meantime, Portuguese translations of Smith's *The Wealth of Nations* were published in Brazil (Rio, 1811; Bahia, 1813), and earlier European editions in Spanish circulated elsewhere in Latin America, where they were cited chapter and verse by exporters trying to break into the protected British market. But literal free trade was not adopted by Latin Americans either; as Brazil's Spanish American neighbors took charge of their own affairs, they followed exactly the same course as had the Portuguese regent on arrival in Rio. Direct trade with all friendly nations was the Latin American position, subject normally to a moderate tariff levied for revenue purposes, although higher, protectionist duties were sometimes adopted on behalf of politically powerful local producers.

The independence won in 1808–1825 was genuine: it ended colonialism in most of the Americas. If a neocolonialism took its place, it was a pale reflection of the real thing. Great Britain, as Brazil's wartime protector, could persuade the Brazilians to lower tariffs on British goods (in 1810 and 1827) but could not prevent them from extending the same low rates to all other nations. Neither Britain nor any other foreign power monopolized the trade of any Latin American country the way Spain and Portugal did before 1808. Under real colonialism, armed imperialist intruders levied taxes on the natives, forcing them to produce or deliver exportable goods in order to meet their tax bills. Britain and other European powers practiced this kind of imperialism in Africa and Asia in the nineteenth century, but not in Latin America. However unfree their domestic economies, Latin American nations traded free of coercion in world markets. If their trading partners often seemed to profit more than did the Latin Americans, this was essentially because of the low level of productivity in their domestic economies.

The wealth of nations, Adam Smith proclaimed, is not the gold or silver they possess but the productivity of their agriculture and industry. Spain owned the silver of Peru and Mexico, and Portugal owned the gold of Brazil, but, as Smith pointed out in 1776, neither was wealthy; they were the most "beggarly" countries in Europe, after Poland. The precious metals of Latin America, contrary to the mercantilist theory that lay at the heart of the Spanish and Portuguese imperial systems, were not the essence of wealth but simply commodities in international trade, whose value in relation to other commodities would fluctuate with the relative abundance or scarcity of each. Bullion was useful as money, in national coinage and for the settlement of international trade balances. As such, it would tend to flow from areas where productivity—goods or services output value for each worker-hour input—was low to areas where it was high. England before the Industrial Revolution had the world's most productive agriculture; consequently, much of the Latin American gold and silver that flowed through Spain and Portugal during the colonial period wound up in England, where it was invested in further productive improvements, including industrial development.

By 1808 Britain, France, much of northern Europe, and English-speaking North America all had far outstripped Spain and Portugal and their colonies in productivity. They were the "rich" nations, and it is unlikely that at any time they would have conspired to hold down productivity in the independent nations of Latin America. Indeed, they stood to gain from a rise in Latin American productivity, insofar as this would tend to increase the supply of any commodities they bought from the region and would lower their prices. The fact is, however, that the rich countries bought little from Latin America in the postindependence period. Latin America produced almost nothing that the Europeans and North Americans did not produce in abundance among themselves and their colonies, and the rich countries found it easier and more profitable to do business with one another. Then as now, a far greater volume of goods moved between rich countries than between poor and rich. The exceptions were few. Most of Europe's sugar came from the Caribbean colonies of Britain, France, and Spain. Spanish Cuba was the most efficient producer and dominated the relatively free sugar markets of continental Europe. Brazilian sugar producers were among those squeezed out of continental European markets by the Cubans. The Brazilians saw their salvation in the opening of the protected British market to their product; as early as 1822 they were willing to immediately renounce the slave trade in return for the free entry of their sugar into Britain. Committed as the British government was to the suppression of the international slave traffic, protection of the unproductive British West Indian sugar industry had a higher priority; the British sugar market remained closed until nearly midcentury. In the meantime, Brazil established itself as the world's foremost exporter of coffee, a hitherto nonessential commodity which it supplied in great quantities to the United States and continental Europe—but not to tea-drinking Britain.

Aside from Cuba and Brazil, the only other Latin American countries whose exports claimed a significant proportion of national production before midcentury were the Río de la Plata and Chile. The Argentine pampas were the source of about a third of Britain's imports of animal hides during 1825–50, while Chile's location on the Pacific Ocean gave it an advantage as a supplier of copper to British India and grain to the fledgling British colony in Australia and, later, to U.S. settlements in California. Chile also exported grain and wine to its Latin American neighbors, while Argentine producers shipped salted beef to Brazil and Cuba to feed their slaves. But this intraregional commerce was a mere drop in the world-trade bucket. And Latin American shipments of tallow, wool, cotton, and lumber to Europe before 1850 were dwarfed by European imports of these same commodities from North America or other European countries. Nevertheless, at the time of their separation from Spain and Portugal, the Latin American nations were perceived as wealthy—they had silver and gold. Mercantilist illusions died hard.

The Limits of the New Imperialism

The North American and European conflicts of 1804–1815 and the Latin American wars for independence that extended into the next decade—with their embargoes, blockades, and privateering—temporarily reduced the volume of imports to Latin America, creating pent-up demand to be satisfied when the hostilities ceased. Foreign trade boomed with the march of liberation across Latin America. In Buenos Aires, cowhides and horsehides and tallow were swapped for imported consumer goods, but most newly independent countries ran a steep trade deficit and paid the balance in silver or gold. The flow of precious metals excited British capitalists, enticing them to invest in silver mines in Mexico and Peru and gold mines in Colombia and Brazil. London bankers were eager to lend money to the governments of these apparently wealthy nations. Then, by the middle of the 1820s, the Latin American demand for imports dried up. Trade goods—wearing apparel, cloth, cutlery, china, clocks, watches, perfumes, beer, wine, spirits—piled up unsold in the warehouses of European and North American merchants in the ports of Latin America. Inventories were liquidated at ruinous prices, and many a merchant-adventurer returned penniless to London, Paris, or Boston. Panic gripped London's financial markets in 1825–26 as Latin America–related securities plunged, precipitating a general sell-off. In the late 1820s, as every Latin American government except Brazil's defaulted on its foreign debt, the bankers joined the merchants on the staggering casualty list of foreign capital's first incursions into independent Latin Ameria. A few of the foreign mining ventures there ultimately paid off but at rates of return far inferior to what the investors could have earned elsewhere. By the end of the 1820s the financial centers of the world had virtually written off Latin America as a field for profitable investment; not until after midcentury could much foreign capital be lured back to the region.

Export production, where it existed in independent Latin America before 1850, was, with few exceptions (e.g., the Peruvian guano trade that got underway in the 1840s), both financed and managed by natives. Outside capital played a greater role in Cuba, and the island remained a political dependency of Spain, but even there economic decision making was largely in the hands of local producers, especially after the Spanish liberal reforms of the 1830s. Indeed, to say that the Latin American countries were economic "dependencies" for whom the decisions that determined their development were made in some far-off "metropolis" is, at best, an exaggeration. Hundreds of thousands of decisions in Germany—to drink coffee and sweeten it with sugar—doubtlessly stimulated the production of those commodities in Brazil and Cuba. But the decisions to respond to this external demand were made in the producer countries; no one forced Brazilian and Cuban planters to produce coffee and sugar. Certainly Great Britain, the premier imperial power of the time, did not. If anything, the British seemed to do their best to ruin the planters of Brazil and Cuba by refusing to buy their products and by trying to cut off their supply of slave labor. The fact that Brazil and Cuba continued until after midcentury to import slaves from Africa in defiance of Great Britain indicates that Britain was far from omnipotent in Latin America. This was further demonstrated when Brazil rejected Britain's request for a renewal of the 1827 commercial treaty and instead raised its tariffs on British imports in 1844. Brazil was not alone in successfully resisting the might of the British Empire: the Argentine provinces, which produced something Britain actually wanted—hides—compelled the British Navy to withdraw from their waters and fire a salute to the Argentine flag in 1848.

For all its economic and naval power, Britain alone clearly was unable to keep Latin America in a state of dependency. Instead, the dependency thesis rests ultimately on the notion that Britain and other advanced capitalist nations worked in concert to maintain the Latin American economies as suppliers of bulk commodities in return for more complex industrial goods and thereby to prolong a situation of relative underdevelopment that in reality (though the fact is sometimes forgotten) antedated independence. Obviously, the means to achieve this result could be much more subtle than brute force and could have been employed almost unconsciously. It has been suggested, for example, that capital itself is somehow attached to a "core" geographical area, to which it is bound to return after forays into "peripheral" lands. The fact that money flows to areas of high productivity, many of which happened to be located near the North Atlantic at the beginning of the nineteenth century, gives the idea a certain plausibility. However, the implication that capital would pass up opportunities for long-term profitable employment in the development of other parts of the world in order to return to the land of its birth—the North Atlantic community—is not supported by the historical record.

The power of attraction of North Atlantic ideas and ways of life for Latin American decision makers is perhaps a better explanation for what happened. The leaders of Latin American society genuinely wanted a closer association, economically and otherwise, with the British, French, and North Americans, and commodity exporting appeared to be the easiest way to bring this about, although it still was not necessarily easy. Latin America's particular economic relationship with the rest of the world thus received the knowing, even enthusiastic assent of most educated, well-to-do Latin Americans at the time of independence. Whether the relationship was wise or not is obviously a different matter, and, as later chapters of this book will suggest, there were both positive and negative effects on the development of individual countries.

In any case, the migration of capital and other forms of wealth is a constant of history, unaffected by sentiment and susceptible to no more than temporary deflection by political action. No geographical or cultural conspiracy determined the flow of money from the Mediterranean to the Baltic and North Atlantic or, more recently, to the North Pacific. In Latin America, capital inflow and accumulation in the first half of the nineteenth century were limited by low productivity. Blaming foreign imperialists for this state of "underdevelopment" is unproductive; reasons for it are to be found in the region itself, in its geography—in the placement of its natural resources and population—and, especially, in the institutions and habits left over from the colonial past.

Society and Economic Development

Spain's most productive colony at the end of the colonial period was Mexico, which in 1800 may have had a per capita income about half that of the United States. The cost of Mexico's membership in the Spanish empire—taxes remitted to Madrid plus value lost through imperial trade restrictions—has been calculated at 7.2 percent of the colony's total output of goods and services at the beginning of the nineteenth century. A much greater burden, it would seem, was laid on colonial Mexico by geography: high mountain ranges and the absence of navigable rivers linking areas of production, domestic markets, and ocean ports greatly increased internal transportation costs, raising the labor input of goods consumed or exported and thereby lowering productivity. Without this geographical disadvantage and "all other things being equal," Mexico's productivity in 1800 should have been roughly equal to that of the United States. John H. Coatsworth speculates about what might have happened if Mexico had been endowed with a system of rivers like those along the eastern seaboard of the United States:

> All other things were not, of course, equal. The viceregal government might well have decided to raise internal customs duties (*alcabalas*) to match reductions in transport costs. Or Madrid could have ordered the colonial government to deny licenses to entrepreneurs clamoring to take advantage of lowered transport costs and ready to invest in new productive enterprise. Or the crown could have decided to make transportation a royal monopoly (*estanco*, from which *estancar*, to stagnate) and control the supply of shipping and charge inflated rates. Or the Council of the Indies might have urged the king to protect the indigenous population by forbidding its employment in the production of goods sold in faraway places. Or, after multiple lawsuits lasting several decades, the Audiencia might have decided in favor of the petitions of muleteers, wagonmasters, and hotel keepers and ordered that all boats, rafts, and canoes in the colony had to be owned exclusively by former muleteers, wagonmasters, and hotel keepers who registered with the authorities and agreed to lend the king ten thousand pesos.[2]

Measures like these actually were adopted at various times during the colonial period in many parts of Spanish America and, to a lesser extent, in Portuguese Brazil. The institutional environment for entrepreneurial activity in most of colonial Latin America discouraged productivity gains. Although planters, mine operators, and other production managers in colonial Latin America were probably as capable, diligent, and enterprising as their counterparts anywhere else in the world, as recent studies have indicated, they operated in a highly politicized environment in which their decisions, while economically rational, were necessarily shaped by nonmarket considerations.

Independence gave the Latin American countries direct access to world markets but did not radically alter the organization of their domestic economies. Madrid or Lisbon no longer could deny licenses to entrepreneurs eager to take advantage of new opportunities, but Mexico City, Lima, or Rio could and did. Some monopolies were suppressed, but others were maintained and some new ones created after independence. The Spanish Council of the Indies lost its authority to protect American Indians, but paternalism survived in the Roman Catholic church and in some postindependence governments. The colonial high courts disappeared, and many guilds—especially those controlled by Iberians—were suppressed, but special-interest pleading continued before new administrative or judicial bodies, often resulting in the reaffirmation of corporate privilege and the denial of benefits to the nation at large. Forced loans, bribes, and purchased "exceptions" to legislation were, if anything, more common after independence than before.

Latin Americans thus made selective use of liberal economic doctrine. They called for unrestricted international exchange of goods but did not abolish tariffs, and much less did they automatically accept or act upon Adam Smith's criticism of domestic monopolies, administered prices and wages, internal customs levies, land entailment and mortmain, and coercive labor systems. For some—those who generally wound up under the label "conservative"—the utility of economic liberalism ended with the elimination of Spanish or Portuguese intermediaries in the export-import business. To carry liberalism further would weaken the structure of Hispanic corporatist society, which to one degree or another conservatives typically wished to preserve. The survival of the traditional regime of corporate privilege required, among other things, the perpetuation of inalienable family, communal, and clerical landholdings; the guarantee of "fair" prices and "just" wages; and the means to compel labor when workers were disinclined to offer it at customary rates of compensation. As for internal customs collection, even liberals—

who in most of the larger Latin American countries tended to be federalists—would recognize this as a convenient means of extracting funds for local or provincial governments, especially those they controlled. The same was true on the national level of theoretically indefensible institutions like the state tobacco monopoly, which was accepted as a sure source of revenue by liberal and conservative governments alike. Internal restraints on trade would not be easily removed in Latin America.

To be sure, movement toward a liberal economy was underway in some colonies before the independence struggle began. The city council of Buenos Aires rejected a step backward by refusing to charter a shoemakers' guild in the 1790s. Peripheral Buenos Aires, unlike the core viceregal centers of Spanish America, never experienced the monopolistic guild system. Also, with no silver mines and few settled Indians—except in Paraguay— the lowland provinces of the Río de la Plata were largely spared the forced labor drafts common in Peru and Mexico. Some work was done by slaves brought in from Africa, but soon after the break with Spain the Buenos Aires government took steps to end the system by outlawing the importation of Africans in 1812 and ordering the phased emancipation of children born to slave mothers after 1813. Similar measures were enacted in other Spanish American countries either during the war of independence or in the next decade, foreshadowing the elimination of black slavery in those republics by around midcentury.

In much of Spanish America, of course, the indigenous population had traditionally met most labor needs. Tied to their villages by inalienable rights to communal land, Indians under the colonial regime were subject to a special head tax, or tribute, which they were required to pay in cash to their Spanish overlords. When the requirement to earn tribute money did not produce the necessary laborers, Indians could be drafted for work on the roads, on plantations, and in the mines. With independence, the tribute and labor drafts were formally abolished in most of Spanish America. The legal basis of this coercion, the obligations of a conquered people, was destroyed with the colonial system. Spanish American conservatives generally agreed with their liberal compatriots—in principle, at least—on the desirability of eliminating Indian tribute and labor drafts. Actually, use of the latter had declined during the late colonial period as employers increasingly resorted to other means of securing needed labor, such as debt peonage. Some even went so far as to offer acceptable wages; in Mexico, after all, the mining industry had long relied primarily on voluntary labor. However, though some of its legal forms were abolished, forced labor hardly disappeared in Latin America in the postindependence period; indeed, chattel slavery expanded in Brazil, as it did in the Spanish colony of Cuba at the same time. In places where slavery was proscribed, Latin American employers often found other ways, illegal and extralegal, to coerce workers. The important difference was that after the separation from Spain and Portugal the coercion was exclusively of domestic origin; it was not generated or directed from abroad.

The colonial system had lasted for three centuries because the people of Latin America generally accepted its corporatist organization and perceived as just the judicial system that was its arbiter. The officially chartered, self-regulated interest groups of the colonial era did not bargain among themselves in a market setting but argued their cases before royal judges, reasonably confident of a decision—though it might be years in coming—that would be fair and would preserve their traditional privileges. Those who proposed changes that might infringe on these privileges were likely to lose in the tribunals. Spanish American Indian communes were notably successful in protecting their lands from encroachments by outsiders in the late colonial period. However, even some of the Indians saw advantages in individual ownership of land, and, with the approval of royal judges, there was limited movement toward the distribution of communal holdings as private property before independence. The trend accelerated after independence as the right to hold private property was enshrined in the constitutions adopted by the new nations—which, however, did not deny the right of communal ownership. All parties continued to look to government to mediate the changes.

Most of the new governments—weak and unstable, shaken by civil strife—were not equal to the task. While property rights were theoretically guaranteed at the time of independence, another quarter-century would pass before even the most stable of nations enacted civil codes setting forth rules for the organization and utilization of private property. In the meantime, property managers had to contend with all the legal uncertainties of the old system plus the likely inability of the new courts to enforce any judgments they might render. With almost any productive change perceived as adversely affecting some corporate interest, entrepreneurs had to secure the favor—through reason, force, or bribery—not only of judges and bureaucrats but also of those who wielded the armed might essential for carrying out judicial and political decisions in societies where habits of obedience to civil authority had been severely undermined. Independence added new dimensions of corruption and coercion in most Latin American countries.

Latin America's financial infrastructure, sorely deficient as a support for enterprise during the colonial period, was little improved in the years after independence. There was no bank in all of Latin America before 1808; from then until midcentury no public institution that accepted deposits and made commerical loans had more than an ephemeral existence, except in Brazil and Cuba. Elsewhere in Latin America, producers were limited to traditional sources of financing: merchants, export-import brokers, guilds, and, especially, the Roman Catholic church and its affiliated organizations. The archbishop of Mexico was, in the words of one visitor from the United States in the 1840s, "the great loan and trust company of Mexico."[3] The archdiocese had real estate and cash—accumulated over the years through donations from the crown and bequests from the faithful—available for lease on easy terms to favored individuals; money was lent at annual interest of six and a half percent. Convents and monasteries also had property to lease and money to lend, not only in Mexico but in many parts of Latin America, including Brazil. And so did the tertiary orders of laypeople—*cofradías* in Spanish America, *irmandades* in Brazil—which were religiously oriented service clubs and mutual-aid societies, chartered by a diocese or a regular order of clergy, and sometimes associated with a particular craft or trade. The cofradías, like other branches of the church, accepted gifts but not deposits; decisions on loans were necessarily influenced by religious principles as well as the desire to promote the collective interests of the cofradía and the individual welfare of the borrower. Indeed, religious perceptions of what was just and fair formed the ideological underpinning of traditional society.

Classes and Interest Groups

The society of colonial Latin America had not been a rigid class- or caste-based system, and neither was that of the independent nations. Birth was important but not solely determinant. Indians born to membership in a communal village might find their birthright more burdensome than advantageous and relinquish it by moving to an unincorporated settlement or to a town or city to work for wages. Similarly, offspring of white landowners with poor inheritance prospects often left the family hacienda or plantation to pursue opportunities elsewhere. Children of various economic and ethnic backgrounds wound up as apprentices in the craft guilds; a few would rise to the position of master. Black slaves remained slaves unless their owners freed them, which occasionally occurred. Blacks who mated with free Indians or poor whites contributed to the formation of a large Afro-Latin American floating population whose members could aspire to serve in the colonial militia or postindependence armies. Even the priesthood, at least on the lower levels, was open to minimally educated men of mixed blood in both Spanish and Portuguese America.

The patronage of relatives or family friends often was indispensable for advancement. Families tended to be broader and more complex than the Victorian nuclear-family ideal. Illegitimate children often lived in the same household with a father's legitimate offspring and sometimes were favored over them. A black slave woman might give birth to a mulatto son destined to receive a large landed estate or to enter one of the professions. In the absence of influential blood relatives, godparents—carefully chosen by a child's parents from a social stratum above theirs—might arrange remunerative employment for a boy or an advantageous marriage for a girl.

But even the godparent system—*compadrazgo*—and all the collective safeguards of Latin American society could not provide comprehensive insurance against catastrophe—against the worst effects of fire, flood, drought, civil war, bad luck, or mismanagement. Cattle died or were stolen, crops failed, mortgages were foreclosed, and landed property changed hands. Some people lost assets, while others gained them. There was more mobility in Latin American society—in both directions—than commonly thought. Legal wives of large landowners could become the mothers of sharecroppers or subsistence farmers. For that matter, male dominance was also less than the conventional harping on Latin American "machismo" would suggest. Upper-class women far outranked lower-class men, and in some communities lower-class women were the normal heads of households. Women managed rural properties, and in urban areas they operated taverns, dry-goods stores, and other retail and service establishments. Even nuns, from behind their convent walls, dealt in real estate, traded slaves, and managed the production and sale of baked goods.

Although the spirit of enterprise was alive in traditional Latin American society, corporatist survivals limited the opportunities for productive investment, discouraged savings, and retarded the emergence of a capitalist "class." Enterprise was channeled repeatedly into unproductive activities: maneuvering to circumvent law and regulations, to preserve or expand group or personal privileges, and to contain or reduce those of others. It is difficult to apply class analysis to this process, which was essentially a struggle for individual advantage within a less than favorable environment. Noneconomic behavior aside, a rational individual may be expected to maximize his or her own utility, whether this means defending the interests of an industry, a trade or profession, a village, a region, a country, a family, a clan, or a class. The claims of the last do not necessarily override those of all the others.

If class is defined strictly in terms of an individual's relationship to the means of production, it cannot wholly explain the dynamics of traditional Latin American society. If class designations are applied to differentiate among categories of people who associate with one another for companionship on a basis of equality, the pattern will be shaped more by consumption than by production. In this case, it is the quantity and quality of the goods and services that a person consumes that largely determine his or her class. Heredity can play a part, but a person born into an upper class who does not maintain a certain level of consumption runs the risk of descending into a lower one. And a person born to a lower class can consume his or her way into a higher one if by hard work, gift, or theft he or she acquires the means to do so. Above the slave and subsistence levels in Latin America, the decision whether to consume or to save was a personal one, to be freely taken. But in the absence of productive investment opportunities—which was usually the case—the rational choice was to consume. This model of class structure more closely reflects the reality of Latin American society and accounts for the mobility within it. That Latin Americans were oriented toward consumption was the result not of some ethnic character defect but of a lack of alternatives under Iberian colonialism—a deficiency that would persist long after independence.

There was a strong correlation between class and race in Latin America, with whites tending toward high consumption and blacks—most of whom were slaves—tending toward low consumption. Indians, whose opportunities were inferior to those of whites, tended toward the low end of the consumption scale, as did persons of mixed blood, who enjoyed few, if any, privileges based on race. As noted above, legally sanctioned racial discrimination came to an end throughout Latin America with separation from Spain and Portugal. The important role played by mestizos in the wars for independence in Spanish America and sensitivity to the racial slurs that Portuguese colonialists had regularly applied to all Brazilians guaranteed the rejection of racism as official policy by the new nations. But discriminatory habits were not easily eradicated, and the correlations between rich and white and poor and nonwhite, though weakened, still held. Nevertheless, Latin America was a far more egalitarian place after independence than before. Indians and mestizos rose to positions of power all over Spanish America after independence. Some, like Rafael Carrera of Guatemala, favored preservation of the colonial corporatist structure, only without its racial bias; others, like Benito Juárez of Mexico, called for thoroughgoing liberal reforms to change that structure. Whites were found on both sides of the issue, as were rich people and poor people.

There is little justification for casting nineteenth-century Latin

American history as a struggle between the elites and the masses. While the latter are fairly easy to identify—those who consumed little or nothing beyond what was required for their own subsistence—it is not so easy to generalize about their class interests, which varied from time to time, from place to place, and within each region and period. The masses were composed of many interest groups. This is no less true of the elites, whom one historian has identified as those who "controlled the government institutions, as well as the commerce, banking, agriculture, and arts" of nineteenth-century Latin America.[4] The definition is self-evidently correct but hardly enlightening: it obscures the varied origins of members of the elites, many of whom sprang from the masses. Aside from the mestizo generals and caudillos whose power and property were acquired through military service, the men of humble origins who gained prominence included civilian politicians like Juárez; some of Latin America's most honored poets, writers, and composers; and Brazil's preeminent financier at the middle of the nineteenth century, Baron Mauá. It makes little sense to say that these people were co-opted by the elites or were their representatives or puppets: they *were* the elites, by every imaginable criterion except birth. The concept of an elite as a single, dominant interest group—self-aware, self-perpetuating, somewhat conspiratorial, committed to incessant class struggle with the masses—is worse than useless. The term *elite* is itself a thin cloak for conceptual poverty; scholarship demands that it be discarded and replaced by more precise designations like "sugar planters," "textile importers," or "higher clergy." The contest was not between the elites and the masses but among interest groups whose membership often cut across class lines.

4

Mexico in Decline
(1821–1855)

Mexico at the time of independence was the most populous country of Latin America, with roughly seven million inhabitants as against Brazil's four million. It was also the largest, at least in terms of land area effectively occupied by European colonizers and their descendants, for the uncharted portions of Brazil's vast Amazon Basin amounted to many more square kilometers than the unsettled desert and mountain fringes of far northern Mexico, which at the time still included much of the later United States. But Mexico was also just plain unwieldy, and it became for a while the prime Latin American example of Murphy's Law, to the effect that what can go wrong will go wrong. Certainly no other Latin American country had to grapple with so broad a range of critical difficulties, whether economic and social, political, or diplomatic. Only some time after Mexico had lost half its territory to its northern neighbor would these problems even begin to be brought under control.

Land and People in the Aftermath of Independence

In 1821, the year Mexico won its independence from Spain, the output of the Mexico City mint was less than six million pesos. In the year before the war for independence began, it had been more than twenty-six million pesos. Thus, there was a drastic drop in the manufacture of Mexico's principal export, money.

The Spanish peso, or piece of eight reales—the model for the U.S. dollar and the standard unit of foreign exchange in China—was minted in Mexico City from silver produced by the mines and smelters north of the capital in Zacatecas and Guanajuato. This area was hard hit early in the independence struggle: mine workers were drafted into the opposing armies; work animals, explosives, and other supplies and equipment were carried off by the belligerents; machinery was wrecked, and mule trains bringing replacement parts were waylaid; pumps failed, and mine shafts were flooded. Though the fighting eventually moved elsewhere, reconstruction of the mining industry was impossible as long as the war continued, disrupting communications and generally taking its toll of the Mexican population and economy.

The drop in mine output produced a corresponding decline in the power of the miners' guild. Its corporate pleading could safely be disregarded by the first Congress of independent Mexico, which dissolved the miners' guild itself and invited foreign capital to rehabilitate the mines. But mining in Mexico, even in the heyday of the Spanish colonial regime, was a relatively small component of the country's economy. The value of agricultural production in 1810 was nearly four times greater than mining output, and roughly seventy-five percent of the Mexican labor force was engaged in agriculture. The government of independent Mexico would be more cautious in dealing with agricultural interests—with Indian communes, private estate owners (hacendados), and the country's biggest holder of rural property, the Roman Catholic church.

The war affected these interests in different ways. The communal landholding villages (*ejidos*, as they were called in Mexico) lost population; perhaps a majority of the half-million or so people who died as a consequence of the conflict were village Indians, many of whom had performed seasonal labor on the haciendas. The hacendados were thus threatened with a labor shortage, and their interests coincided with those of the Indians to the extent that they required that the diminished Indian population be induced to remain in the traditional villages by the perpetuation of communal property and the elimination of the head tax, or tribute. The direct tax that the hacendados themselves were obligated to pay for support of the church—the tithe, or ten percent levy on gross agricultural production—was largely evaded in the confusion of the war years. The hacendados were generally unwilling to accept the reimposition of this burden; they wanted it officially eliminated or made voluntary. Finally, the church, deprived of most of the proceeds of the tithes and subjected to forced loans imposed by both colonial and national governments, lost much of its working capital in the countryside—along with many of its personnel, who had fled to safety in the cities—and chose to rent out most of its rural properties rather than administer them directly in the unsettled postindependence period.

Large estates, including those leased from or administered by the church, accounted for most of Mexico's production of corn, beans, wheat, sugar, beef, mutton, work animals, hides, wool, sisal fiber, and pulque, the fermented drink made from juice extracted from the maguey plant. Small-scale farmers—including ejido Indians, who made up about a third of Mexico's population and whose mode of production was individual rather than collective, the communal village lands being actually farmed in small separate plots—produced most of the fruits, tomatoes, chili peppers, pork, goats, poultry, eggs, honey, silk, and cochineal, a dye made from cactus bugs. Tending small animals (including insects) and raising garden produce were labor-intensive operations which offered little prospect for cost reduction through economies of scale. Depending on local conditions or the enforcement of monopolistic legislation, tobacco, wine, and cotton might be produced either by communal villages and small landholders or by large estates.

Mexico's farmers—commune dwellers as well as hacendados—responded readily to economic conditions and, where government interference was kept to a minimum, generally maintained a rational division of labor. Hacienda records show that estate owners invested in new productive capacity in periods of prosperity and curtailed their operations in periods of economic decline. In the hard times that descended on Mexico with the war for independence, many hacendados simply sold their estates or divided them into tenancies and rented them out; where buyers or tenants did not appear, estates were abandoned. The general trend, which began in 1810 and was not reversed until after midcentury, was the gradual disintegration of large estates into smaller units.

More than anything else, it was the lack of low-cost transportation that inhibited the growth of large landholdings, or *latifundios*, in Mexico in the first half of the nineteenth century. Precarious wagon roads ran from Mexico City north to Zacatecas and east to Puebla and Veracruz, but commerce in most of the country moved by mule train, at rates considerably higher than wagon-freight charges. Transportation costs limited the supply radii of provincial cities and made the expansion of production uneconomical beyond the radii. The silver-mining center of Guanajuato, for example, was supplied with corn by producers located no more than fifty-five kilometers from the city; the cost of shipping corn to Guanajuato from a greater distance would exceed forty percent of the delivered sale price of the grain and preclude any producer profit. There was no incentive to amass landholdings for commercial agriculture beyond the supply radii of market centers.

Between provincial capitals like Guanajuato, with populations numbering in the tens of thousands, were towns of one to three thousand where marketing fairs were held on one or two days each week. These towns were the principal points of contact for Mexico's two cultures—the Indian and the Hispanic—in the broad highland valleys where most Mexicans lived, from San Luis Potosí in the north to Oaxaca in the south. Spanish-speaking whites and mestizos—shopkeepers and impresarios—sold utensils, trinkets, tobacco products, and pulque to, and staged cockfights and gambling games for, the Nahuatl- or Zapotec-speaking Indians who trudged in from the countryside loaded with farm produce, charcoal, firewood, woolen blankets, and other handicrafts intended for sale at the town fair. The arrival of the Indians on foot underscored their status as peons (*peones*: literally, pedestrians) in contradistinction to the Spanish-speaking *caballeros*, or horsemen. Many of the Indians would go to the town church for mass, which was seldom said in their villages where priests visited only intermittently. Indians with nothing to sell might come to town to spend the silver or copper coins they had earned for work on a nearby hacienda.

The haciendas sold their surplus production to town and city merchants, to wholesalers in the larger transactions. But most of what the haciendas produced—especially in times of economic recession—was consumed on the estates by the hacendados and their families, their servants, and other employees or tenants. The haciendas were largely self-sufficient. Resident artisans produced everything from saddlery and furniture to horseshoes and nails to roofing tiles and pottery, while tenants and hired hands supplied the estate community with produce from their gardens and meat from the populations of pigs, goats, chickens, turkeys, ducks, geese, pigeons, quail, and tortilla-fed dogs that they maintained in and around their homes. A portion of a hacienda's acreage would be allotted to the production of forage and feed grain for the estate's horses and mules, which were usually housed in stables attached to the hacendado's residence, typically a fortresslike adobe or stone structure that faced inward onto a patio, with one or two wings designated as storage areas for food, supplies, and equipment. The quarters of the hacendado's family and domestic servants would be furnished with amenities comparable to those available in upper- or middle-class urban residences, while the outlying homes of field workers were similar to those found in Indian villages: one-room adobe or wattle and daub huts, sparsely furnished, in which family members slept on straw mats spread out on dirt floors; smoke from cooking or warming fires escaped through a hole in the tile or thatched roof. The hacienda, like the ejido, usually had a chapel but seldom a resident priest.

Internal exchanges on the haciendas and within the ejidos usually took the form of barter; the economy of the rural communities was essentially a natural one. Money was earned for surplus production sold in towns or cities and paid to seasonal workers on the haciendas, but this represented only a small fraction of the total income of rural Mexico. Savings were nonexistent or minimal, and country folk were subjected to one of the most precarious social conditions imaginable: dependence on their own nonliquid community resources. A flood, a drought, an insect plague, an epidemic, or a rampaging army could tax these resources beyond their limits, wreaking utter havoc on communes and private estates alike. Whole areas might be devastated, with natural or man-made disasters overwhelming the charitable institutions of the market towns and devouring the meager public and private capital available there. But the perils of dependency were evident even in normal times, as thin markets magnified the inevitable imbalances of supply and demand. Lack of liquidity reduced the recovery options of private estates and communes alike; the natural economy was hardly a secure one. Producers who had ready access to Mexico's stultified provincial and national markets were not much better off, unless they belonged to a politically favored interest group—like the tobacco growers of Veracruz Province, who traditionally monopolized the production of tobacco for the entire country.

The most privileged economic interests were based in that region of the country most favored by geography and government spending: the Valley of Mexico surrounding the capital and the area along the Camino Real (royal highway) that ran east to Puebla before descending in two branches, via Jalapa and via Córdoba, to the city of Veracruz, the port for about ninety percent of Mexico's foreign commerce. Transportation costs in this central region were the lowest in the country. Corn and wheat from the Valley of Mexico's lakeside haciendas were shipped to the capital in boats and canoes at minimal rates that maximized the profits of producers, who received payment on delivery to distributors at government-decreed prices. Puebla, a major population center since before the Spanish Conquest, shipped ceramics and cotton cloth made in its *obrajes* (workshops) over the paved Camino Real to Mexico City. To ensure a steady supply of raw material for the obrajes, and in keeping with mercantilist principles, monopoly privileges were granted to cotton planters in the Puebla area. Similarly, farmers in the vicinity of Córdoba in Veracruz Province had the exclusive right to sell tobacco to the government-owned cigar-, snuff-, and cigarette-making concern in Mexico City, the country's largest manufacturing enterprise which employed thousands of factory workers and legally monopolized the production and distribution of tobacco products throughout the country. The state tobacco monopoly was, in fact, a key pillar of the revenue system. Mexico's second largest manufacturer was another state enterprise, the government mint in the capital city; many of its silver coins went to Veracruz to pay for European imports or to Acapulco to buy Chinese silks and lacquerware shipped from Manila. This international trade dwindled as mint production declined during the war years. The Asian commerce virtually ceased once the mule trail to Acapulco was interdicted by insurgents and, later, by bandits.

But in a few areas far distant from the capital, international trade was increasing at the time of Mexican independence, though on a modest scale. The hacendados of Yucatán found lucrative markets for their sisal fiber in New Orleans, which was almost as close to them as Veracruz, where prices for their commodity were not nearly as high. Similarly, ranchers in Coahuila and Texas found it profitable to sell hides and live cattle and horses to the nearby United States. New Mexico supplied mules and equine breeding stock, progenitors of the Missouri mule, to Kansas City and St. Louis via the Santa Fe Trail. In New Mexico and elsewhere on the northern frontier, from San Antonio, Texas, to San Francisco, California, church missions— usually manned by Franciscans—mediated between the native Indians and small settler populations and generally kept the peace in the vast region. The peace and modest prosperity of these peripheral provinces contrasted with the political turmoil and economic decline in much of the rest of Mexico.

From Monarchy to Republic

The army that liberated Mexico from Spain in 1821 numbered more than fifty thousand officers and men. It included Mexican troops who had defended Spanish rule in the preceding decade, native insurgents who had fought consistently for independence, and even some Spaniards who, lamenting the turn of events in their native land following the liberal revolt of 1820, cast their lot with the new nation. Virtually all the forces that had been fighting each other since 1810 plus thousands of last-minute volunteers came together in 1821 to form the largest military establishment Mexico had ever seen—at least since the time of the Aztecs. The ex-insurgents were outnumbered in the consolidated armed forces by their former enemies, who largely shaped the institutional attitudes of the national military. The army would jealously guard its corporate privileges, or fueros, which exempted its

personnel—including off-duty militia officers—from the jurisdiction of civilian courts in all matters, criminal and civil. The
government of independent Mexico was in no position to deprive
the military of its privileges.

The position of the church, which enjoyed fueros similar to
those of the military, was almost as strong as that of the armed
forces in postindependence Mexico. The power of the church
derived from its spiritual hold over the Mexican people, the
conspicuous participation of members of its clergy in the independence movement, and, especially, its extensive liquid assets.
While the last attribute also made the church a prime target for
forced loans, it gave the hierarchy the means to influence officeholders and extract concessions from the government in return
for the mandatory cash advances. Like the army, the church was
determined to preserve its corporate privileges, and both institutions found ready defenders in those who wanted to maintain the
same kind of regime, administratively centralized and socially
corporatist, bequeathed to Mexico by the Spanish colonialists.
Conservative centralists saw in the church and the army the
indispensable instruments for maintaining order in the provinces,
while the bureaucrats, concessionaires, and privileged producers
of the Mexico City–Puebla–Veracruz axis continued to enjoy
their monopolistic advantages—which provincial producers and
consumers could not help but recognize as detrimental to their
own interests. Not all centralists in early postindependence Mexico were conservatives; some were liberals who believed that a
strong concentration of political power on the national level
would be necessary to extinguish the old order and guarantee
individual rights. However, conservative domination of Mexico's
first national government, which was centralist, virtually ensured
the identification of the vast majority of liberals with federalism.

Generalísimo Agustín de Iturbide, armed forces commander-
in-chief and architect of Mexican independence, presided over
the five-man junta that replaced the Spanish colonial government
in Mexico City in September 1821. The executive junta—staffed
by high-ranking clerics and other notables, a majority from the
Mexico City–Puebla region—was joined by a legislative body
when Mexico's first Congress, composed of representatives of
the country's incorporated cities and towns, convened in the

capital in February 1822. The new regime courted the favor of
the people by cutting the retail prices of tobacco and pulque,
thereby reducing government revenue from the sale of those
monopolized items at a time of mounting public expenditures—
to pay for the huge army, expanded bureaucracy, and other
excesses of an inexperienced and insecure regime. To meet the
demands of the national treasury, Congress approved emissions
of paper money and forced loans on the church. On the other
hand, Congress suspended a forced loan on large, mostly Spanish
mercantile houses that had been decreed earlier by the junta and
was resulting in a massive flight of capital from the country.
Congress and the junta were agreed that independent Mexico
should be a monarchy. After Spanish King Ferdinand VII rejected their offer of the Mexican throne and the Cortes in Madrid
refused to recognize Mexico's independence, most congressmen
seemed to favor continuing the search among the royal houses of
Europe for a suitable prince willing to become their sovereign.
Iturbide, however, backed by his junta colleagues and the army,
grabbed the crown for himself in May 1822. The generalísimo
appeared before Congress, with his supporters packing the gal-
leries and his soldiers standing by outside, and induced the intim-
idated legislators (who lacked a quorum) to proclaim him Agustín I, constitutional emperor of Mexico. The church hierarchy
and the people of Mexico City were quite enthusiastic about their
native-born monarch, and few dissenting voices were heard from
the provinces. In fact, the rulers of the six provinces of Central
America—formerly the captaincy-general of Guatemala, nominally subordinate to Mexico City under the Spanish colonial
regime—were so impressed with the prospects of the new Mexican Empire that they elected to join it. Thus, the realm of Emperor Agustín I bordered Panama at one extreme and Oregon at
the other.

Cracks in the imperial facade appeared soon after the corona-
tion of Agustín I, amidst immoderate pomp and ceremony, in
July. Congress, which was intermittently working on a constitution for the monarchy, declared that the press should be free in
Mexico. The emperor disagreed and began closing down newspapers and jailing writers who criticized or mocked him—for the
extravagance of his administration or for his nonregal origins

(born in the provincial city of Valladolid, now Morelia, he was the son of a Basque merchant and a Mexican mother). Members of Congress spoke out against the emperor and were arrested. Finally, in October, Agustín I dissolved Congress and announced that he would rule by decree. Within two months, in the port city of Veracruz, where an isolated Spanish garrison was still holding out, the commander of the besieging Mexican forces, General Antonio López de Santa Anna, declared in favor of a republic and called for the overthrow of the upstart emperor.

Santa Anna's rebellion began in December 1822 and picked up important support in the first weeks of 1823. Several prominent ex-insurgents joined the movement, which became federalist as well as republican by the time the rebels issued their Plan of Casa Mata in February. This somewhat veiled call for the establishment of a federal republic (national sovereignty, it declared, resided exclusively in the Congress that Agustín had dissolved) was a bid for support from the provinces, and also from the United States, which might be induced to lend Mexico the money necessary to meet the continuing financial crisis if the latter adopted a form of government more compatible with its own; the first official U.S. envoy to Mexico, who had visited the country at the end of 1822, had strongly implied that this was the case. Emperor Agustín hoped to arrange a loan from Great Britain, but the revolutionary outbreak hardly reassured the prospective lenders. While the church stood by the embattled monarch, it was reluctant to invest more money in him. The best the hierarchy could do for its beleaguered protégé was to persuade the rebels to guarantee him safe passage out of the country and a generous pension in exile if he would abdicate—which he did in March 1823. As Agustín de Iturbide left Mexico, so did five of the six provinces of Central America; only Chiapas remained to become a state of the Mexican federal republic.

Congress was reconvened upon the abdication of Agustín I and sanctioned a new executive junta composed of three generals: Guadalupe Victoria, an ex-insurgent of obscure origins (probably a mestizo from Durango) who had established himself in Veracruz, an avowed federalist; Nicolás Bravo, also an ex-insurgent but from a prominent white family of the south of the province of Mexico (now Guerrero), a centralist; and Pedro Negrete, a Spaniard who had joined the Mexican independence movement in 1821. The last was chosen to reassure wealthy natives of the mother country that they were still welcome in Mexico; the first two represented the two forces contending for control of the post-Empire government. The centralists gained an advantage with the appointment of the able Lucas Alamán, a mining engineer from Guanajuato, to the post of foreign minister under the junta. A conservative in the mercantilist tradition, Alamán secured for Mexico a loan of ten million pesos from Great Britain, providing at least a temporary solution for the financial crisis and outmaneuvering the federalists who sought the patronage of the United States. The federalists, however, carried the day in the constituent Congress that convened in the capital in November 1823 and proceeded to write a constitution for the Mexican republic that bore a striking resemblance to that of the United States.

The first Mexican constitution, which was formally adopted in 1824, provided for a union of nineteen "sovereign" states and four territories. The states (formerly provinces) were to qualify voters and choose their own governors and state legislatures. The national Congress in Mexico City, like the one in Washington at the time, was to be composed of two houses: a Senate whose members were elected by the state legislatures and a Chamber of Deputies chosen from electoral districts. The federalism of the Mexican constitution exceeded that of the U.S. model in that the states of Mexico were given equal weight in the voting for president and vice-president of the republic: these offices were to be awarded to the candidates endorsed by a majority of the nineteen state legislatures. In liberalism, however, Mexico's Constitution of 1824 fell short of its U.S. counterpart. There was no full-scale bill of rights for individuals in the Mexican document, no guarantee of equal treatment under the law. The system of corporate privilege, the special jurisdictions—including the military and ecclesiastical fueros—remained largely intact under the 1824 constitution. Roman Catholicism was constitutionally established as the religion of Mexico, and the practice of other faiths was prohibited.

Masonic Politics and Corporatist Reaction

In the first national elections under the 1824 constitution, Guadalupe Victoria won the presidency, and Nicolás Bravo was named vice-president. There were as yet no political parties. Politics became the business of secret societies, as deals were made and conspiracies hatched behind the closed doors of Masonic lodges. The president and other prominent federalists belonged to the Mexico City York Rite Masons (*yorquinos*) whose lodge charter was brought from the United States by U.S. Minister to Mexico Joel R. Poinsett. The vice-president and his centralist colleagues congregated at the Scottish Rite Lodge (they were the *escoceses*) established in the Mexican capital under a charter from Britain, supplied by British Minister to Mexico Henry G. Ward. Neither Masonic group had much use for ex-Emperor Agustín I, who inadvisedly returned to Mexico from European exile in 1824 and was promptly arrested and executed by a federal firing squad— an event, however, that centralist Lucas Alamán would later lament in his literary efforts to confer quasi-martyrdom on the architect of Mexican independence. Alamán himself was on treacherous ground as a centralist in Victoria's federalist administration. He was forced out as foreign minister in 1825. Two years later, Vice-President Bravo and the *escoceses* attempted a military coup against the Victoria government. They failed and were driven into hiding or exile.

In the meantime, government finances had taken a turn for the worse. The proceeds from the British loan of 1824 had been expended, and, with Alamán gone from the foreign ministry and London financial markets reeling from the 1825–26 crash, there was no prospect of further aid from that source. U.S. financiers, Poinsett's good offices notwithstanding, were unwilling to follow their British colleagues into the Latin American quagmire. In 1827 Mexico, like many of its southern neighbors, defaulted on its foreign debt. The federal government's revenues did not equal its expenses: customs collections were down because of falling commerce and rising corruption, and federal income from the tobacco monopoly had virtually disappeared because of a federalist reform enacted in 1824 by which the proceeds from the sale of tobacco products were shared with the states. About the only recourse left to the federal government was to manufacture more money—out of copper, because silver was in short supply and people had come to distrust government paper. By the end of Victoria's four-year presidential term, Mexico was flooded with copper coins carrying face values far in excess of their intrinsic worth; they would be heavily discounted.

In the first seven years of Mexican independence not much had changed in the provinces—or states, as they were now designated. Local economies generally continued to function— that is, stagnate—as before. There were no appreciable investments in human capital, no improvements in education, and no arrivals of skilled immigrants, except in Texas. British investment in silver mining had sparked a mild upswing of economic activity in Zacatecas, but in most of the rest of the republic the picture remained bleak. The transportation system deteriorated as roads and bridges fell into disrepair. Neither federal nor state governments could find the funds to make the improvements and repairs that all agreed were necessary. Public employment, however, increased as new bureaucracies were created on the state level. Efficiency suffered. Under joint federal-state administration, the tobacco monopoly was being driven into bankruptcy. Members of the state legislatures were aware of the disparity between the promise and the reality of liberal federalist rule. Few wanted to return to a centralized system of government, in which their offices would be abolished, but majorities in ten of the nineteen legislatures favored a change in Mexico City. When the time came to choose a new president, they rejected the nominee of the outgoing Victoria administration, another ex-insurgent mestizo general, and voted for a creole lawyer and general who had served the Spanish cause until 1821.

Manuel Gómez Pedraza, the president-elect in 1828, a self-styled moderate (*moderado*), was unacceptable to the "pure" federalists (*puros*), who gathered at the York Rite Lodge and plotted his downfall. Outgoing President Victoria, defeated presidential candidate Vicente Guerrero, and General Antonio López de Santa Anna joined in a military movement to set aside the election results and put Guerrero into the presidency. Gómez Pedraza tried to seize the presidency in a preemptive strike before inauguration day, but after four days of bloody fighting and much looting and wanton destruction in Mexico City in December 1828, a compromise was reached: Guerrero would become president, and Gómez Pedraza would leave the country, but the vice-president-elect, General Anastasio Bustamante, a centralist, would take his office as scheduled. Bustamante, like Santa Anna, was a royalist combat veteran of the pre-1821 campaign against the insurgents. He was also a conservative creole from Michoacán, so that his presence in the government provided a small measure of comfort to the upper classes of the federal capital, who were badly shaken by the postelection events; not since the fall of the Aztec empire had Mexico City been the scene of such destructive violence.

Seated in a hostile capital, saddled with an unreliable vice-president, his treasury empty, President Guerrero faced dim prospects. While most of the state legislatures that had backed his opponent were persuaded by military force to switch their votes and ratify his election, new troubles appeared on the horizon. In Texas, a district of Coahuila State, uncontrolled Anglo-American immigration was reaching alarming proportions, and in Cuba a Spanish army was being assembled for the invasion and reconquest of Mexico. To make Texas less attractive to slaveowning migrants from the southern United States, Guerrero pushed through Congress and signed, in September 1829, a law abolishing slavery throughout the Mexican republic. To counter the Spanish threat—to deprive the anticipated invaders of local collaborators—Guerrero ordered the expulsion from Mexico of virtually all native Spaniards. The exodus began early in 1829, as thousands of Mexico's best educated and most skilled residents departed through Veracruz, withdrawing from the republic their considerable human capital and whatever financial and tangible assets they managed to take with them.

The invasion was expected at Veracruz, where Spanish holdouts in the fort of San Juan de Ulloa had surrendered to the Mexicans only four years before. But the Spanish landing was four hundred kilometers to the north, at the small port town of Tampico, in July 1829. Mexican forces under General Santa Anna rushed to Tampico, where they pushed the invaders back to their beachhead, put them under siege, and eventually accepted their surrender in October.

With the Spanish threat removed, President Guerrero still re-fused to relinquish the emergency wartime powers Congress had conceded to him. In December 1829, accordingly, Vice-President Bustamante rose up in the name of constitutional govern-ment and took power in Mexico City in a bloodless military coup. Guerrero bowed to reality, gave up the presidency, and retired in January 1830 to his hacienda in the "hot country" south of the capital. Victoria and Santa Anna also accepted the situa-tion: the federalist partners of 1828 were willing in 1830 to let the centralists try their hand at solving Mexico's intractable prob-lems.

Bustamante, a competent and respected general of strong character, was eager to meet the challenge—with the assistance of Lucas Alamán, his minister of foreign and internal affairs. The new administration moved to shore up public finances by selling the deficit-ridden tobacco monopoly to a group of wealthy Mexi-can merchants. Ending direct government administration of the monopoly stopped a drain on the treasury, which at the same time received an infusion of cash from the sale, but it also eliminated a substantial number of public jobs and created a class of disgruntled ex-bureaucrats who would pose problems for the regime in the future. Other savings were made by reducing the size of the army, at the cost of further swelling the ranks of the unemployed and discontented. The stern measures of the Bustamante-Alamán administration impressed British bankers and investors, who agreed to a renegotiation of the government's defaulted debt and extended new credit to public and private borrowers in Mexico. Alamán personally invested in British min-ing ventures in Mexico, and he committed public funds to the government development bank that he organized in 1830, the Banco de Avío, which financed the subsequent industrialization of textile production in Puebla.

Alamán was a developmentalist, but he was no liberal. He despised the masses, feared economic and political freedom, and promoted development through government partnership with selected private interests—through the preservation, rationaliza-tion, and refinement of the colonial corporate state. National resources were transferred through the Banco de Avío to favored textile producers of Puebla to enable them to buy foreign machinery and switch from the handicraft to the industrial mode of production. Tariffs were raised to protect the textile industry from foreign competition. The coercive power of the state was leased to the new owners of the tobacco monopoly to enable them to streamline their operations and maximize profits in the absence of foreign or domestic competition. Consumers continued to pay inflated prices for inferior goods, while producers of raw materials—cotton and tobacco— were squeezed by the manufacturing monopsony, notwithstanding their own corporate privileges as exclusive suppliers.

The revitalization of the corporatist system required the restoration of strong central authority in Mexico. Alamán and Bustamante did not formally abolish federalism, but they used the considerable force available to them—thanks to the president's high standing in the military—to impose their will on the states: federalist governors were deposed, and legislatures were purged. In Mexico City federalist congressmen received similar treatment, public dissent was suppressed, puro newspapers were closed down, and U.S. Minister Poinsett was declared persona non grata and ordered out of the country. The Roman Catholic hierarchy was courted, Protestantism from the north was identified as the principal threat to the nation, and the Texas border with the United States was ordered closed to further immigration and commerce.

Ex-President Guerrero prematurely took up arms against the repressive government at the end of 1830. His forces were defeated, and he sought refuge on a foreign ship in Acapulco. Betrayed by the ship's captain, an Italian, for fifty thousand pesos, he was delivered into the hands of his enemies. Guerrero was executed by a firing squad, presumably on the orders of Alamán in January 1831. The fallen hero's many friends, admirers, and comrades from the war for independence vowed vengeance; within a year they were joined in overt opposition to the central government by displaced bureaucrats and other interest groups injured by the policies of the Bustamante-Alamán regime, including textile importers and tobacco growers in Veracruz. In that state General Santa Anna pronounced against the government early in 1832. He defeated the forces sent against him and, with rebellion spreading throughout the country, marched on Mexico

City, seized the government, sent Bustamante and Alamán into exile, and installed the moderate Gómez Pedraza in the presidency to which he had been elected four years earlier. Gómez Pedraza served for only three months; during that time elections were held, and the state legislatures chose Santa Anna to be president for the 1833–37 term.

The Era of Santa Anna

The career of Antonio López de Santa Anna represents one of the more conspicuous stumbling blocks in the way of those who would explain nineteenth-century Latin America's political divisions as the manifestation of underlying divisions between socioeconomic groups whose views and interests were supposedly best represented by either liberal or conservative parties. Alternately liberal and conservative in affiliation, this one Mexican leader did not change social class or economic sector every time he changed parties, so that in light of his performance it is easier to disprove than to prove those interpretations that automatically associate liberalism with commercial interest and conservatism with landholding (or some other contrasting pair of occupational categories). Neither, of course, did his socioeconomic interests remain wholly static over time. He instead exemplifies the tendency of talented individuals to acquire both new opinions and new interests, and to discard old ones, as they move up or down the rungs of power.

The son of a minor bureaucrat, Santa Anna was born in Jalapa, Veracruz, in 1794. He embarked on an army career at age sixteen, when he became a cadet at the Spanish military academy in Mexico City. As a Spanish colonial officer, he distinguished himself in combat against Mexican insurgents. In 1821 he joined Agustín de Iturbide in the independence movement. In 1822 Santa Anna launched the republican revolt that destroyed Iturbide's empire. Santa Anna carried out various military assignments for the Mexican republic and simultaneously accumulated extensive landholdings near his birthplace in Veracruz; tens of thousands of cattle bearing the ALSA brand roamed his Manga de Clavo hacienda, which eventually would cover nearly half a

million acres. Santa Anna helped suppress Bravo's escocés revolt
in 1827, and the next year he joined the military movement that
denied the presidency to the moderado Gómez Pedraza and
gave it to the puro Guerrero. In 1829 Santa Anna defeated the
Spanish invaders at Tampico. After Bustamante's 1829 coup,
Santa Anna bided his time, tending to his political and military
power base in Veracruz. In 1832 he pronounced against Bustamante, overthrew the centralist regime, and restored federalism
to power in Mexico. In this movement and in all the previous
ones in which he had played a leading role, Santa Anna, as ex-
U.S. Minister Poinsett noted, had sided with "liberty."

Santa Anna's victory in 1832 opened the door to liberal reform
in Mexico. Inaugurated as president on April 1, 1833, Santa Anna
soon tired of the office and retired to his hacienda in Veracruz,
leaving the national government in the hands of his most fervent
supporters, the federalist puros. Under the oppression of Bustamante's proclerical dictatorship, they had strengthened their
commitment to liberalism. They now were prepared to mount an
assault on the privileges of the Roman Catholic church, the
central focus, they believed, of a corporatist spirit (espíritu de
cuerpo) that they swore to eradicate. The attack was led by Vice-
President Valentín Gómez Farías, a physician from Zacatecas,
who was acting president during much of 1833 and 1834 in the
absence of Santa Anna. Assisting Gómez Farías were Lorenzo de
Zavala, a mestizo journalist from Yucatán, and José María Luis
Mora, a liberal publicist and professor from Guanajuato. Zavala
served the liberal regime as governor of the state of Mexico;
Mora was federal minister of education. Zavala had played a key
role in the Guerrero administration and had supported the expulsion of the Spaniards from Mexico in 1829. The more reflective
Mora had deplored that action on both philosophical and practical grounds. In the 1830s both Mora and Zavala favored the
promotion of European immigration to Mexico.

Congress, controlled by the puros in 1833, gave the new administration most of the legislation it asked for. Education was
made the responsibility of the state, and Mora closed down the
national university in Mexico City because it was run by clerics.
Franciscan missions on the frontier were secularized, and their
property was appropriated by the federal government. Legisla-

tion was enacted to disentail some other church property, too, and to allow clergy—including monks and nuns—to renounce their vows and abandon the religious life. The payment of tithes was made voluntary. The special interests of the church, however, were not the only targets of the puro reformers. Under the Gómez Farías administration, manufacturers lost tariff protection, the national tobacco monopoly was suppressed, and the size of the federal army was reduced. A law was passed putting military personnel under the jurisdiction of civilian courts. By 1834 Congress was considering proposals to abolish the federal army and replace it by a system of civilian militias supported by the states.

Strong voices were raised against the Gómez Farías administration, and they were heard by President Santa Anna on his hacienda in Veracruz. The tobacco farmers of the president's state, who had clamored for suppression of the national tobacco monopoly two years earlier, found themselves worse off under free trade: Mexican consumers preferred imports from Cuba or the United States, the liquidation of the huge stocks of the former monopoly drove down prices, and in some states locally produced tobacco entered the market and undersold the Veracruz product. Similar complaints were heard from cotton producers and textile manufacturers in nearby Puebla. Investors in monopolistic enterprises, generals, bishops, and their myriad retainers appealed to the president for the restoration of "religión y fueros." In June 1834 Santa Anna answered the call, marched to Mexico City, and reassumed the presidency. In short order he expelled Gómez Farías and his principal collaborators from the country, purged Congress of its puro majority, and secured the repeal of most of the liberal legislation. Compulsory tithes, however, were not reinstated; Santa Anna and his fellow hacendados, whatever their philosophical orientation, generally were happy to see that tax wiped off the books.

In 1835 Santa Anna suspended the federalist Constitution of 1824, announced that state governors henceforth served at the pleasure of the president, and instructed Congress to devise a new, centralist constitution for the Republic of Mexico. The new order was not acceptable to Yucatán, Zavala's state, where sisal producers had thrived under the federalist regime; nor to Gómez

Farías's state of Zacatecas, relatively prosperous from revived silver mining; nor to the part of Coahuila known as Texas, which had aspired to statehood under the 1824 constitution. These more productive areas of the Mexican republic feared the confiscation of their assets by the national capital in a centralized system. They declared themselves in revolt against Santa Anna's unconstitutional regime.

Secession and Foreign Wars

Santa Anna left the government in Mexico City in the care of a conservative-centralist vice-president in 1835 and marched north with his troops to suppress the federalist revolts in Zacatecas and Texas. The Zacatecan uprising was put down with great brutality, after which the centralist army moved into Texas, at the beginning of 1836. While Santa Anna was besieging the federalist garrison at San Antonio, a group of Texans and outsiders met on the banks of the Brazos River and declared the independence of the Republic of Texas. Among the outsiders was Zavala, who accepted the post of vice-president of Texas. Zavala had become convinced that Yucatán, Texas, and the northern Mexican states would be forever disadvantaged in any union with conservative central Mexico; these areas should rule themselves as independent republics or, if necessary, join the United States. Zavala died six months after he signed the Texas Declaration of Independence and did not live to see the incorporation of Texas and much of northern Mexico into the United States. But his native state of Yucatán maintained its independence from Mexico City for more than a decade and returned to the Mexican union only after the United States rejected its petition for annexation.

The man who was supposed to save Mexico from the dismemberment envisioned by Zavala was Santa Anna. At first, Santa Anna seemed equal to the task: he overran the Texan stronghold (the Alamo) at San Antonio, drove from there to the Gulf of Mexico, and marched rapidly along the coast toward the U.S. border—storming rebel positions, taking hundreds of prisoners, shooting most of them, leaving terror in his wake, and spreading panic before him. But then, in April 1836, the Texans surprised

Santa Anna at San Jacinto, routed his army, and took him prisoner. To save his life, the defeated general, as president of Mexico, signed a treaty recognizing the independence of Texas. Santa Anna was escorted from Texas to Washington, D.C., where he reaffirmed his recognition of Texan independence. But on his return to Veracruz in 1837, Santa Anna disavowed his treaty with Texas, on the reasonable grounds that it was made under duress, and promised to reconquer the area for Mexico.

By this time Anastasio Bustamante was again president of Mexico, having been elected under the centralist Constitution of 1836, adopted during Santa Anna's absence. The states of the former federal union were redesignated as departments and were to be presided over by governors appointed by the president of the republic. The centralization, however, was largely illusory: President Bustamante had less real power in 1837 than he had had in 1830. Seven years of reform and counterreform, army coups and countercoups, provincial revolts, secession, and disastrous military campaigns had left the entire nation weaker, so that in fact no one had much power. For this very reason, on the other hand, Bustamante's personal position as president was somewhat more secure in 1837 than it had been in 1830. Santa Anna was in disgrace. Other generals and provincial potentates were so concerned with simply trying to maintain their own status as the economy eroded everywhere that they paid little attention to proposals that they get together and seize the central government. The resources of that government were so meager as to make such an effort bootless.

The government in Mexico City could decree higher import tariffs, but it was the bureaucrats on the spot in Veracruz who collected the duties, received bribes from smugglers, paid off local extortionists, and decided what proportion of the revenue would be remitted as tribute to the capital. With its income from customs collections falling, the Bustamante government in 1837 recreated the national tobacco monopoly. But the proceeds the government received from the sale of exclusive privileges to grow and process tobacco were more than offset by the expenses it incurred in trying to carry out its obligations to the monopolists; the weak state lacked the power to drive illegal producers and distributors out of the tobacco business.

The Banco de Avío, brainchild of Lucas Alamán, was on its way to insolvency by 1837, and the Bustamante government lacked the resources to keep it afloat. Alamán himself, because of the various interests he had offended during the 1830-32 Bustamante administration, was denied participation in the new centralist government. As an outsider, Alamán complained about the leadership of the conservative restoration, which he regarded as hopelessly ineffectual, though it did achieve two objectives he had long sought: diplomatic recognition of Mexico by Spain and by the pope in Rome. Elsewhere on the diplomatic front the situation was grim. The United States recognized the independence of Texas, and France demanded reparations from the Mexican government for losses French citizens had suffered in Mexico because of the national government's inability to maintain law and order.

The bill France presented to Mexico included charges for pastries stolen from a French bakery in Mexico City. The conflict that erupted in 1838 when French forces occupied Veracruz to collect the debt became known as the Pastry War. Bustamante belatedly agreed to pay the bill, six hundred thousand dollars, but the French then demanded an additional payment of two hundred thousand to cover their occupation costs. The added humiliation was too much for the Mexican government to bear, and when Santa Anna emerged from retirement to offer his services in expelling the invaders, the offer was accepted. Santa Anna attacked the French in Veracruz in December 1838. The Mexican general lost his left leg in a hard-fought engagement in which his troops drove the invaders back to their ships. France then agreed to accept six hundred thousand dollars as payment in full and withdrew its warships from Veracruz, and Santa Anna regained his reputation as hero of the Mexican republic.

Santa Anna stood with Bustamante when, in 1840, Dr. Gómez Farías returned from exile and attempted a federalist coup in Mexico City. After eleven days of destructive combat in the capital, an agreement was reached that left Bustamante in the presidency and allowed Gómez Farías to leave the country: nothing was changed. The social and economic fabric of the country was in tatters and threatening to unravel completely. The Mexican republic, whether centralist or federalist, was inherently unstable, a prominent conservative observed to Lucas Alamán in a letter published in the Mexico City press in 1840; the country could be saved only through the legitimation of power, by the restoration of monarchy. Alamán clearly agreed, but the time had not come for him to say so publicly. Indeed, his correspondent was driven into hiding as Bustamante, Santa Anna, and other eminent Mexicans reaffirmed their devotion to republican principles.

In 1841 General Manuel Paredes, restless commander of the Guadalajara garrison, persuaded Santa Anna to join him in overthrowing Bustamante. There was considerable maneuvering and some fighting before the rebels—whose political orientation was unclear—captured Mexico City and drove Bustamante into exile. After Santa Anna, Paredes, their troops, and their collaborators had been paid off, neither general was eager to hold the reins of the bankrupt government. Paredes returned to the barracks and Santa Anna to his hacienda, while moderates and conservatives in Mexico City tried to form a viable government. A constituent assembly in 1843 adopted a new constitution that assigned virtually unlimited power to the president; the document was tailormade for Santa Anna, who was lured away from his hacienda to govern the republic. For nine months Santa Anna ruled despotically and extravagantly in Mexico City. He survived that long because of his influence in Veracruz, which enabled him to increase customs remittances to the central government. Then, in 1844, he was overthrown by an uprising of moderates and was banished to Cuba.

General José Joaquín Herrera, who led the 1844 revolt against Santa Anna, was, like the president he overthrew, a professional army officer and a native of Jalapa, Veracruz. He was a moderate federalist, a moderado of the stripe of Gómez Pedraza. In 1845 Congress elected Herrera president under the 1843 constitution. The regeneration of Mexico, Herrera believed, required the promotion of responsible government on the state level and the avoidance of the divisive anticlericalism propounded by the puro federalists. Herrera's regenerative program, however, was disrupted by trouble with the United States.

Mexico officially protested when the United States annexed Texas early in 1845, although President Herrera was willing to negotiate with the United States on the Texas question. Before Mexico could recognize U.S. possession of Texas, however, that state's border with Mexico would have to be established. The former Republic of Texas had claimed but had not occupied all of the formerly Mexican territory east of the Rio Grande, from the Gulf of Mexico to Santa Fe. The administration of U.S. President James K. Polk insisted on the Texas claim and went on to demand that Mexico sell California, and the United States proceeded to bait Mexico into war. U.S. troops were ordered into the disputed territory between the Rio Nueces and the Rio Grande, and, when Herrera failed to react forcefully to the aggression, General Manuel Paredes deposed him and seized power in Mexico City in January 1846, vowing to defend the country against the Yankee invaders. The war began in April with a clash between U.S. and Mexican troops east of the Rio Grande.

U.S. troops crossed the Rio Grande from south Texas and drove on Monterrey, while other Yankee forces seized California. Paredes, unable to deliver on his promise to stop the invaders, was overthrown by a popular uprising in Mexico City in July 1846 led by Gómez Farías. His faction, the puros, pledged to mobilize national resistance to the invasion; they restored the 1824 constitution, requisitioned church property for the war effort, and summoned General Santa Anna home from Cuba to take command of the Mexican army. Santa Anna was eager to save his country, but he faced the likelihood of being captured by the U.S. Navy, which was blockading Mexico's ports, if he attempted to sail home from Cuba. He solved that problem by making a deal with the United States through its consulate in Havana: in return for a monetary consideration and safe passage through the blockade, Santa Anna agreed to make peace on U.S. terms once he was in charge of the Mexican army and government.

Santa Anna double-crossed the United States. He landed at Veracruz at the end of 1846 and passed quickly to Mexico City, where he was warmly received by Gómez Farías; the general agreed to serve as president and commander-in-chief of the army in the field, while the puro physician accepted the vice-presidency and the responsibility for running the government. Santa Anna then marched north to Coahuila and, in February 1847, fought a drawn battle with General Zachary Taylor at Buena Vista, where the Mexicans captured two U.S. battle flags. Santa Anna returned immediately to Mexico City with the war souvenirs and claimed a great victory. He proceeded to depose Vice-President Gómez Farías, place a proclerical conservative in charge of the government, and take personal command of the Mexican troops that were resisting a new invasion via Veracruz. Church officials, who greatly resented Gómez Farías's confiscations, contributed somewhat more willingly to Santa Anna's war chest.

U.S. forces under General Winfield Scott seized Veracruz in March 1847 and during the next six months fought their way to the outskirts of Mexico City. Mexican resistance was determined but futile. The cadets of the Mexican Military Academy made a gallant stand at Chapultepec, but their position was overrun in September 1847. With the fall of Chapultepec, Mexico City lay at the mercy of the invaders. Santa Anna resigned the presidency and fled into exile as the Yankee army occupied the Mexican capital.

A new Mexican government was formed north of the capital under the protection of the moderado General Herrera. Peace negotiations got underway at the end of 1847 and resulted in a treaty signed at Guadalupe, Hidalgo, in February 1848. Texas, with its border at the Rio Grande, was recognized as U.S. territory, while California, New Mexico, and the vast unsettled region between those two provinces were ceded to the United States in return for a fifteen-million-dollar payment. The Treaty of Guadalupe Hidalgo was promptly ratified by the U.S. Senate, and occupation forces were withdrawn from what was left of Mexico in July 1848. Earlier that year the United States had rejected a petition from the autonomous state of Yucatán for U.S. annexation of that nominally Mexican territory.

The peninsula state of Yucatán, separated from the rest of Mexico by practically impenetrable jungles and the waters of the Gulf of Mexico, had maintained its independence from the governments in Mexico City since 1835. When Mexico went to war with the United States, Yucatán declared its neutrality; the principal market for the peninsula's sisal fiber was New Orleans, and Yucatecan producers and exporters were determined to continue this profitable commerce despite the war. But the main threat to the Yucatecan export economy, as it turned out, was not external but came from the peninsula's indigenous Maya Indian masses. Export agriculturalists had been steadily encroaching on Indian lands since the fall of the Spanish colonial regime in 1821; this fed Mayan resentment of the peninsula's Spanish-speaking whites and mestizos and set the stage for the outbreak in 1847 of Yucatán's Caste War. Mayan insurgents seized control of most of the countryside, laid waste the sisal plantations, and drove the Spanish-speaking population into a few fortified towns. The Yucatecan authorities appealed for U.S. troops to put down the rebellion and asked to be annexed by the United States. When Washington turned down their requests, the beleaguered Yucatecans had little choice but to appeal to Mexico City. General Herrera, now president of Mexico and strengthened by the U.S. payment of fifteen million dollars, welcomed Yucatán back into the federal union and dispatched troops to the peninsula. State and federal forces eventually succeeded in liberating the sisal planting area and confining the Mayan rebels to the scrub country of eastern Yucatán.

Rise of the Conservative Party:
The Monarchist Alternative

The recovery of Yucatán was a major achievement of the moderate President Herrera. Elected for a two-year term in 1848, he turned over the presidency to his constitutionally elected successor (the first time that had happened in Mexican history) in 1850. Herrera served out his term despite the hostility of puros who accused him of truckling to the church and of conservatives who denounced him for selling out to the United States. When a military revolt headed by General Paredes failed to oust Herrera in 1848, the president's conservative opponents organized a formal political party—Mexico's first—to compete more effectively in the electoral process. Candidates of the new Conservative party swept the 1849 elections in Mexico City, but moderate federalists retained control of most state legislatures and chose moderado General Mariano Arista to serve as president for the 1850-54 term.

President Arista would not complete his term. The Conservative party, dominated intellectually by Lucas Alamán, worked diligently to bring about the president's downfall, by whatever means available, to prepare the way for the restoration of legitimate monarchy in Mexico. Alamán's brilliant *Historia de Méjico*, five volumes published between 1849 and 1852, shaped the Conservative party's perception of past and present: the Mexican republic had demonstrated that it was incapable of maintaining the standards of security and well-being that had been guaranteed by the Spanish colonial regime, the corporate order was dissolving into anarchy, and universal poverty loomed on the horizon. There had been no caste wars when Hapsburg or Bourbon kings ruled Mexico, Alamán's readers might reflect; indeed, for more than two and a half centuries after the Spanish conquest, Mexico had not needed an army for internal security. Habits of obedience could be restored, the Conservatives believed, by the legitimization of state power—not through constitutions and elections but through the consecration of a genuine prince of royal blood as sovereign of Mexico.

Alamán and the Conservative party were willing to take advantage of any opportunity to advance their monarchist project. When President Arista tried to cut the military budget and reduce the size of the army, Conservatives encouraged disgruntled officers to revolt against him. Arista was overthrown in a military coup early in 1853; the officers who deposed him received assurances of more generous appropriations for the army from the Conservatives, to whom they entrusted the government. Alamán then sought out the strongest authority figure available for the Mexican presidency, one who could hold on to power in Mexico while Conservative envoys searched Europe for a prince willing to mount a Mexican throne. In Colombia exiled General Santa Anna agreed to return to Mexico and accept the position of stand-in for a future monarch.

Santa Anna was sworn in as president for the fifth time in April 1853. The death of Alamán two months later removed a restraining hand, and Santa Anna's rule degenerated into tawdry despotism. The Conservatives were stuck with Santa Anna and had no choice but to rally around him when moderados and puros rose in arms against the dictatorship in 1854. The commitment of highly motivated Conservatives to Santa Anna ensured that he would not be easily ousted. Also, the dictator could draw on ten million dollars he received from the United States in 1854 for the sale of the Mesilla Valley—or the Gadsden Purchase, a tract on Mexico's northern frontier through which the United States planned to build a transcontinental railroad.

The windfall from the north helped Santa Anna resist the revolution for more than a year. Finally, in August 1855, he slipped out of Veracruz for exile in Colombia, leaving his Conservative allies in Mexico City to face the forces that were closing in on the capital from several directions. Three months later the Conservatives surrendered the national government to a coalition of moderados and puros, who then launched the country on a course of thoroughgoing liberal reform that is known in Mexican history as La Reforma. The era of Santa Anna ended with his departure for exile in 1855; two decades later the ex-dictator, penniless and senile, would be permitted to return to Mexico to die.

5

Andean South America to Midcentury: Consolidation of Independence

The nations of Andean South America, from Venezuela in the north to Chile (which shared the Andes mountains as a frontier with Argentina) in the south, were a heterogeneous grouping whose component parts after independence had many common goals and common problems but pursued those goals and sought to overcome those problems in several different ways. The differences reflected, among other things, different experiences in the war of independence itself, a variety of social and cultural patterns, and the realities of postwar production and trade. Except for Chile, none of the countries could be accounted a model of successful nation building, but neither did any have quite the string of frustrations that afflicted Mexico. And in the immediate aftermath of independence, the united republic formed by Simón Bolívar out of the Spanish viceroyalty of New Granada— Gran Colombia, as it has come to be known, corresponding to the modern Venezuela, Colombia, Panama, and Ecuador—was a natural leader of Spanish America, if only because of the prestige of Bolívar himself. (In its time it was simply called the Republic of Colombia. The "Gran" was added by later historians to distinguish it from the smaller Colombia of today.)

The Abortive Colombian Union

The personal influence of Bolívar had been one reason for the creation of Gran Colombia. On the broader Spanish American scene, he was content to press for a loose network of alliances among the former Spanish colonies, but for that part of Spanish America where he was born and where he first won his reputation as Liberator, he wanted a tighter unity as a single nation-state. Indeed, as leader of an army composed indiscriminately of Venezuelans like himself and patriots from New Granada to the west, he had moved back and forth at will across the boundary of the two former colonies until he defeated the royalists in both. Military unity already existed, and political unity seemed a natural corollary. Moreover, when the union was first proclaimed in 1819 in the aftermath of the decisive victory of Boyacá, and even when a supposedly permanent government was set up by a constituent congress meeting in 1821 at Cúcuta on the Venezuelan–New Granada border, the war with Spain was not yet wholly finished, so that political unification had apparent military advantages in ensuring a coordinated war effort. Not only were there parts of Gran Colombia itself still to be cleared of royalist troops, but Spanish armies in Peru and the Spanish West Indies still posed a potential threat. And creation of the larger nation did attract favorable attention abroad, as Bolívar had assumed it would. Gran Colombia was among the first batch of Latin American nations to receive diplomatic recognition from both the United States in 1822 and Great Britain in 1825. Though not much came of it, there was further evidence of Gran Colombia's international prominence in the Panama Congress of 1826, the first inter-American gathering of states and Bolívar's particular brainchild, held on what was then Colombian soil.

The formal constitution that Gran Colombia adopted in 1821 provided, at least on paper, a highly centralized regime with no trace of federalism, which Bolívar bitterly opposed. In practice, political centralization was never wholly effective, as the central government located in Bogotá had neither the human nor the material resources to impose its will evenly through such a vast territory. Bolívar was naturally elected first president—or, to be more precise, converted his status from that of revolutionary

supreme chief and acting president to constitutional chief executive—but he then went off to finish the war with Spain, ultimately fighting his way down to Peru and Bolivia. Real control of
government was meanwhile left in the hands of the vice-president, Francisco de Paula Santander, whose position assumed
unusual importance.

Himself a native of New Granada, Santander had left his law
studies after the start of the independence movement to go to
war, and he seems to have become a reasonably competent
military officer, but he showed greatest ability as administrator
and organizer of newly liberated territories. He complemented
Bolívar perfectly both in talents and in regional origin, and somewhat the same can be said regarding the basic political orientation of each man. Bolívar, on his part, is best classified as a
moderate conservative, not so much because of any abstract
political convictions—he had only contempt for doctrinaire theorists—as because his innate realism made him skeptical of the
practical possibility of rapidly transforming Spanish American
society. Santander's outlook was more typically liberal, in that he
wanted to see a wide range of political, economic, religious, and
other changes, and in order to attain these he was more willing to
experiment with new laws and institutions. But Santander, whose
personal background was that of provincial landed gentry, was a
rather pragmatic liberal. The difference between the two was
only of degree.

Actually, a first installment of liberal reform was enacted in
1821 by the constituent congress itself. The first measure of any
sort that it issued was a free-birth law for the gradual elimination
of slavery; no one in future could be born a slave, though existing
slaves were out of luck except insofar as the state might purchase
the freedom of a select few with the proceeds of special taxes
earmarked for that purpose, and even the free offspring of slave
mothers were ordered to work for their mothers' masters until
age eighteen to repay the cost of their early upbringing. For the
Indians, there was abolition of the colonial Indian tribute and
affirmation of their full equality with other citizens, plus a law
calling for division of communally owned village lands into private parcels. The latter was supposedly in the Indians' interest so
that they could use their lands most efficiently, but at the same

time it would make them more vulnerable to outside land grabbers. It was not something the Indians themselves had asked for, and in the short run not much was done about carrying it out; it simply remained on the statute books as a sign of what non-Indians thought was good for them.

Also important were certain measures taken with respect to the church. The Inquisition was abolished for good, although this did not amount to establishment of full religious toleration; it meant only that dissenters would henceforth be dealt with by other civil or ecclesiastical tribunals. More controversial was a law suppressing the smaller male convents (those with fewer than eight friars) and taking over their property, which was to be used for the support of public secondary education. This was a good bit more serious than abolishing the Inquisition—which had few defenders—because it was a precedent for possible further confiscations of church assets and because the friars did have supporters.

As acting executive in Bolívar's absence, Vice-President Santander was the person initially charged with both implementing the reforms of the constituent congress and establishing the new government itself on a sound footing. The task was in many respects beyond the capability of any human, but Santander nevertheless turned in a quite creditable performance. He was a hard worker with an eye for detail; he even liked to correct the spelling and literary style of laws passed by Congress, as nothing was too small for his personal attention. But he was aware of his responsibilities as a constitutional ruler. He could be ill-tempered and self-righteous, and he had the custom of writing critical articles against his opponents that he published behind a thin veneer of anonymity in the progovernment press. But at least he did not lock them up. He was likewise respectful of the rights of Congress. Santander tried to get specific legislative authorization for every important measure, even if it meant wasting precious time while Congress debated. This last trait rather annoyed Bolívar, who did not share Santander's liking for legal formalities and found himself more than once waiting impatiently at the head of his armies for reinforcements while Santander was twisting arms in Bogotá to get the legislators' approval before filling

Bolívar's requests for men and supplies. But Congress usually came through in the end.

Even economic conditions seemed superficially promising at first. With an economy overwhelmingly agricultural, recovery from the ravages of war was mainly dependent on time and weather. In Venezuela, which had suffered most, the cacao plantation belt around Caracas never did return to prewar levels of production, but this was offset by the growing importance of coffee, which did not take as long after planting to yield a crop and for which world market conditions were favorable. In western New Granada, Gran Colombia further possessed what had been the Spanish empire's leading center of gold production, an industry that suffered nothing like the damage done to Mexican silver mines in the war of independence. Gold extraction was mostly alluvial, with little equipment to be destroyed, and the main impact of the struggle was the taking of slaves for military service; though production was down somewhat, for this and other reasons, the problem was far from critical.

Gran Colombia also succeeded in raising a thirty-million-dollar loan in London in 1824, which went partly for the consolidation of earlier obligations incurred during the independence struggle but was still a sign of the confidence that Bolívar's republic enjoyed in the financial marketplace. In addition, private foreign entrepreneurs were joining in numerous ventures to open up mines, bring in European settlers, and carry out such useful projects as the introduction of steamboats on the Magdalena River, which was the main access route to central New Granada. Most of these ventures ended in failure, including the first steamboats, which were ill adapted to the river and tended to get stuck on sandbars—just as was also happening in other Latin American countries, where a first flush of optimism concerning prospects for development caused foreign speculators to overlook the many practical obstacles. Investment schemes, however, were one relatively minor aspect of the general opening up of the region to foreign economic contacts. Trade was also facilitated, to the annoyance of domestic artisans and manufacturers, especially in highland Ecuador, a center of hand-loomed production of woolen textiles that felt more and more pressed by foreign competition. And in many cases import-export trade came to be handled by merchants from western Europe and the United States, who settled in the main commercial centers and in effect took over the role of Spanish-born merchants displaced by revolution. From the standpoint of local traders, this was no unmixed blessing, but the prevalent attitude among Gran Colombian leaders continued to be one of welcome to both capital and skills from overseas.

Neither the positive nor the negative effects of foreign trade and investment had much meaning, however, for the great majority of the population that was engaged in little more than subsistence agriculture and associated domestic chores. For most people, furthermore, economic stagnation was compounded by sheer physical isolation in a huge and mountainous country so deficient in transportation infrastructure that there were places where horses and mules could not pass and travelers went by means of chairs strapped to the backs of human carriers. It soon became apparent that the confidence of foreign investors was somewhat misplaced. The Gran Colombian economy could not come close to generating the additional government revenue needed to maintain service on the foreign debt, even though it amounted to less than one dollar per inhabitant per year, and after just two years the 1824 loan was in default. And funds were not available to carry out all the ambitious programs of internal improvement (from educational expansion to agricultural credit) that had been launched in the first euphoria of nation building and in the hope that borrowed English money would help directly or indirectly to pay the bills. The loan itself was far from enough, particularly as much of it went to cover military requirements. Even so, there were wild insinuations that Santander and his collaborators had somehow siphoned off the proceeds.

Another cloud of controversy arose in the field of education, where Santander did in fact make some visible progress, above all at secondary and university levels. What annoyed the more devout citizens was both that the progress was being financed in considerable part at church expense (i.e., with the assets of suppressed convents) and that the schools were being used, it seemed, to spread all manner of unorthodox ideas among the young. Particularly obnoxious to them was the introduction of legal texts by the English philosopher of utilitarianism, Jeremy Bentham, who happened to be a great favorite of Santander. As the name of his doctrine suggests, Bentham made utility the central criterion by which to judge laws and institutions, and this approach had great appeal to Latin American liberals of the period as it seemed to offer a systematic way of analyzing—and revamping—their colonial institutional heritage. But the Benthamite philosophy was anathema to the religiously orthodox because of its materialistic point of departure. One priest predicted that God would send fire and earthquake to punish Colombia for having its young read Bentham, and when a serious earthquake did hit Bogotá in 1826 some observers were not at all surprised.

Potentially even more disruptive were certain questions that pitted not liberal innovators against proclerical conservatives but Venezuelans against New Granadans against Ecuadorans. Above all, there was disaffection in Venezuela, which complained ceaselessly, though without much real justification, of neglect and discrimination at the hands of the central authorities. In the cabinet of Santander half the positions were regularly held by Venezuelans, and if the latter were less prominent in other offices it was in part because so many Venezuelans did not want jobs in the national capital even when offered. In addition, Venezuelans made up for the lack of civil posts by virtually monopolizing the top army commands; because Venezuela was where the war of independence had raged hardest and most continuously, Venezuelan officers had an accumulated backlog of military seniority that guaranteed them the upper hand in the military for years to come.

The one wholly valid complaint made by Venezuelans had nothing to do with government policies but only with the basic geography of the country. Because of the obstacles of distance and terrain, it took the mails about a month to get from Caracas to Bogotá, and ordinary travelers took longer. This caused inconvenience for individual Venezuelans who had business with the central government. It was also an obvious reason why Venezuelans did not want jobs in Bogotá—getting there was just too difficult—or failed to take the seats to which they had been duly elected in the Gran Colombian Congress and then complained that Venezuela was underrepresented in the legislative branch. Ultimately, though, the suspicion of Venezuela toward anything that smacked of Bogotá did not rest chiefly on concrete grievances, real or imagined. The basic trouble was a feeling that any true subordination to a government in Bogotá was a humiliating step downward; and so it was, in the sense that the colonial captaincy-general of Venezuela had not been thus subject to the viceroy of New Granada based in Bogotá but had normally taken orders directly from Madrid. The affront might still have been tolerated if union had brought practical benefits, but Venezuelans could not see any, particularly after the fighting for independence drew to a close.

The one place where popular disaffection was justified by immediate, concrete grievances was Ecuador, the smallest and weakest of the three main sections, which really was discriminated against. There was never a single Ecuadoran cabinet minister or even an Ecuadoran-born general, and top civil and military officials in Ecuador tended to be carpetbaggers from other parts of Gran Colombia. Ecuador also had a grievance over tariff policy. The textile manufacturers of Quito and other highland cities were demanding protection against European imports, but the Santander administration and Congress at Bogotá, in line with the conventional liberal principle that tariff protectionism was an arbitrary government interference with economic laws, turned a deaf ear. (Yet exceptions to that same principle were sometimes made in favor of agricultural interests of Venezuela and New Granada.)

The unraveling of Gran Colombia began, however, in Venezuela, where the highest military commander on the spot, José Antonio Páez, in April 1826 announced his open defiance of Bogotá. Though lacking both social graces and formal education, Páez—the self-made chieftain of the *llaneros*, or cowboys of the Orinoco plains—had in fact been behaving quite well, until suddenly he was called to Bogotá to face charges before Congress that he had sent out soldiers to round up peaceful citizens for militia service at bayonet point, authorizing them to raid houses and even shoot if need be. The charges appear to have been exaggerated, but this was the kind of thing the military had in fact been doing all too often, so it was easy to believe the worst.

Congress unwisely decided to force the issue just then, and force it with Páez, in a sense to see who was boss, the generals or the civil authorities. Congress soon found out. Páez refused the summons, and most Venezuelans rallied around him, often less because they supported Páez than because they opposed Bogotá. Vice-President Santander decided to wait and see what position Bolívar, who was still engaged in organizing the new governments of Peru and Bolivia, would take in the dispute, for he did not want responsibility for shedding the first blood, and he hoped Bolívar would use his influence in behalf of the legal government. However, Bolívar did not react the way Santander hoped. He had been hearing of unrest back home and had come to the conclusion that much of the trouble resulted from an attempt to push reforms too far and too fast. Bolívar was not against reforms on principle, but he felt caution was needed. And he not only wanted to slow the pace of innovation but also had his own panacea for what ailed Colombia in the form of the constitution he had personally drafted for the new nation of Bolivia. This Bolivian constitution, which he hoped could be adopted in some form in Gran Colombia too, was a curious and unworkable document—providing for a three-house congress and other complications—but its key ingredient was a president elected for a life term and with power to choose his successor. The legal powers of the president were limited, but his life tenure and ability to groom his successor would give him a vast amount of influence over and above his stated powers. The plan was obviously a camouflaged version of monarchy, and it represented the final evolution of Bolívar's political thinking.

At length Bolívar tore himself away from Lima and went back home to try to set things right. His first step was to make a deal with Páez whereby the latter received full pardon for rebellion in return for recognizing the supreme authority of Bolívar. The latter then stayed for a while in Venezuela, waiting apparently for a powerful movement in favor of his own pet ideas. But none developed, since doctrinaire liberals rejected the Bolivian constitution as a betrayal of republicanism and numerous others had doubts about its practicality. Santander disliked it on both grounds. And what actually happened was the appearance of increasingly bitter criticism of Bolívar on the part of the vice-

president and his immediate circle, until Bolívar finally broke off
relations with him and returned to Bogotá to take direct charge
of the government himself. By gradual stages, Bolívar proceeded to set up a conservative
dictatorship. It was a mild one but still a dictatorship in that
Bolívar dismissed Congress and ruled by decree. Moreover, he
used his power to roll back quite a few of the liberal measures
adopted in Gran Colombia since 1821. Bolívar allowed the
smaller convents to reopen, and Bentham was tossed out of the
curriculum. Tariffs were raised, which pleased Ecuador. And
though Bolívar did not seek to abuse his dictatorial authority, in
outlying regions that authority had to be delegated, usually to
some powerful general or colonel whose main qualification was
undying loyalty to the Liberator. These generals and colonels
sometimes behaved rather badly, while, right in Bogotá, Bolívar's last and most famous mistress, Manuela Sáenz, once livened
up a party by staging a mock execution of Santander. Tensions
rose, culminating in September 1828 in an attempt to assassinate
Bolívar. Fortunately, Manuela, who was in the presidential pal-
ace with him, heard the noise and roused Bolívar in time for him
to jump through a window and escape. The army restored order,
and a number of conspirators were executed. Even Santander
was sentenced to death, on the unproved allegation that he had
been involved in the conspiracy, but Bolívar grudgingly agreed
to commute the sentence to exile.

Suppression of the September 1828 conspiracy did not bring
peace to Gran Colombia. A brief war broke out with Peru over
the southern boundary and various lesser disputes. Colombia
won, but the war was not popular, and it cost money. Nor did the
outbreak of foreign war ward off either a number of sporadic
internal uprisings by the adherents of Santander or a steady increase of unrest in Venezuela, the very place where Santander
previously had most difficulty. Venezuela rebelled under Páez in
1826 against Santander essentially because it wanted more autonomy from the government in Bogotá; it had not been seeking a
conservative dictatorship, also operating out of Bogotá, which is
what the nation now had. The last straw came when Bolívar's
cabinet launched a move to establish an openly monarchical government under a European prince, sounding out European go-

vernments concerning their possible reaction to such a scheme. The idea apparently was to let Bolívar serve as president as long as he wished, but when he died or retired he would be followed by a genuine monarch. Bolívar was not in Bogotá when this rather desperate maneuver was being hatched, and there is no proof that he directly inspired it, but he got the blame. Venezuela rose in rebellion again at the end of 1829, once more under the leadership of Páez, and this time went all the way to formal secession. Venezuela even went so far as to forbid Bolívar to set foot in his own homeland. The revolt of Venezuela both encouraged New Granadan liberals to come out into the open in opposition to Bolívar's government and set an example for Ecuador, which withdrew from the union in mid-1830. But even before he heard the news from Quito, Bolívar himself resigned from office in despair, planning to go to Europe to self-imposed exile. He never made it, dying near Santa Marta on the coast in December 1830.

The Successor States of Gran Colombia

After the breakup of Gran Colombia, northern South America consisted of three distinct sovereign states: Venezuela, Ecuador, and the Republic of New Granada, as the central core (present-day Colombia plus Panama) now called itself. But they did not turn their backs on each other overnight, as they continued to share not just the legacy of a common past but a number of current problems. An obvious example is the body of laws of Gran Colombia that remained in force in all three unless specifically modified or repealed. Included were such key measures as the 1821 free-birth law, which as a matter of fact was amended rather quickly in Venezuela to extend by a few years the period that technically free offspring of slave parents had to work for their mothers' masters. A legacy and common problem at one and the same time was the public debt incurred by Gran Colombia, which was in default when the union dissolved but which everyone agreed, in principle, must be paid off. A great deal of haggling ensued as each of the successor states tried to unload as much as possible of the burden on the others, but an agreement dividing up the debt was peacefully worked out by 1837.

Another common bond was provided by the personal associations of many of the current leaders, who knew each other or shared mutual acquaintances as a result of joint participation in the armies or civil government of Gran Colombia. This was particularly true of the military, which initially provided the bulk of top-level leadership of the new nations. The dominant figure and first elected president of Venezuela was inevitably General José Antonio Páez. Almost as inevitably, the dominant figure and first regularly elected president of New Granada, after a string of provisional presidents, was General Francisco de Paula Santander, who had been both collaborator and antagonist of Páez. Most striking of all, the first president of Ecuador was General Juan José Flores. He was not only another old wartime comrade but a Venezuelan by birth, and he surrounded himself with numerous other nonnative military men who in much the same way had helped expel Spanish forces from Ecuador and then stayed on after the fighting ended. In the long run, most became assimilated into the local upper class, often marrying Ecuadoran wives in the process. Flores was no exception in that respect. He was of undistinguished social origins in Venezuela, but in Ecuador, where he first came on the scene with troops at his command and wearing a colonel's uniform, he propelled himself by marriage directly into the Quito nobility.

A further point about all three countries is that, relatively speaking, they enjoyed a fair degree of internal stability during the first ten to twenty years of going their separate ways. They certainly enjoyed more than Mexico, or than themselves at certain later periods. This was especially true of Ecuador, which during much of the twentieth century became a pacesetter for rapid changes of government but from 1830 to 1845 got by with just two presidents, one of them Flores. Even when he stepped down for one term to let someone else be president, Flores stayed on as head of the army; for the entire fifteen years he remained in ultimate control.

During those fifteen years, Flores's Ecuador was almost an oasis of tranquility in Spanish America, although it was a tranquility resulting less from good management than from intermittent bursts of repression combined with long-term economic stagnation. At least the highlands were stagnant. The cacao export economy in the coastal region of Guayaquil was expanding, but the coast still contained only a sixth of the population, and its situation did not fundamentally alter the general picture. Flores himself was aligned more with the traditional landed aristocracy of the Andean highlands than with the incipient coastal plutocracy. He did his best to keep the peace, and he did nothing to disturb the creole magnates in the possession of their estates or exploitation of the Indian masses, who for the most part comprised a semiservile tenant class. Neither did he touch the privileges of such powerful institutions as the church, which was the greatest landowner of all, or the army, of which he personally was a member. And, on their part, the highland aristocrats came to regard Flores virtually as one of themselves.

New Granada: Modest Expectations, Modest Achievement

New Granada, largest of the successor states and—with a population of roughly a million and a half—the third most populous of Latin America, had the greatest difficulty getting started. For one thing, it had the most formidable geographic obstacles separating one part of the country from another and a range of economic, social, and cultural differences to match. The central highlands around Bogotá were a region of predominantly mestizo population, of large estates and peasant *minifundios* devoted to subsistence farming and the supply of nearby towns. The Caribbean coastal region and Isthmus of Panama had a particular interest in overseas commerce, a triethnic population with a strong African component at the lower social levels, and patterns of popular culture and even speech that had more in common with the Caribbean generally (including coastal Venezuela) than with the Andean interior. The province of Antioquia, in the northwest, was notable for its broken terrain, small and medium landholdings, and enterprising merchant class which had gradually accumulated capital over the colonial centuries by serving the nearby gold mines.

Other sections had their own distinctive patterns; what all had in common was poverty and isolation. In New Granada, wealthy merchants and landowners enjoyed material conditions comparable to those of the comfortable middle class in England or France. As late as 1850, the highest income enjoyed by anyone in the province of Bogotá was assessed at fifteen thousand pesos, roughly equivalent to dollars of that same period but still quite unimpressive. The rural masses were for the most part only marginally linked to the money economy. And the economy as a whole was marginal to that of the world outside. The one reliable export year after year was gold, whose production involved few people, and, even with miscellaneous other items included, the yearly volume of export trade in the 1830s and 1840s was around two dollars per person, which in turn set a definite limit on what could be imported. It also set a limit on government revenue and official programs, because customs duties were far and away the principal source of state income; there was not even much worth taxing, apart from foreign trade.

Other problems also had to be faced. The collapse of Bolívar's final dictatorship had allowed the generally liberal supporters of Santander along with assorted moderates to take control of the governmental apparatus in Bogotá, but there were hard-core Bolivarians still entrenched here and there, especially in the military. There was also for a time the real threat that certain outlying provinces might secede and that New Granada itself would disintegrate after the dissolution of the Gran Colombian union in the manner of Central America following its separation from Mexico. Panama for almost two years enjoyed de facto independence, the far south toyed with joining Ecuador, and the eastern plains flirted with Venezuela, which loyally refused to accept an offered annexation.

In the end, these challenges were overcome. The antagonism between followers of Bolívar and Santander degenerated into a brief armed confrontation decisively won by the Santanderistas. Indeed, their opponents never had a chance, since so many were Venezuelans like Bolívar. Ecuador might passively accept the rule of Flores and his foreign-born cohorts, but New Granada felt quite able to get along without the help of Venezuelan generals and colonels. Santander then returned from exile to assume the presidency in 1832, by which time New Granada had given itself a conventional liberal constitution and most of the secessionist threats had been safely overcome, by peaceful intrigue or force of arms.

Santander remained as president until 1837, and he, too, kept the peace rather successfully. Though faced with a number of conspiracies, he never had to cope with outright rebellion, and conspirators learned that Santander, who had defended the right of revolution against the dictatorship of Bolívar, could be a quick man with a firing squad when plotting was directed against himself. The difference, of course, was that he was a *constitutional* ruler, and he drove home the point by attending executions in person and then lecturing the troops and anyone who cared to listen about the majesty of law and how terrible it was to conspire against the legal authorities. As for those enemies who stopped short of conspiracy, Santander treated them (as he had done as vice-president of Gran Colombia) to uncomplimentary articles in the press.

Apart from reestablishing a climate of constitutional order, Santander sought to improve the quality of administration and even, very roughly, balanced his budget. He economized partly at the expense of the military, whose share of the budget kept declining until eventually it came to less than fifty percent of the total. The size of the military was limited, too, fixed by law at some three thousand, or roughly one per five hundred inhabitants. The military had further lost its fuero or judicial privileges by decree of New Granada's constituent congress, and all these measures pointed to a reduction in status and influence of the professional military that would be one of the enduring characteristics of New Granada (and modern Colombia) in comparison with Latin America as a whole. One reason, initially, was that the military institution had become too closely associated with Venezuelan influence in the closing days of Gran Colombia—and with the political fortunes of Bolívar. But upper-class civilians generally were wary of a powerful, overgrown army as a possible avenue of upward mobility for too many men of humble or middling family origins and a threat to their own control of political life. Civilian supremacy over the military in effect underwrote traditional social patterns at the same time. It was a tenet of liberal constitutionalism, and on that ground wholly acceptable to President Santander, a liberal general whose close collaborators were almost all civilians.

It must nevertheless be noted that Santander accomplished less in the way of liberal reforms as president of New Granada than did the so-called Conservative Oligarchy then ruling Venezuela (as will be seen shortly). From his own experience of exile and from his observation of the state of New Granada, he had learned to be more cautious. He had also frankly changed his position on foreign trade; he no longer sought to promote economic growth through reduction of external trade barriers, as he had in Gran Colombia, but supported an inward-directed strategy of moderate protection for local industries. He tried to reinforce this policy by personal example, ostentatiously wearing native fabrics in preference to European textiles; but in practice it was high transportation costs and a national scarcity of foreign exchange that mainly ensured the survival of domestic spinners and weavers.

The one area in which Santander still practiced a militant variety of liberalism was education. Hence, the works of Jeremy Bentham and other heterodox writers, which he had first introduced as vice-president of Gran Colombia and Bolívar had then removed, were again assigned reading for students. The result was more violent protests and predictions of divine punishment, but Santander stood his ground. The next generation, he was determined, would be properly indoctrinated with whatever new intellectual currents were fashionable in France, England, and the United States and as a corollary would be in a position to enact the liberal program lock, stock, and barrel. This is in fact what happened. In addition to liberalizing the content of the curriculum, Santander expanded the size of the educational system. At the elementary level, the number of students attending state schools went from twelve thousand to twenty-five thousand under his administration, which was still a minute portion of school-age population but in terms of percentage increase a rather notable accomplishment.

At the end of his term, Santander delivered the presidency to a former collaborator, Dr. José Ignacio de Márquez, whom he had not, however, supported for the position. There was little difference between the two in matters of policy, but there was a difference in style. Márquez was a quiet and unassuming figure who conspicuously failed to share the former president's intense hostility toward all (or almost all) who had collaborated in Bolívar's dictatorship, some of whom were now taken into the government. This in itself was enough to turn Santander into a vehement critic of the Márquez administration and opposition spokesman in the Chamber of Representatives, in which he, exactly like his contemporary John Quincy Adams, chose to continue a political career after leaving the nation's highest office. Márquez eventually had to face an outbreak of civil warfare far more serious than the miscellaneous troubles that had followed the breakup of Gran Colombia. It all began when Congress ordered the closing of certain small convents in the isolated and ultra-Catholic province of Pasto in the far South. The people of Pasto rebelled in protest and were defeated, but in early 1840 the rebellion was revived with the help of a regional caudillo, General José María Obando, who proclaimed himself "Supreme Chief of the War in Pasto, General in Chief of the Restoring Army, and Protector of the Religion of Christ Crucified." Obando himself was an ex-royalist guerrilla leader turned ardent liberal republican, of socially questionable antecedents (related by an illegitimate line to the aristocracy of Popayán, the leading city of southern New Granada), and widely accused of having engineered the assassination in 1830 of Bolívar's heir-apparent, General Antonio José de Sucre. He nevertheless had a certain charisma and a strong personal following and had even been Santander's choice in the election held to pick his successor—which Obando lost. It was, in any case, slightly ludicrous for Obando now to rise up against the decent, middle-of-the-road government of Márquez as defender of Christ Crucified; but his example was followed by a number of liberal leaders in other parts of the country who rose in rebellion, dubbed themselves Supreme Chief of this or that, and caused the whole confused movement to be known in Colombian history as the *Guerra de los Supremos*, War of the Supremes. Ex-President Santander took a somewhat dim view of it, but death in May 1840 removed his potentially restraining hand.

The one really concrete grievance of the liberal revolutionary bands against Márquez was the way he had let certain ex-Bolivarians back into government. But, significantly, they were also making federalist-sounding noises, calling for a larger measure of provincial autonomy vis-à-vis Bogotá. This is something New Granada's liberals had felt no great need for as long as they had full control of the central government themselves, but as they turned against Márquez they found the idea of provincial autonomy increasingly attractive. It was likewise the one logical connecting link between the ultra-Catholic reactionaries of Pasto and their strange bedfellows.

In due course the revolution was suppressed, but it was quite a struggle, and naturally it unbalanced the budget. Moreover, it marked the true birth of the present Colombian two-party system. On the one hand, it drove a deep wedge between the more militant liberals who backed the revolution and the moderate faction represented by Márquez. On the other, it greatly furthered the rapprochement already begun by Márquez between proadministration moderate liberals and the ex-Bolivarians, to whom he turned for support in suppressing the challenge. Indeed, the main work of fighting on the government side was done by a group of generals who had been closely associated with Bolívar and served his dictatorship. These two components of the official coalition in effect merged to become the Conservative Party, though it did not formally assume that title for a few years. And the "liberal" label was now left in exclusive possession of the government's opponents.

The essential nature of New Granadan and later Colombian conservatism was made perfectly clear in the administration that followed Márquez from 1841 to 1845. The president was Pedro Alcántara Herrán, one of the Bolivarian generals. His most influential adviser was the secretary of interior, Mariano Ospina Rodríguez, who in the 1850s would become a Conservative president in his own right. The son of a middle-rank landowning family, Ospina Rodríguez had started out as a hotheaded young radical, even taking part in the attempted assassination of Bolívar in 1828. He then went through roughly the same evolution as Márquez, from liberal to moderate liberal to a final stand as Conservative. In its political ideology, the Conservative Party owed more to these former supporters of Santander than to those who had followed Bolívar through thick and thin. It stood for representative, republican, constitutional government as much as anyone, and though it carried out a reform in 1843 somewhat enlarging the powers of the national executive as against both Congress and the various provinces, it was scarcely guilty of the tyrannical intentions its opponents charged it with. Neither were there significant differences between Liberals and Conservatives in economic policy: both groups represented upper-class interests, and within the upper class itself there were as yet no real conflicts between economic subsectors. But a measurable difference did appear in religious and cultural orientation. Under the guiding hand of Ospina Rodríguez, the Conservative administration launched an educational reform which sought to curb avantgarde ideologies (Benthamite or otherwise) and to promote both Catholic orthodoxy and politically neutral yet practically useful technical education. This reform was not wholly successful, particularly where promotion of technical studies was concerned, but it was logically complemented by the return of the Jesuits to New Granada in 1844. They were ardently desired both for their reputation as proficient teachers and for their doctrinal orthodoxy. The lifting of the exile decreed against them by Spain's enlightened despot Charles III thus formed part of an effort—undertaken in the aftermath of a ruinous civil conflict—to check the seeming advance of social and political disunity by strengthening the traditional religious values that were seen as one of the few forces binding all citizens together.

Otherwise, the Conservatives were not much interested in making changes: true to their title, they were content to conserve. Under the presidency of Tomás C. Mosquera, however, from 1845 to 1849, they did undertake a costly series of public works, from roads and bridges to the start of construction of the Colombian capitol building whose neoclassic symmetry and grayish yellow stone frame one side of the Plaza Bolívar at the center of Bogotá. Mosquera gave support to the final inauguration of regular steam navigation on the Magdalena River, the principal artery of internal communication. He further sponsored the adoption of the metric system and signing of the Bidlack-Mallarino (or Mallarino-Bidlack) Treaty of 1846 with the United States, which prepared the way for construction of a railroad across the Isthmus of Panama and also provided for a U.S. guarantee of both freedom of transit and New Granadan sovereignty over the Isthmus. The railroad was completed in the mid-1850s, the first anywhere in the nation; and if one clause of this same treaty was later cited by Theodore Roosevelt to justify the role of the United States in preventing Colombia from suppressing the Panamanian revolution of 1903, it was not necessarily Mosquera's fault.

Mosquera himself, though the member of a patrician family of Popayán and another former Bolivarian general, was in other respects a rather untypical Conservative. In his administration he gave employment to a number of crypto-Liberals, one of whom as secretary of finance sponsored both an across-the-board reduction of tariffs and an act providing for final liquidation of the state tobacco monopoly inherited from the colonial regime. These measures would have their chief impact only after Mosquera left office and the Liberal Party took power; but they were not the only ones whereby this ostensibly Conservative administration gave New Granada a foretaste of the great burst of reform activity that was just around the corner in the 1850s.

The Páez System in Venezuela: Military Upstarts and Traditional Elites

The most dynamic economically of Gran Colombia's successor states was Venezuela, which also achieved a degree of relative stability under the leadership of José Antonio Páez. Páez succeeded in forging a symbiotic relationship between the military (including self-made generals like himself) and surviving members of the Venezuelan creole aristocracy not unlike that between Juan José Flores and the landed magnates of highland Ecuador. However, the Páez system was both milder and more liberal, in which respects it also had something in common with New Granada.

By the time Venezuela finally emerged as a separate country with Páez as president in 1830, the economy was well on the way to recovery from the damage suffered in wartime, though recovery did entail certain changes. As already noted, cacao production had not maintained its colonial primacy and was giving way to coffee as the principal export crop, and, since cacao production had been traditionally dependent on slave labor and coffee in Venezuela was not, this represented, among other things, an adjustment to the decline of slavery as an institution. Yet obviously it did not lessen an orientation to the world economy that was much stronger than in Ecuador or New Granada, neither of which had yet developed an equal stake in commodity exporting. Foreign trade per capita was usually twice or more that of the other two countries. This in itself was a circumstance favoring consolidation of the new political order. However, the fact that in no major part of Spanish America had the war of independence been harder fought meant that Venezuela was also left with several troublesome legacies. Slaves and free pardos whose hopes for freedom and equality had been raised during the struggle and then only partially satisfied had by 1830 returned (most of them) to outward conformity; but, having once been stirred up by leaders on one side or the other, they remained one potential focus of unrest.

The military constituted another such focus. Venezuela had supplied a disproportionate number of the officers who led Bolívar's armies, and though some (like Flores) never came home even if they survived the fighting, Venezuela still ended up with more than its share of generals and colonels. Most of these were now out of active service, but whether they took civil government positions or went back to live on their estates, it often was not difficult to induce them to ride off to battle again at the least sign of political commotion. Not only that, but the veterans of independence had a generally high opinion of themselves on the basis of their service to the freedom of the fatherland, and they were not slow to avenge apparent insults to their personal honor or to their honor as a group. Obviously, too, officers were not the only potential troublemakers. Most common soldiers had been demobilized soon after the war ended, and in the absence of any real system of veterans' benefits—the land bonus they were promised having proved almost wholly illusory—they naturally formed another potential focus of unrest. Perhaps their old jobs no longer existed or no longer seemed appealing. Either way, many veterans turned to banditry and cattle rustling or waited around for somebody (it did not necessarily matter who) to start a revolution they could join. The fact that many of the former soldiers were pardos meant, of course, that the veterans' problem and the racial problem tended to overlap.

Despite the number of combustible elements on hand, of which the foregoing is hardly a complete list, these were juggled so successfully by Páez that for most of the 1830s and 1840s

Venezuela stood out as one of Latin America's more "stable" countries. To be sure, that may not be saying a great deal, and there were in fact a few outbreaks of conspicuous instability. One was an epidemic of minor revolts in roughly the first two years following dissolution of Gran Colombia, and in 1835 a major revolution had to be put down. In each case, the leaders were mostly retired officers who had some odd idea about putting Gran Colombia back together or had taken offense at something done by Páez's administration or were just getting bored with inactivity, and their followers were personal retainers and/ or discontented veterans. There were some other outbreaks, too, but they usually did not amount to much. Through it all, Páez served as president in his own right from 1830 to 1835 and again from 1839 to 1843; at other times he remained on the sidelines but ready to take a hand when needed, for he was always the ranking caudillo of Venezuela. Indeed, it did not make much difference whether he was holding the title of president or not, for even when he was he left the real work of governing to his ministers. As the Venezuelan historian José Gil Fortoul has expressed it, Páez's mode of operation was essentially that of a constitutional monarch: he tried to keep himself apart from the bothersome details of politics and administration and would merely step in to arbitrate when major disagreements arose. If his supporters came to blows with each other, or if the regime was threatened from another source, Páez was prepared to do more, even to direct military operations in person. But that was not often, and commonly the losers were pardoned or else allowed to go into exile on some pleasant Caribbean island.

Though sometimes referred to as a dictator, Páez allowed Venezuela to enjoy substantial press freedom, and arbitrary official actions were more the exception than the rule. Moreover, the Venezuelan government in the age of Páez functioned with a level of honesty and efficiency that may not have been outstanding by any absolute measurement but would not have been matched by many other Latin American republics at that point. Year after year, the treasury even managed to take in more than was spent, and the national debt kept getting smaller as the surplus was channeled into debt retirement.

A large part of the secret of Páez's success was the personal prestige he enjoyed as a result of his service to the cause of independence and his close rapport with the llaneros in particular. After all, it was as a leader of these tough cowboys of the Orinoco plains that he got his start as a revolutionary hero and by dint of sheer physical bravery and leadership skills rose to a degree of power and influence exceeded in Venezuela only by Bolívar—who was never *in* Venezuela after 1827. Páez, by contrast, never left his home ground. Neither did he lose his common touch, and as president he happily rubbed shoulders with the masses at the Caracas cockfighting arena. He was even happier, though, to retire to his properties on the plains, where one moment he might take a machete to clear away brush, working side by side with his ranch hands, and the next might be demonstrating his skill at bull tailing before his friend the British consul.

Most of the rest of the explanation of Páez's success is the identity of interest between him and the country's traditional upper class, composed of both large landowners and import-export merchants. This class had been somewhat depleted by exile, death, and economic disasters in the course of the war for independence, and in its weakened state it was delighted to have a figure like Páez come along who was prepared to keep down disorder and give needed protection to property rights. Páez was especially suited for the job since he had become a great landowner himself, thanks to the operation of the military land bonus—which greatly favored higher officers—as supplemented by further private speculations. He remained a man of few social or cultural pretensions, but members of the aristocracy gladly served in his governments and treated him with sincere respect.

The understanding between Páez and the Venezuelan upper class did not entail any blind adherence to the status quo. That upper class was in fact rather liberal-minded, in nineteenth-century terms, clearly reflecting its interest in commodity exporting and resultant economic and intellectual ties to western Europe. Thus, in 1834, during Páez's first presidency and with remarkably little opposition, Venezuela legally adopted religious toleration, becoming one of the first Latin American countries to do so. Venezuela likewise compiled a quite liberal record in economic matters, which, as liberalism was then understood, meant a policy of laissez-faire and elimination of arbitrary government interference. Such a policy suited the interests of large landowners and merchants perfectly well, and it led, for example, to the abolition of the tobacco monopoly as early as 1833. Even more suggestive is the measure of 1834 known in Venezuelan history simply as the Law of the 10th of April, which removed all limitations from the rate of interest. To a large extent, this only legalized what was already the practical situation, for the colonial restrictions on interest—themselves derived from the medieval Catholic condemnation of interest taking as usury—were disregarded on every hand. Nevertheless, the measure had symbolic importance as an affirmation of liberal principles in defiance of both Catholic theology and the presumed economic interest of debtors, and in due course it was to become a key political issue. Finally, not even the corporate interest of the military was immune to the assault of liberal principles. Hence Venezuela, which for many years would enjoy the reputation of a classic spawning ground of military caudillos, abolished the military fuero in 1830, actually a bit sooner than New Granada. Páez himself subsequently followed a policy of limiting the size and cost of the military establishment as far as possible, and the maintenance of domestic order was entrusted preeminently to a militia rather than the regular army.

Despite the above-mentioned liberal reforms—and others not mentioned—the long domination of Páez is generally referred to by Venezuelan historians as the "Conservative Oligarchy." The term is confusing when one considers that these Conservatives were doing the very kinds of things that self-professed liberals were calling for elsewhere in Latin America. Nor was the label originally adopted by the Conservatives themselves. Instead, they were stuck with it when about 1840 Antonio Leocadio Guzmán, a former collaborator of Páez, broke away to organize a formal opposition and preempted for his own group the title of Liberal Party. However, the terminology correctly reflects the fact that Páez, having risen up the socio-economic ladder himself, proceeded to identify himself with the traditional upper class; thus, his rule was socially conservative, whatever it may have been in other respects.

It is also true that the liberalism of the Conservative Oligarchy did not extend to the abolition of slavery; on the contrary, the most glaring exception to its moderately liberal orientation was the measure already mentioned that watered down the free-birth law inherited from Gran Colombia. This, however, was not one of the points raised by Guzmán and his fellow Liberals as they increasingly assailed the Conservative regime for its neglect of the interests of the popular majority; both parties dragged their feet on the slavery question. Guzmán criticized the government for such things as using the treasury surplus to reduce the national debt—taking money out of circulation to be shipped to London for foreign creditors—instead of using the funds for public works, agricultural credit, or other programs to benefit people at home. He also raised a hue and cry over the Law of the 10th of April, portrayed as an iniquitous device to penalize the poor on behalf of the rich and furthermore as a contributing cause of the economic hard times which did in fact descend on Venezuela in the early 1840s. One reason for economic distress was a decline in the export price of coffee, which could hardly be blamed on any one piece of Venezuelan legislation, but the removal of limitations of the rate of interest did worsen the plight of farmers who had borrowed money at high interest to expand their plantings and were hard put to repay it when the price fell. Their situation had been aggravated by companion legislation that facilitated foreclosures and forced sales of debtors' property.

Since those mainly hurt by the debtors' crisis were agriculturalists, and their creditors mainly of the merchant class, that crisis and the political use to which it was put by the Liberals tended to drive a wedge between two elements that had previously functioned as partners in and of the Conservative Oligarchy. Not only this, but the continued rule of Páez and his circle caused increasing resentment among all those who did not have a share of power and spoils. The prestige of Páez accordingly entered a decline, until the president who took office in 1847 with his blessing—General José Tadeo Monagas—turned suddenly against Páez, threw off his tutelage the following year, and introduced what Venezuelan historians have called the "Liberal Oligarchy." This term was an even greater misnomer, perhaps, than Conservative Oligarchy, but that is another story.

The "Portalian" State and Rise of Chile

The oligarchic constitutionalism exemplified in varying degrees by Venezuela and New Granada after the breakup of Gran Colombia was nowhere as successfully practiced as in Chile. Indeed, Chile in any number of ways became the principal success story among the former Spanish colonies. Its success was particularly obvious in comparison with, and was achieved in part at the expense of, the adjoining nations of the central Andes, Bolivia and Peru.

Though Chile stretched from the southern tip of the continent to the Atacama Desert—initially not as far into the Atacama as later on—its effective national territory was little more than the central valley that measured about six hundred kilometers from north to south but seldom as much as eighty in width between the Andes to the east and a lower coastal range on the west. This small, compact area came close to optimum size for a Latin American nation in the last century, particularly as land routes up and down the valley could be supplemented by coastal shipping for ease of transportation and communication. The land was generally fertile and the climate temperate. Beyond the central valley to the north lay a barren and virtually uninhabited desert coast. To the south, apart from a few enclaves of Hispanic settlement, one entered what for most purposes was still the independent domain of the Araucanian Indians.

The society of the central valley was fairly uncomplicated. The dominant group was a creole landed aristocracy, whose great estates took in perhaps eighty percent of the good land, for a rate of land concentration matched in few other parts of Latin America. The rural lower classes, largely mestizo, had little choice but to accept a dependent position, whether as service tenants (*inquilinos* in Chilean terminology) or as a floating landless population whose members served as day laborers in harvest or other times of peak labor demand in return for little more than a temporary abundance of food and drink and associated fiesta-type entertainment. The capital city, Santiago, was an administrative center of around thirty thousand people at the time of independence, with few cultural or other amenities. There was some mining of silver and copper on the mountain rim and an export trade of wheat to Peru, although the independent Peruvian government tended to place more restrictions on this commerce than the former viceregal authorities had done.

Chile had been a backward outpost of the Spanish Empire, then a secondary theater of the independence struggle; it now had the outward appearance of a rather stolid and sleepy Latin American republic. Nevertheless, the new political order was accompanied by a number of other changes, not all of them foreseen. One was the emergence of Valparaíso, the port of Santiago, as a major commercial entrepôt, used by a growing colony of foreign (mainly British) merchants as a way station for trade with the entire Pacific coast. There was also an entirely new trans-Pacific trade, as Chilean metals found new markets in India and East Asia. The fact that Chilean mines, unlike those of Mexico or Peru, had not been seriously affected by damage or neglect during the war of independence was a favorable circumstance.

New ideological currents were also evident, as would-be liberal reformers sought to bring Chile into line with the political and other advances of the North Atlantic world. The first such reformer was the father of Chilean independence, Bernardo O'Higgins, Chilean-born son of an Irish father, educated partly in England, who headed the first postindependence government. O'Higgins encouraged the opening of Chile to foreign trade, prohibited the bullfights that offended British sensibilities, and even authorized the establishment of a Protestant cemetery, though not freedom of worship. (Religious toleration in Chile was for dead Protestants only.) He further decreed the prohibition of entailed estates, the system whereby a landowner would bind his descendants forever to pass on a property intact from oldest son to oldest son—only to have the measure suspended by the senate, whose members he himself had appointed. The strength of opposition to that one measure, which was a very modest blow against the concentration of landownership and one adopted in other parts of Latin America with little controversy, suggests how resistant Chilean society was to liberal innovation. The authorization of Protestant burials also proved controversial. Yet O'Higgins was at the same time criticized because of the autocratic and highly centralist nature of his rule—because, politically, he was not liberal enough—and in early 1823 he was forced into exile.

For the next few years, the pace of innovation briefly accelerated. In 1823, Chile became the first Spanish American country to completely abolish slavery. Some blows were struck against ecclesiastical property and privilege, and entails were now formally prohibited. Moreover, though early Chilean liberalism was once described as little more than a fad among the brighter members of the aristocracy itself, it did have regional importance in outlying areas, notably in Concepción at the southern end of the central valley, where it was associated with demands to loosen the political control of Santiago. Liberalism in Chile, as in Mexico and a number of other countries, thus took on a federalist hue, and a federal constitution was adopted in 1826. The federalist experiment did not work very well, however, and it did not last long. Indeed, the political scene came to be marked by a general air of confusion and conflict, inevitably adding to pressures for a conservative reaction.

The reaction, when it came, was masterminded by Diego Portales, an able businessman whose yearning for greater political stability was enhanced by personal resentment over the cancellation of a contract entrusting to him and his associates the administration of the state tobacco monopoly. Portales turned a very confusing revolt of late 1829 into a movement that established a new government nominally headed by General Joaquín Prieto but in which he was the dominant figure, even if serving only as cabinet minister. There is no reason to believe that Portales at any time seriously wanted to become president himself or otherwise to occupy the limelight—in which respect he was far from being a stereotypical caudillo. He did believe in strong government; he merely wanted it to rest on institutional mechanisms rather than on personal loyalties and connections.

Portales's commitment to impersonal institutions and the rule of law did not prevent him from taking often dictatorial measures as short-run expedients, to get Chile's house sufficiently in order so that the rule of law might then take hold. He purged the bureaucracy and armed forces not just of those who were too liberal but of others whose only fault was to be dishonest or incompetent. He was prepared to bribe and muzzle the press, and he was a firm believer in the death penalty for conspirators (as was Santander in New Granada). He also organized a civic guard or national militia which came under the civil authorities and largely took over from the regular army the task of keeping internal order. He took this approach because he knew the military were often a source of disorder as much as order and because, by commissioning businessmen (like himself) and landowners as officers of the guard, he could directly associate those who had most at stake in domestic tranquility with the task of maintaining it. He similarly proposed to make the church a partner, and he accordingly countermanded various anticlerical measures adopted by liberal rulers of the previous decade, though not O'Higgins's Protestant cemetery. Portales was not personally a religious man, but he recognized that the clergy were useful people to have on one's side. As he once observed to a more devout political associate, "You believe in God, and I believe in priests."[1]

As soon as Portales felt things were well in hand, he gave up national office and returned to his business, though his influence was still felt. In 1833, Chile adopted a new constitution, with a view to placing the government on a sound permanent basis. It provided for a highly centralized state, a strong but hardly omnipotent executive, and a suffrage that was limited (albeit not unusually so for the period). The standard guarantees of individual rights definitely did not include freedom of worship, and another article once more legalized entails. The Constitution of 1833 was to prove remarkably enduring; it lasted until 1925, by which time it had been considerably altered by both amendment and reinterpretation. Even in its original form, as a matter of fact, it was a bit too liberal for Portales's taste, not because it offended his principles but because he seems to have felt Chile was not quite ready for it. In any case, it became the charter of what has been loosely termed the Portalian state—a regime capable of turning back all challenges to its authority but which relied for the most part on impersonal legal means rather than brute force and on the close support of social and institutional vested interests. Certainly Portales had no trouble accepting the constitution once issued, and, under it, Chile became a much-admired model of political stability in Latin America.

Creation and Destruction
of the Peru-Bolivian Confederation

The admiration and even envy evoked by the Chilean model was also partly caused by Chile's spectacular success in turning back the external challenge of the Peru-Bolivian Confederation of 1836 which brought together Peru and Bolivia under a single government and which Chilean leaders chose to regard as an intolerable threat to their own nation's security. In reality, to be sure, the confederation was an unstable union of two countries that, even taken singly, were somewhat artificial conglomerations of disparate peoples and regions. Each had a largely creole dominant minority, disenfranchised Indian majority, and growing mestizo population in between. The Indians in both countries were further subdivided into Quechua, Aymara, and other ethnic groups whose members did not necessarily understand each other much better than they understood the Hispanicized ruling class. There were regional rivalries between different highland areas, and in Peru between highlands and coastal plain. (Bolivia, too, had a coastal plain at this stage, but it was too undeveloped to become a focus of regional rivalry.) To complicate matters further, the two countries' silver mining was in decline because of the impact of the independence struggle together with—in Bolivia, at any rate—unfavorable long-term factors. This process of decay was really a benefit to the Indian masses; there was less need for their labor, and they were more likely to be left to their own devices. But the crisis of the mining industry was a serious matter for the merchant class and government treasuries.

In the immediate postindependence years, both Peru and Bolivia did some experimenting with institutional innovations, but aside from the abolition of the *mita* system of officially mandated Indian forced labor and a remarkably thorough assault on the assets of the religious orders in Bolivia, the reforms adopted were mostly superficial and short-lived. Typical was the way in which the Indian tribute, having been abolished here as elsewhere as a gesture of redemption of the native people, was quickly reinstated; in the case of Peru, it was merely renamed "contribution of indigenes," a term less likely to conjure up memories of Spanish oppression. In either country, political power came to rest ultimately with the army, reflecting both the weakness of civilian politicians and the feelings of insecurity of the upper socioeconomic strata, which looked to the military for the maintenance of order.

By their internecine quarrels, military leaders in practice often undermined the very stability they were upholding, although it is true that these directly involved only a minute portion of the total populace. And in Bolivia, at least, the earlier military rulers compiled a better record than those who were to follow. The first president was Venezuelan-born Antonio José Sucre, Bolívar's favorite lieutenant, who tried against tremendous odds to function as an enlightened reformist. After a brief interregnum, he was followed by Andrés Santa Cruz, Bolivian-born and part Indian, who originally served as officer in the royalist army. Having turned patriot, he became another loyal supporter of Bolívar, and he was left in charge of Peru by the Liberator when he went home to Gran Colombia in 1826. Bolívar's Peruvian enemies soon caused the collapse of Santa Cruz's government, whereupon he transferred his operations to Bolivia and, after becoming president in 1829, gave that country some modest progress in education and public works as well as an interlude of order maintained by sometimes dictatorial means. Yet Santa Cruz had not abandoned his interest in Peruvian affairs, and in 1836 he combined his own country with Peru, the latter broken down into separate northern and southern states, in a loose confederation.

In a hemispheric perspective, the Peru-Bolivian Confederation ranks with Gran Colombia and the Mexican Empire of Iturbide as one more attempt to form a larger nationality cutting across former colonial subdivisions. Certainly Peru and Bolivia had in common, historically and culturally, as much as or more than the component parts of those other unions. Nevertheless, there were Peruvians, in Lima especially, who looked askance at their country's being cut in half as two distinct states of the confederation, not to mention Bolivians fearful of being overshadowed in any larger union. At the same time, Chile and, to a lesser extent, Argentina rightly or wrongly considered the union a threat to themselves. As far as Chile was concerned, there was a quite real economic threat, in that the government of Santa Cruz set out to displace Valparaíso from its role as Pacific entrepôt by placing discriminatory duties on goods shipped by way of the Chilean port. Chile did not hesitate to go to war to break up the confederation and, with the aid of Peruvian opponents of Santa Cruz, brought about its collapse at the battle of Yungay in 1839. By then, Argentina had likewise declared war, but it had little to do with the outcome. Peru and Bolivia then reverted to the status of separate nations, under mostly military leadership and in a situation of economic stagnation that would continue for Peru until midcentury, longer for Bolivia.

Chile after Portales

In Chile, an upsurge of political tensions and alarms had brought Diego Portales out of retirement even before the struggle with Santa Cruz, which he stayed on to manage. He again displayed frequent high-handedness, but he served simply as member of the cabinet and did not intend his return to be permanent; however, in practice it was permanent, because in 1837 he died by assassination while still in office. What happened then was the best indication of how well Portales had done his work. Not only did Chile go on to win the war, but at home government continued to function about as smoothly as when the strongman was there in person. Needless to say, without an effective governmental apparatus, Chile could not have prevailed over two opponents that together had considerably more than twice the population and had more of most other resources, too, at least on paper. The war itself, in addition, contributed to a growing sense of national unity, and when the next presidential election took place, the winner, appropriately enough, was Chile's principal war hero, General Manuel Bulnes.

Bulnes served two consecutive terms exactly as Prieto had done before him, then likewise turned the presidency over to a constitutionally chosen successor. The regime was becoming steadily more tolerant of dissidents, including the non-Catholics who received de facto, if not legal, permission to establish Protestant chapels. Even so, the Chilean government's effective control of the nation was never in question. In elections, official slates rolled up comfortable majorities, if necessary by regimenting the vote of the civic guard rank and file, made up of artisans, small shopkeepers, and other members of the lower middle sectors. The working masses themselves were mostly disenfranchised and were in the main ignored, safely as it turned out. As Portales himself said, in perhaps the best known of his political aphorisms, "The social order is maintained in Chile by the weight of the night, and because we do not have men who are subtle, capable, or prone to take offense."[2] By "the weight of the night," he meant the sheer ignorance and passivity of the great majority, while a lack of subtle thinkers meant that people would not be stirred up by constant political agitation. Of course, Portales had still preferred to take no chances on the latter score, so that the definitive mellowing of the "Portalian state" came only after his death.

The solidity of the Chilean system derived also from steady economic growth. The continuing expansion of mining output—silver production in 1846 was already six times the average of 1801–10, and copper was becoming even more important—generated revenues for the state and foreign exchange both to support the expansion of commerce and to permit regular servicing of the foreign debt. The latter was an uncommon circumstance in the Latin America of the 1840s. By the end of that decade, a new surge in agricultural exports had begun, supplying wheat to gold-rush California. These developments inevitably set in motion still other forces that in the end produced political changes as well, and so did the influx of political refugees from other countries— paradoxically including many both subtle and capable—who were attracted to Chile precisely for its stability and rule of law.

The most eminent of all immigrants to Chile during the period was Venezuelan diplomat and man of letters Andrés Bello, who arrived in 1829 not really as a political exile but in search of tranquility and professional opportunity. Of moderate conservative leanings both politically and philosophically, Bello quickly gained a niche for himself as public official, journalist, and educator, becoming in 1843 rector of the University of Chile. For his adopted country, he wrote grammatical and philosophical texts, and he helpèd draft its first legal codes. In the 1840s especially, Bello was joined by other notable figures, such as the later liberal presidents of Argentina Bartolomé Mitre and Domingo F. Sarmiento. The presence of these newcomers contributed to a general quickening of intellectual life in Chile, which in turn led to greater criticism of prevailing policies and ideas. Symptomatic in this respect was the sudden notoriety of a young Chilean, Francisco Bilbao, who in 1844 published a treatise in which he boldly called for the repudiation of Hispanic and Catholic traditions and did not except even the institution of matrimony.

Bilbao's work was ordered burned by the authorities as blasphemous. Nevertheless, Chile retained its reputation as an oasis of freedom and moderation in postindependence Spanish America. The Chilean model was perhaps less unique than sometimes thought, for other countries came close to matching it at times, but they never matched it consistently, and the land from which Mitre and Sarmiento had fled did not match it at all.

6

The Road to Dictatorship in the Platine Area

In the early twentieth century, the area of southeastern South America drained by the Río de la Plata and its tributaries became the most prosperous and highly developed part of Latin America. At the dawn of independence, such was far from being the case, even though the port of Buenos Aires, with sixty thousand inhabitants, was already one of the largest cities of the hemisphere. Its hinterland was thinly inhabited and to a significant extent still the domain of semi-independent groups of Indians. Potentially the wealthiest part of Buenos Aires' zone of influence was the fertile, well-watered Argentine pampa, a plain stretching several hundred kilometers inland from the port and almost entirely unobstructed by natural barriers to transportation. The pampa was the choicest stretch of agricultural land in Latin America. But with the principal exception of a farming enclave in the vicinity of Buenos Aires itself, the pampa's only industry was ranching, in which the operation of settled estancias was supplemented by catching wild cattle on the plains and then slaughtering them for hides and other by-products, less frequently for meat. Uruguay, just across the Río de la Plata from Buenos Aires, was smaller in size than the pampa and had a rolling terrain but was similar in its economic basis. Also forming part of the Platine area but farther to the north lay Paraguay, between the river of the same name and the Paraná River, an oasis of fairly dense

117

agricultural settlement that was isolated by both distance and politics and played a somewhat marginal role as a result. (Geographically, the Platine basin contained portions of both Bolivia and Brazil, but historically these faced away from rather than toward the Río de la Plata.)

Before independence, this had been a relatively neglected corner of the Spanish Empire, both because it lacked significant quantities of precious metal and because of still limited European demand for the commodities it could produce. The pace of development began to quicken toward the end of the colonial period, and it quickened further with the coming of independence, which put an end to the last of the Spanish commercial regulations that hampered trading in hides and other articles with non-Spanish ports. Coincidentally, thanks in large part to technical and managerial advances, the independence period saw a rapid growth in the export of jerked beef to plantation areas of Brazil and the West Indies. This dried and salted meat product was nutritious but tough and not especially appetizing; Europeans would not eat it. Brazilian or Cuban slaves, however, had less choice, and *saladeros* (meat-salting plants) began to spread along the Río de la Plata and the Paraná and Uruguay rivers. Because of the opportunities provided by export markets for both hides and meat, it was not uncommon for a rancher in the 1820s to obtain a yearly return on his investment of better than thirty percent. A less favorable circumstance was the cutting, by independence itself, of the political connection which in late colonial times had made Upper Peru or modern Bolivia a dependency of Buenos Aires and oriented it to use the Platine gateway for its exports of precious metal and imports of European merchandise. The merchant commissions and tax revenues generated by that traffic now went mainly elsewhere. Even so, conditions seemed favorable for steady economic growth, provided a severe problem of political disunity and disorder could somehow be overcome.

The Roots of Political and Sectional Conflict

As of 1820 the Portuguese were consolidating the control over Uruguay that they had seized during the wars of independence (and that Brazil would soon inherit), and Paraguay enjoyed autonomy from Madrid and Buenos Aires alike. In practice, both provinces were already lost to what eventually became the Argentine nation, although most Argentines did not yet recognize the fact, and there would be a war to fight with Brazil before the status of Uruguay was defined for good. The rest of the Platine area, meaning those provinces that had accepted the authority of the revolutionary regime set up in Buenos Aires during the independence struggle, were in principle ready to form a single nation. Yet their readiness was often only skin-deep. In fact, during the same year, 1820, all national authority simply collapsed as armed conflict within and between provinces created a general state of disorder.

Ostensibly, much of the conflict was over form of government, whether to organize the new nation as a centralized republic tightly controlled by authorities in the national capital or as a loose federation of provinces. Buenos Aires, on its part, with close commercial and other ties to western Europe and the United States and possessing a disproportionate share of the wealth and brains of the country, felt destined by nature to "civilize" the more isolated and backward interior. Its political leaders thus tended to favor a centralist solution, in which they would naturally have the upper hand, and came to be known as *Unitarios* (literally unitaries) in Argentine political terminology. Federalism, in turn, drew strength from the resentment of the interior against the domineering ways of Buenos Aires and of its inhabitants, the *porteños* (people of the port).

The federalist alternative also appeared to many to be a natural response to some very real regional differences—economic, social, and cultural—for not only was Buenos Aires at odds with the interior on many issues, but the interior was not even united within itself. In the north and west (around Salta, Tucumán, Mendoza), the economy featured a significant amount of agricultural production and handcraft manufacturing for domestic consumption or export to Chile and Bolivia, and independence had both created new barriers to trade with the two neighboring countries and lowered those that previously limited the competition of European wines and manufactures in the Argentine market. The resulting economic stagnation served to accentuate the relative isolation of the northern and western provinces from the latest currents in material and intellectual culture, and somewhat the same could be said of Córdoba, at the nation's geographic heart, whose capital city, with about twelve thousand people, was still the second-ranking urban center after Buenos Aires. Córdoba-made ponchos faced the competition of English factory textiles, and Córdoba's role as a hub of internal commerce was hurt by the economic depression of other interior provinces. A somewhat different situation prevailed in the provinces upstream along the Paraná from Buenos Aires, predominantly devoted to livestock raising, as was the province of Buenos Aires itself, and, like it, having direct access to the water. But their interests were not identical with those of Buenos Aires, because the latter was intent on maintaining the monopoly of overseas commerce that it enjoyed in the colonial period and accordingly insisted that the riverside provinces use its port even though they had ports of their own that could be reached by sailing ships of the period. The remaining interior provinces were little concerned with this port question, but they did want tariff protection of their local industries, whereas the provinces along the Paraná (with the partial exception of Corrientes) had virtually no industries to protect and were almost as interested as the porteños in trade with foreign countries.

Buenos Aires province also was divided internally. The port city lived by commerce and aped European fashions, but the ultimate source of its wealth was the countryside, where a small number of *estancieros* possessed vast estates that extended as far to the south and west as appeared safe at any moment from the depredations of the pampa's Indian nomads. These ranchers normally had homes in the city as well, and they shared the same essential economic interests as the urban merchants and professional middle groups, yet they were more conservative in social and cultural outlook, and they sometimes differed in tactics. And they were not the only element of the rural population to be reckoned with. In the Buenos Aires countryside, as thoughout the livestock-raising regions, including Uruguay, the landed elite was in turn dependent on the services of the local *gauchos*, or cowboy population, who shared many of the traits of the Venezuelan llaneros. Generally mestizos, untouched by formal schooling and indifferent to both civil laws and church precepts, they had developed a subculture that revolved around fighting, horses, and gambling—especially horses, because almost everything was done on horseback. Hence the gaucho who supposedly observed that he was too poor to work, meaning too poor to have a horse, for no gaucho would think of doing anything on foot. As a distinguishable element of society, the gaucho had first attracted notice in the late colonial era, with an image of smuggler and cattle rustler. Social deference was not one of his characteristics, and he was intrinsically difficult to control. Buenos Aires city slickers such as the principal Unitarios were especially unlikely to win his confidence.

However, the gaucho's particular skills made him indispensable to all factions in the independence struggle and in civil wars thereafter, as well as to the expanding livestock business. For the latter, the problem was to attach him to a given employer long enough to do some good. The more skillful estancieros accomplished this through the development of strong patron-client ties, which were supplemented by the general adoption of a pass requirement whereby rural inhabitants had to possess (and show on demand) a *papeleta* certifying that they were gainfully employed. In its absence, a standard punishment was military service, something that gauchos found less to their liking than waging spontaneous knife fights with each other but for which there was almost always a requirement somewhere in the Argentina of the first half of the last century.

The Unitario Experiment in Buenos Aires

The most important province of all, Buenos Aires, was one of the most afflicted by the turmoil of the "terrible year twenty," as traditional Argentine historians dubbed the year 1820, when national unity dissolved. Taking a somewhat loose definition of *governor*, it was later said that Buenos Aires went through twenty of them in that one year, including as many as three on a single day in June. Toward the end of the year, however, with the advent of a temporary respite from civil strife, a new provincial government headed by Martín Rodríguez began to restore a climate of order. Rodríguez himself was an estanciero and military officer who had the tacit or open support of most others of his class; but in order to create a more efficient provincial administration, he wisely enlisted the help of a team of urban business and professional men of Unitario leanings, whose representative figure, Bernardino Rivadavia, he made chief minister.

A porteño merchant and lawyer who had been active in the independence movement from the beginning, Rivadavia had also traveled abroad and was really better acquainted with Europe than with the interior of his own country. He was rather self-important, but he was able, and he had an exceptional corps of collaborators with whom he now set out to remake Buenos Aires as far as possible in the image of western Europe so that it might serve as a fit model and nucleus around which to organize a whole new Argentine nation as soon as the time was ripe. Working in his favor was the relative prosperity of Buenos Aires province, particularly as compared to the Argentine interior or, for that matter, most of Latin America in those years. The lack of a true national government in Argentina meant further that such inherently national taxes as the customs duties on foreign trade went directly into the provincial treasury, which had something like seven times the amount of revenue per capita to work with that independent Mexico produced.

Rivadavia and his friends set to work. They slashed the size of the regular army, both to save money for more useful purposes and to weaken a potential rival of civil authority. They stripped both army and clergy of the fuero, and they endowed Buenos Aires with such presumably modernizing institutions as a university and a stock exchange. The University of Buenos Aires gave young men an alternative to the University of Córdoba, which had been the only university in Argentina before the revolution and was deemed to be too steeped in clerical influence. In somewhat the same way, Rivadavia transferred control of hospitals, cemeteries, and various other welfare and educational institutions from the hands of the church to those of the state or to a privately run though state-sponsored *Sociedad de Beneficencia* (Welfare Society). Buenos Aires did more to lessen the role of the church, however, than merely prune away some of its educational and welfare functions. The province ended compulsory payment of tithes, reduced the number of monasteries, and took over both their assets and assorted other church properties, although there was no general confiscation. The provincial legislature in 1825 even introduced freedom of religious worship. These measures affecting the status of the church were similar to yet went substantially farther than those elsewhere in Latin America in the immediate postindependence period. Both Haiti and Brazil (though not any of the former Spanish colonies) had established religious toleration before Buenos Aires, but only there did it form part of a systematic program to reduce the power and influence of the Roman Catholic church in society.

The most important policies of Rivadavia and his collaborators had to do with economic development, which they sought to promote by eliminating the *alcabala*, or colonial sales tax, and assorted nuisance taxes, while improving the collection of those that were retained. Like other governments of the period, they raised an English loan, supposedly to be used for port improvements and other useful works, though in practice the outbreak of the war with Brazil over Uruguay would cause its proceeds to be diverted to other purposes. Above all, they sought to integrate Buenos Aires more closely into the economic sphere of western Europe by encouraging foreign trade, investment, and immigration. Trade was fostered by, among other things, the adoption of a moderate revenue tariff, and it did grow rapidly; with Great Britain it nearly doubled in value from 1821 to 1824, though with imports greatly exceeding exports. The promotion of capital investment and immigration was rather less successful, since European capitalists were interested above all in gold and silver, which Buenos Aires lacked, and potential immigrants found the United States both more attractive and easier to get to. Actually, for skilled craftsmen, Buenos Aires had much to offer. Labor was in relatively short supply, and therefore wages were high even by European standards; one of the complaints of local producers calling for tariff protection against foreign manufactures was that they could not compete with cheap English wages. On the other hand, the need and consequently the incentives for a mass influx of unskilled laborers were not yet present, and the effort to bring groups of agricultural settlers under government-sponsored immigration contracts was badly mismanaged. Some of the hapless recruits were actually taken to the Argentine countryside, where they found conditions to be not quite as promised; they did not stay there long.

In general, nevertheless, things went sufficiently well in Buenos Aires that the Unitarios got up their courage for a new attempt at national organization. The call went out to the interior provinces to send delegates to a constituent congress at Buenos Aires, whose function would be to devise a permanent system of government for the entire country. The call was accepted, and the congress, opening in 1825, made Rivadavia head of a provisional national administration with the title of president. Unfortunately, in the same year, a serious complication appeared with the outbreak of the struggle against Brazil over Uruguay. The Uruguayans had risen in rebellion against Brazilian rule and moved to rejoin Argentina, if only because they knew they could not defeat Brazil on their own. The Argentine authorities accepted the offer of incorporation, and war between Argentina and Brazil inevitably followed.

On land, at least, the war favored the Argentines and Uruguayans, who cleared most of Uruguay of Brazilian forces and even carried the war into the southernmost Brazilian province of Rio Grande do Sul. However, a Brazilian naval blockade caused serious economic hardship to Buenos Aires, and fighting the war also cost money. To make matters worse, the Unitarios seized upon the foreign conflict as one more evidence of the practical need to give Argentina the very kind of government they had been advocating all along. The constituent congress agreed and adopted a rigorously centralist constitution in 1826, under whose terms provincial governors were to be appointees of the national executive. Opinion in the interior provinces themselves, however, was still strongly federalist, and it was hostile to Unitario leadership on other grounds as well. Rivadavia's anticlerical moves had not been truly popular even in Buenos Aires; in much of the interior they were viewed as the work of the Antichrist. The adherence to a strictly revenue tariff policy, moreover, had antagonized weavers and wine makers and various other local producers. The interior simply did not accept the new constitution. Another round of civil warfare broke out, in the midst of which the national government dissolved again, and in mid-1827 Rivadavia headed off to exile. A year later the war with Brazil finally petered out, as with the help of British mediation Argentina and Brazil both accepted the principle that Uruguay should become an independent state.

The great experiment of Rivadavia and the Unitarios to bring Argentina, starting with Buenos Aires, rapidly into the mainstream of world progress thus ended in failure. It failed largely because of their own grievous misjudgment about what their countrymen were prepared for; they were one or two generations ahead of their time. Nevertheless, not all their work was in vain, for some of their accomplishments in the one province of Buenos Aires would be retained even under the long dictatorship of Juan Manuel de Rosas, the man who quickly moved to fill the power vacuum left by the Unitarios' collapse. And the spiritual and intellectual heirs of the Unitarios, who were often their physical heirs as well, were destined to preside over Argentina during its golden age of rapid economic and political development in the late nineteenth and early twentieth centuries.

The Estanciero as Dictator: Juan Manuel de Rosas (1829–1852)

Rosas ranks without question as one of the great dictators of Latin American history, and in his own country today it is almost as easy to get an argument going over Rosas as over whoever happens to be occupying the presidency at the moment. His portrait has yet to grace a postage stamp, and all moves to return his remains from the cemetery where they still rest in exile in Southampton, England, have so far been resisted; yet he is a cult figure to extreme nationalists, and even those who do not like him recognize the consummate skill he displayed in consolidating his rule.

Rosas personally was one of the wealthiest members of the landowning upper class of Buenos Aires province. With various partners, he held extensive estancias and operated saladeros, effecting a vertical integration of the livestock business whereby he raised cattle, slaughtered and processed them, and finally sold the products for export. He would be a notable figure in entrepreneurial history even if he had not also made a mark in politics. But the former claim to fame came first and was really the basis

for his political success. His ranching operations not only made
him a spokesman for the most powerful single economic interest
group in Argentina, but they also, since he took pains to master
every detail of the business from the ground up, gave him an
unequaled ascendancy over the gauchos of the hinterland. Rosas
was no gaucho himself, but he could practice any of the arts of
the gaucho, and, unlike such a figure as Rivadavia, he knew how
to speak the gaucho's language and win his trust. Among the
many stories about him is that one day he saw a swirl of dust on
the horizon that he instantly recognized as caused by a rustler
making off with some of his cattle. He jumped on his horse, took
off in pursuit, captured the rustler, and brought him back to be
given a hundred lashes. The punishment having been administered, he invited the man to join him at table for lunch and
offered him a job as ranch foreman on the spot. The astonished
gaucho readily accepted and, needless to say, became a devoted
follower of Rosas ever after. Some Rosas stories, possibly including this one, are apocryphal, but they faithfully mirror the reputation he built up and the respect he enjoyed among the mass of
rural inhabitants.

Rosas himself had at one point respected the administrative
ability of Rivadavia, but he had no sympathy for the Unitarios'
attempt to create a tightly centralized national government,
which he saw as wholly impractical and a source of nothing but
trouble. Rosas was accordingly a federalist, as far as national
political alignments were concerned, but he was not much interested in the country as a whole—only in the province where he
lived and had his business. And, since he was convinced that
strong personal authority was needed to restore peace and
prosperity to Buenos Aires, he insisted on being given dictatorial
powers when he finally emerged as governor of the province in
1829. He proved to be a good administrator of public as well as
private affairs—with a keen eye for detail and willing to keep
poring over papers on his desk until early-morning hours—and
thus governed quite ably in most respects. Indeed, he was successful to the point that the provincial legislature felt dictatorship
no longer necessary and allowed his extraordinary powers to
expire. In 1832, Rosas retired from office and went off to head a

military expedition against the nomadic tribes still taking up good cattle land on the southern pampa.

Rosas's Indian campaign was successful in adding tens of thousands of square kilometers of land to that available for ranching operations. It also earned him the loyalty of those who obtained estancias for themselves in former Indian territory in the form of military bonus. In his absence, moreover, his wife, Doña Encarnación, and other close supporters had been effectively leading a campaign of agitation against the governors who followed him in office, all federalists as he was but of a more moderate variety. By the beginning of 1835, the province was ready to take Rosas back on his own terms and made him governor again, this time with "the sum of public power," by which was meant the concentration of supreme executive, legislative, and judicial authority in this one man. To strengthen his position further, Rosas insisted on having this grant of sweeping personal power confirmed by a popular plebiscite, which he won handily, receiving 9,316 votes in the city of Buenos Aires to a mere four cast against him. Obviously, it was not an election by secret ballot, and one of the "Buenos Aires four," a retired general, was soon on his way to exile. However, it is true that Rosas started out with great personal popularity. Many people were so tired of disorder in 1835 that they yearned for a strong hand to restore stability by any means whatsoever.

Rosas allowed the legislature to stay in session, but it was not tempted to withdraw his powers again, and he could in practice now run the province exactly as he pleased. In economic matters, his policies were framed strictly to suit the interests of his own estanciero class. In addition to the tracts given away to those who had accompanied him on his Indian expedition, other large chunks of the public domain were sold on easy terms. Rosas discontinued the experimental policy introduced by the Unitarios in the 1820s of distributing public lands only on the basis of long-term leaseholds; those who had earlier received estates on that basis were allowed, even encouraged, to buy them outright. It is not too much to say, in fact, that the Argentine landed aristocracy whose power and prosperity won the attention of Europe and America during the boom years of the late nineteenth century really took shape in the era of Rosas, with his direct aid and encouragement. The Anchorena family, who were relatives and political supporters of Rosas, did best of all, accumulating more than three hundred square leagues of land in Buenos Aires province by the end of the 1840s.

Rosas also protected the interests of the landowning class in his handling of financial matters. Because of both domestic and foreign complications (of which more below), his government faced some heavy expenditures, and to a considerable extent he met them simply by printing paper money as needed. He probably deserves the title of first great Latin American inflationist, although his fame in this respect would pale by comparison with many recent Argentine rulers; currency in circulation increased a mere six times over, from 1837 to 1851 (Rosas's last full year in power). The peso fell in value as a result, but the printing press allowed Rosas to pay his bills without imposing significant taxation on the estancieros, and they were not hurt by inflation at all. They had hides and other products which were sold abroad for pounds sterling or other foreign currency, and as the local currency declined in value, the exporters' foreign earnings were automatically exchanged into a larger number of pesos. If anything, they benefited, since the exchange value of the peso tended to fall faster than their wage bill and other peso costs were rising.

It is, however, the political aspects of Rosas's regime that loom largest in any catalogue of his sins, whether drawn up by opponents at the time or by later critics. Unlike the Unitarios, he had no ambitious programs of reform to carry out, and the *Registro Oficial* of Buenos Aires province, in which all laws and decrees were published, grew thinner and thinner during the years of Rosas's power, consisting in some months of nothing but a statistical appendix. Apparently, Rosas had not even bothered to issue one executive decree or to prod his rubber-stamp legislature into passing a single law. At the same time, though, Rosas did bother to conduct an intermittent reign of terror against his adversaries, who consisted of both Unitarios and dissident federalists. One of the former calculated—with highly dubious precision—that Rosas had caused 722 people to be assassinated, another 1,393 to be shot, and 3,765 more to be put to death by having their throats cut. The prominence of throat cutting was naturally ascribed to Rosas's rancher mentality: he had people put to death in the same way as cattle, by the knife. Of course, his opponents could wield a pretty mean knife, too, and it would not make much sense to try to figure out who had actually started the round of atrocities and counteratrocities. It is enough to say that Buenos Aires was not a safe place to be if you were a known or suspected enemy of Rosas and that Montevideo in Uruguay, the first stopping place for most political exiles, was home to an ever larger number of Argentines.

Yet murder and exile do not exhaust the list of methods of the Rosas dictatorship. Rosas also made expert use of propaganda, agitation, and political symbolism, in often quite modern-looking ways, to whip opinion into line behind him and to maintain political fervor at a constant high pitch. His propaganda and related tactics were geared especially to the common man, appealing to his incipient nationalism and antiforeignism while associating Rosas's Unitario enemies with foreign customs and interests. He was one of the very first Latin American rulers to court popular backing in systematic fashion. However, even members of the porteño intelligentsia, if they did not go into exile, were required to proclaim at least outward support for the regime by such means as wearing a red ribbon affixed to their clothes, red being the official color of Rosas's federalists. These ribbons were first inscribed with the slogan "Death to the Unitarios," but the message kept getting longer until eventually it read, "Death to the Vile, Filthy, Savage Unitarios." The same slogan had to be used on the masthead of newspapers and appeared as a heading on all laws, decrees, and official correspondence. To be sure, it was omitted from diplomatic correspondence. What would the British Foreign Office or the State Department in Washington have thought on opening a message that started out with the words "Death to the Unitarios"? In a way, the Unitarios were as essential to the designs of Rosas as the Jews were to Hitler—if there had not been any, he would have had to invent them, because literally anything that went wrong was blamed on their intrigues. And actually, the charges of treason conventionally leveled against the Unitarios were not, as we shall see, wholly unfounded.

In his regimentation of public opinion, Rosas went so far as to have his portrait placed in the churches and to require the clergy to wear federalist red ribbons while saying Mass, although they were allowed to omit the slogan calling for physical destruction of the Unitarios. They were mostly quite willing to go along with this, as Rosas consciously promoted ecclesiastical influence in education and elsewhere, rooting out religiously unorthodox textbooks and the like while targeting the University of Buenos Aires, founded by Rivadavia as a bastion of secular enlightenment, for repeated economy drives. Not all priests supported Rosas; there was a liberal minority even within the clergy. But the bishop was an unconditional Rosas supporter, and a majority of priests had undoubtedly greeted his coming to power with a sigh of relief, seeing it as deliverance from the liberal, anticlerical tendencies of the Unitarios. The high point in Rosas's cultivation of closer ties with the church was, or rather was intended to be, his invitation to the Jesuits to return to Argentina. He hoped that those skilled preachers and educators would help to instill traditional values and political obedience in the young. When the Jesuits turned out to be too independent for Rosas's taste, wanting to do things their own way and making clear that their first loyalty was to Rome and not to the governor of Buenos Aires, the latter suddenly discovered "Savage Unitario" leanings even among the Jesuits and evicted them again himself.

His treatment of the Jesuits was only one of a number of indications that Rosas's support of church interests was not quite unconditional. Not only did he fail to repeal the grant of religious toleration made by the Unitarios, but as governor he presented to the British community the lot in downtown Buenos Aires on which it built the first Protestant church in Argentina. He did this, obviously, not from any philosophical commitment to toleration but because he valued and hoped to tighten still further the close economic relationship between Buenos Aires and members of the foreign business community, many of whom were Protestant. And just as the province's agro-exporting economy dictated a minimum degree of hospitality for non-Catholics, it also ruled out any bona fide adoption of tariff protectionism. Rosas did for a time lend an ear to the protectionist demands of the interior and of certain manufacturing interests in Buenos Aires itself, to the extent of raising tariffs on some categories of imports and flatly prohibiting others. It would seem, however, that he did this in part simply as a tactical maneuver, to gain political support while still consolidating his rule. After all, the interests of his own estanciero class required the exchange of the products of the land for foreign manufactures, with as few artificial restraints as possible. Thus, as the years went on, Rosas made exceptions or failed to keep adjusting duties upward in line with depreciation of the currency, so that in the end the tariff under Rosas was not greatly different from what it had been with Rivadavia—a moderate revenue tariff. To the extent, then, that Rosas's dictatorship represented a reaction against the innovations of his predecessors, it was a rather selective reaction.

Rosas as National Ruler

Since the great majority of foreign goods consumed in Argentina entered through the port of Buenos Aires, the tariff policy of Rosas had to affect other provinces as well, at least indirectly. He set that policy, however, merely in his capacity as governor of Buenos Aires, because ever since the failure of the Unitario experiment, Argentina once again lacked anything that could be called a true national government, whether federal, centralist, or otherwise. Nor did Rosas propose to create one. But he did join with the other provinces in what was called the Argentine Confederation. This was a confederation that had no president, no congress, and much less a confederate bureaucracy; all it did was authorize the governor of Buenos Aires, as head of the single most important province, to act in the name of all in matters of defense and foreign relations. At least on paper, that was all it did. For the rest, Rosas entered into friendly compacts with sympathetic provincial leaders, paid subsidies from the Buenos Aires treasury to some, and intervened in neighboring provinces with Buenos Aires troops from time to time. By such methods he obtained respect for his wishes as number one caudillo of Argentina and eventually managed to bring about a greater measure of internal peace than the country had known for years; but what this mainly amounted to was a mechanism of personal power and influence, operating largely outside legal mechanisms.

Much less did Rosas try to use his influence in other provinces to dictate their policies (if they had any) in regard to social welfare or economic development, or to tell them how to raise their taxes or clean their streets. In the rest of Argentina he was concerned with little more than internal security, so that he kept after other governors to evict suspected Unitarios from their territory, and Jesuits too, once he himself had broken with them. He would also send out circulars saying, for example, that a certain libelous, infamous book had been published over in Chile by a notorious loco Unitario traitor so-and-so, and if copies turned up in your province you should be sure to seize them and duly punish whoever brought them in. As already mentioned, he did take note of the protectionist sentiments of the northern and western provinces and made some concessions to them in formulating Buenos Aires' tariff policy, but in the end he gave little more than lip service. Neither was he more inclined than the Unitarios had been to open the Paraná River to direct trade with foreign countries. He insisted that all overseas trade pass through Buenos Aires, and in the interest of the Buenos Aires trade monopoly, he even took a jaundiced view of transandean trade between Mendoza and Chile.

Trade relations with Chile were suspect in part, of course, because of those "libelous, infamous books" that sometimes got mixed in with other merchandise. There were Argentine exiles in Bolivia, too, and concern over their activities was one reason why Rosas joined with Chile in the war of 1837 to destroy the Peru-Bolivian Confederation. Yet Uruguay was the neighboring country that always caused the greatest problems, for it harbored the chief concentration of Unitario exiles, and they intrigued ceaselessly to obtain Uruguayan support for their own efforts to topple the Buenos Aires dictator. They won the ear principally of the Uruguayan faction known as *Colorados* (or Reds), who were bitter rivals of the opposing *Blancos* (Whites), not over fundamental differences of policy or principle but mainly because of differences of style and personality. Rosas, on his part, felt therefore that he had no choice but to support the Blancos, and the result was that both parties in either country became entangled in the civil conflicts of the other. It was especially confusing in that party colors were reversed when one crossed the Río de la Plata: the Argentine "Reds," namely Rosas's federalists, were allied with the Uruguayan "Whites" *against* the Uruguayan "Reds," who in turn were allied with Argentina's "Blues," that being the color of the Unitarios. With the help of their Uruguayan allies, the Unitarios succeeded in giving Rosas a number of rather bad scares, including one invasion that penetrated uncomfortably close to the city of Buenos Aires. But by 1843 Rosas and *his* Uruguayan allies succeeded in penning the Colorado-Unitario forces up inside the city of Montevideo, where they remained under siege for eight long years until 1851.

Rosas also faced complications with two European powers, Great Britain and France. One problem, which really involved only the French, concerned allegations of unfair treatment of their citizens in territory under his jurisdiction. Another, which was of greater concern to the British, was Rosas's intervention in Uruguay, which seemed to pose a long-range threat to Uruguayan sovereignty and also annoyed the British merchant community in Montevideo. The British government was not legally committed to protect the independence of Uruguay, but it felt a vague moral obligation as a result of its role in the negotiations that led to the creation of Uruguay as a separate state. There was also a dispute over Rosas's insistence on closing the Paraná to foreign commere. The European powers (and Brazil, for that matter) argued that the Paraná River system as a truly international waterway should not be subject to the whim of a single one of the interested parties. The argument had some merit, as the Paraná system was the only outlet to the sea for one independent nation, Paraguay—not that any Argentine government until after the fall of Rosas formally recognized its independence—as well as the most convenient gateway to and from a large part of interior Brazil.

Then, last and also least, there was the problem of the Falkland Islands/Islas Malvinas. The first settlement there had been made by the French, but they yielded their rights to Spain, whose eventual heir was Argentina. The British also made a brief attempt at settlement in the colonial period, but they were induced to withdraw and did not return until 1833, when a British expedition forcefully rounded up and evicted every Argentine resident and planted the colony that continues to this day amid continuing Argentine protests. Rosas was not in office as governor when the British seized the islands, and he didn't lose much sleep over the question. He offered to give up all Argentine rights if only the British in return would cancel the unpaid balance of the loan Argentina had raised in London in 1824. The British unwisely turned down the offer, which would have cost them far less than fighting the South Atlantic War of 1982.

Though he was prepared to negotiate on the Falklands and other issues, too, there was a limit to the concessions Rosas was prepared to make. There are even grounds to suspect that sometimes he did not try quite as hard as he might to reach an accommodation, since these foreign complications served him well, allowing him to stand forth as a champion of Argentine nationalism and giving him a further excuse for dictatorship at home. In any case, the Europeans proved unable to humble him. The French by themselves in 1838–40 and Britain and France together after 1845 blockaded the coast of Argentina, with warm moral support and encouragement from the Unitarios ensconced in Montevideo. Real hardship was caused, but Rosas stood his ground each time while skillfully sowing seeds of distrust among his opponents. His generally good relations with British merchants doing business in Buenos Aires itself paid off in the form of some effective lobbying to convince opinion at home that their government's feud with Rosas was an irrational show of pique.

In the end, neither European power cared enough about the Río de la Plata to expend the resources that would have been needed to bring the Argentine dictator to his knees. The British withdrew with none of their aims accomplished, although they did keep the Falklands. The French had little choice but to follow suit, and Rosas's success in defying the European blockaders is undoubtedly the most important single reason for the widespread admiration he enjoys in present-day Argentina. Paradoxically, though, his victory over foreign enemies was his undoing, because he could no longer convincingly use foreign dangers as an excuse for domestic tactics, and even some of his erstwhile allies within

Argentina came to the conclusion that the time had arrived to adopt a real constitution, in which matters would be set down on a regular legal basis, and everyone, not just the governor of Buenos Aires, would have a say in how the country was run. When Rosas refused to go along with demands for change, one of those who proceeded to desert him was Justo José de Urquiza, an estanciero like Rosas who had been serving as governor of Entre Ríos, one of the provinces up the Paraná. Though ostensibly allied to Rosas, Urquiza had been violating Rosas's commercial regulations to trade directly with foreign shippers, but he also wanted the regulations changed for the sake of his province generally. For this and other reasons, on May 1, 1851, Urquiza replaced "Death to the Unitarios" as the official slogan of his province with "Death to the Enemies of National Organization," by which he meant just one in particular—Rosas. He made peace with the Unitarios, and he enlisted the aid of Brazil, which in effect took the place of Britain and France in the anti-Rosas coalition. The Brazilian government did not content itself with a mere blockade but provided troops as well. And that was that. Rosas was defeated in battle in February 1852 and departed on a British ship, to spend the rest of his years among his former European adversaries.

Though it was some time after his overthrow before Rosas became the object of a nostalgic hero cult, it must be emphasized in conclusion that his accomplishments amount to considerably more than successfully defying the British and the French. He was, after all, the first postindependence ruler who really ruled over all of Argentina. This makes him, as much as anyone, the architect of Argentine national unity, even though he did not create formal national institutions. Furthermore, the relative stability provided by his regime, regardless of the methods by which it was imposed, was a circumstance that favored continued economic expansion in Buenos Aires province (where by midcentury wool had emerged as still another major export industry), as well as somewhat less pronounced and uneven progress among the interior provinces. His conquerors, as a result, would face an easier task in finally organizing the nation than he had faced in recreating it.

The Distinctive Paraguayan Path:
Paternalism and Isolation

Though it is easy to discuss the affairs of Uruguay during most of the nineteenth century as a sidelight to the history of Argentina (or Brazil), Paraguay just as clearly stands apart. Except briefly in the 1860s, when it challenged the combined forces of Argentina, Brazil, and Uruguay in the War of the Triple Alliance, Paraguay did not play a key role in affairs of the Platine area. It nevertheless followed a sufficiently distinctive course of development to require treatment as a special, deviant case within the context of Latin America as a whole, particularly as the Paraguayan path is held up by some as a model of what other countries should have done but failed to do.

Colonial Paraguay had been a frontier province politically dependent on Buenos Aires and a supplier of tobacco and yerba mate—sometimes known as Paraguay tea—to other parts of the viceroyalty of the Río de la Plata. It was also the site of early and unusually thorough racial and cultural mixing between Spaniards and Guaraní Indians, resulting in a basically mestizo society whose lingua franca was Guaraní, not Spanish. Members of the small minority of more or less pure European extraction did use Spanish among themselves and felt part of the same cultural universe as the people of far-off Buenos Aires, but the great majority of Paraguayans felt no kinship whatever with the porteños. Linguistic peculiarity reinforced sheer geographic isolation to give Paraguayans a strong sense of separate identity.

The chief architect of Paraguayan independence, José Gaspar Rodríguez de Francia, was a university-educated creole who nevertheless established an instinctive rapport with the masses. A congress in 1816 had declared him (somewhat redundantly) "perpetual dictator of the republic during his life," and he did in fact retain a position of absolute supremacy until his death in 1840. He had no further need of congresses even to rubber-stamp his measures, and neither did he bother to give the country a window-dressing constitution. With the help of one or two subordinates, Francia personally set tax rates, tested weaponry for the armed forces, and in special cases issued licenses to marry. He assumed personal control of the church to the extent that for most practical purposes Paraguay was made independent of Rome. While he was at it, he suppressed all monasteries, seizing their property for the state, and closed the ecclesiastical seminary, which as the only institution of higher education in the country also served lay students.

Any who questioned Francia's rule or were merely suspected of working against him could expect no mercy. Virtually all those apart from Francia himself who had played a significant role in the independence movement were eventually executed on grounds of real or imaginary conspiracies. They may have been luckier than those other critics who were consigned to dungeons, aboveground or below, and there left to rot; Francia was inclined in such cases simply to "throw away the key." Still others were able to gain the safety of exile. Repression did not, however, touch the ordinary Paraguayan, who was quite content to leave governing to the dictator. It fell heavily instead on Francia's own class, the creole elite, and to an even greater extent on the small but once influential peninsular minority. The latter Francia set out to eliminate altogether as a factor in Paraguayan society, which he accomplished by decreeing that its members could henceforth marry only Indians, mestizos, or mulattos. The creole upper class was not quite eliminated, but its ranks were decimated, and a great part of its land and other property passed into the hands of the state by way of fines and confiscations. The result was the closest Latin America came to true social revolution between the Haitian slave insurrection and the victory of Fidel Castro in 1959: a general tendency toward equalization of social status, effected through the leveling down of what had been the dominant groups.

Social equalization went hand in hand with a primitive form of state socialism. Francia was no doctrinaire foe of private enterprise, but when he seized the property of his enemies, he did not turn around and sell or give it to someone else. He added it to the existing national patrimony and either exploited it directly or leased it to mostly small operators. This both restricted the scope of private ownership in the economy and gave the state itself a high degree of economic independence. Government estates supplied the army with beef cattle and other provisions, while the steady income from rent payments allowed Francia even to reduce the burden of taxes. A final dimension of Francia's policy was his isolation of Paraguay from neighboring countries. This was in part an effort to insulate Paraguay from the troubles afflicting the latter, especially Argentina, and it was reinforced by Francia's deep distrust of the intentions of both Brazil and Argentina. Not only did those countries have disputed borders with Paraguay, but the authorities at Buenos Aires had never reconciled themselves to the loss of Paraguay, insisting that it was rightfully a province of the Argentine Confederation. Isolation was not total, as some trade continued, but it was a trade strictly controlled by the state and not of great importance for the Paraguayan economy, which had been largely self-sufficient to begin with and under Francia became even more so. Other contacts were limited, too, but could not be avoided altogether. One constant threat to the isolation policy was the stream of refugees from Argentine civil wars seeking safety on Paraguayan soil.

Protected from those same civil wars, subject to minimal taxation, and owing personal allegiance to a paternalistic state rather than a class of private land barons, the Paraguayan masses genuinely revered their dictator, or *El Supremo* (The Supreme One) as he came to be known. And when in 1840 he became *El Difunto* (The Dead One, as some people still preferred not to call him by name), there was no immediate change in the situation. After a brief transition, one of the surviving members of the creole upper class, Carlos Antonio López, emerged in control and, until he died in 1862, retained most of the essential features of the Francia regime. He deigned to issue a rudimentary constitution, and he kept slightly fewer political prisoners, but he was not more tolerant of genuine opposition than Francia had been. Though casually unassuming in manner, quite capable of dressing in shorts to receive a foreign visitor, López did not share Francia's strict financial austerity and enriched his family greatly. Yet the accumulation of vast landholdings by the López clan really had the same effect as Francia's expansion of state farms, in that it kept those lands from falling into the hands of a new landed oligarchy capable of either challenging the state or exploiting the peasantry.

On another front, López founded many primary schools as well as the first Paraguayan newspaper, the latter so that his subjects might have some official propaganda on which to practice their newly acquired literacy. And by sponsoring a free-birth law in 1842, he began the process of abolition of slavery. This was something that Francia, for all his patriarchal interest in the masses, had signally failed to do. Indeed, Francia *increased* the extent of slavery in Paraguay by reducing to slave status numerous free black or mulatto workers of estates that he confiscated from political opponents.

The most notable characteristic of López's rule, however, was his conscious effort to modernize Paraguay technologically with the aid of foreign, mainly British, experts. An iron foundry, an arsenal, a shipyard, even a railroad (begun in 1858) were among the projects undertaken. In each case it was the Paraguayan government that took the initiative, contracting for the services of foreign technicians and paying the costs out of current revenues. The fact that López at the same time opened the gates somewhat wider to foreign trade helped to increase the state's disposable income. By this means, in any case, Paraguay modernized without slipping into a state of dependence on foreign loans or foreign capital investment—at most on foreign technology.

It is the relative autonomy of Paraguay's chosen course together with the relative well-being enjoyed by the average Paraguayan—whose basic needs were satisfied more adequately than those of most other Latin Americans, albeit without exceeding a comfortable level of rustic simplicity—that have drawn favorable attention to the Paraguay of the first half-century after independence as a "model" of what Latin America could and should have become.[1] Until the 1860s, moreover, Paraguay continued with minor exceptions to enjoy peace within as well as on its borders, not to mention a slowly rising prosperity. Yet it must be emphasized that modernization as promoted by López was to a great degree defensive in purpose, to make the Paraguayan nation better able to ward off threats from its larger neighbors. Thus, special attention was given to building up the armed forces—with most unfortunate results when Paraguay's military might emboldened López's oldest son and successor, Francisco Solano López, to take a more active role in the affairs of the

Platine region. The outcome would be the disastrous war of 1864-70 (see chapter 11). In sum, the Paraguayan model of autonomous development under guidance of an authoritarian state had much to recommend it, but, exactly as happened with the Rosas system in Argentina, its very success brought on its destruction.

A ranch hand who made
good: José Antonio Páez
of Venezuela. (Litografía
Venezolana, c. 1847.)

Beggar (licensed) on
horseback: Buenos Aires
in the days of Rosas.
(Woodbine Parish, *Buenos
Ayres and the Provinces
of the Río de la Plata*,
Buenos Aires, 1958.)

Mendigo a caballo.

Upper- and lower-class travel in the Colombian mountains (1850s).
(Biblioteca Nacional, Bogotá.)

Slave auction in Rio de Janeiro, about 1850. (Nineteenth-century etching.)

Encounter of two cultures:
Josefa Juárez (sister of Benito) posing for portrait by
latest technology.
(*Epistolario de Benito
Juárez*, ed. Jorge I. Tamayo,
1957.)

Natural obstacle successfully
overcome, on the rail line
Veracruz–Mexico City. (The
Harry Ransom Humanities
Research Center, University
of Texas at Austin.)

THE PHILATELIC RECORD.

(a) Bernardino Rivadavia, trail-blazer of Argentine liberalism and the face most often seen on stamps issued by Mitre and Sarmiento. (Private collection.)

(b) Stamp issued by the sovereign state of Antioquia. (Private collection.)

(c) Stamp issued by Antonio Guzmán Blanco, with portrait of Bolívar and earmarked for support of schools ("Escuelas"). (Private collection.)

Pedro II in late career and full regalia. (Livraria José Olimpio Editora)

Cuban slaves pounding sugar into boxes (1860s). (Samuel Hazard, *Cuba with Pen and Pencil*, 1871.)

7

The Rise
of the Brazilian Monarchy
(1822–1850)

The history of Brazil has diverged in many respects, both great and small, from that of its Spanish American neighbors (which, for that matter, have diverged in many ways from one another). Its sheer size and wide range of climatic and ecological zones would be enough to guarantee its distinctiveness. So would the fact of its being the product of Portuguese, not Spanish, colonization. In the nineteenth century it stood apart still more obviously by virtue of two "peculiar institutions"—monarchy and large-scale plantation slavery—which it shared only with the Spanish Caribbean colonies of Cuba and Puerto Rico which had not yet attained their independence. Nevertheless, Brazil was inevitably exposed to the same external influences, and it shared with its immediate neighbors many of the same problems of nation building. It merely surmounted those problems more successfully than most—from the standpoint of its upper social strata, if not of its enslaved masses.

Life and Work in Imperial Brazil

Aside from sugar, Brazil's principal manufactured export during the colonial period was ships. At the time of Brazilian independence in 1822, the largest ships in the Portuguese navy were products of the royal shipyards in Bahia, Brazil. Brazilian ship-builders had been favored within the Portuguese seaborne empire; they lost that artificial market advantage with independence, which coincided with the onset of a period of rapid technical change—the first world revolution in maritime technology since the one the Portuguese had launched four centuries earlier. Sailing their ships was a job that Brazilians generally left to the Portuguese before independence and to various foreign nationalities afterward. In Brazil there was no cultural imperative to design, build, and sail ships as there was, for example, in North American ports from Marblehead to Baltimore. With the separation from seafaring Portugal, Brazil's shipbuilding industry withered.

Except for shipyards, sugar mills, and a few textile workshops, manufacturing enterprises were prohibited in Brazil before 1808, the year the Portuguese royal court took up residence in Rio de Janeiro. In 1808 the crown removed the mercantilist restrictions and began to actively encourage new economic activity in the colony, which soon was raised to the status of kingdom, coequal with Portugal. The industrial production of pig iron in Brazil began with the inauguration of a government-owned mill in the province of São Paulo in 1818. The crown promoted Brazilian agricultural development by the introduction of new varieties of sugarcane, coffee, and tea, all of which were grown experimentally at the Royal Botanical Gardens in Rio and distributed as seedlings to interested planters. The tea from China did not survive in Brazil after independence, which cut off Brazilian access to skilled labor and expertise from Canton via the Portuguese colony of Macao. Sugarcane from Mauritius had a more lasting effect in increasing the productivity of Brazil's long-established sugar industry, though not enough to enable it to meet the challenge of Cuban competition in world markets. It was the Portuguese government's promotion of coffee cultivation in Brazil that had the most profound consequences for Brazilian economic and social development in the postindependence period.

Some coffee had been exported from Brazil as early as the middle of the eighteenth century, following the crop's introduction into northern Brazil from French Guiana. Coffee moved south in Brazil and appeared as a minor export of the Rio de Janeiro area by the turn of the century; about half a metric ton of coffee was shipped from Rio in 1800. Production and export of the commodity soared after the Portuguese crown arrived and began handing out nursery stock and land grants near Rio to potential coffee planters. In 1820 coffee exports from Rio amounted to 6,763 tons; the yearly export figure doubled to 13,286 tons in 1825, and by 1828 it had doubled again to 26,703 tons. Almost concurrent with Brazilian independence, coffee became the mainstay of the economy of the southeastern provinces of Rio de Janeiro, Minas Gerais, and São Paulo.

Southeastern Brazil offered not only ideal soil for growing coffee but also an available pool of slave labor and an extensive transportation network, both left over from the eighteenth-century mining boom. By the early 1800s most of the mines were exhausted, and labor originally allocated to gold and diamond extraction could be switched to coffee cultivation, while mules that once carried precious minerals from across the mountains into Rio could pack coffee beans instead. Well-policed trails, with regularly spaced waystations providing rest and maintenance facilities for animals and drivers, ran from Rio across the Rio Paraíba to the mining towns of Minas Gerais, and through the Paraíba Valley into the province of São Paulo, the intermediate source of most of the mules employed in southeastern Brazil. The original sources of the draft animals were the far south provinces of Uruguay and Rio Grande do Sul, whence mules and equine breeding stock were driven to the Paulista town of Sorocaba, where they were sold to buyers from all over the southeast at Brazil's largest livestock fair.

As sugar prices weakened in the 1820s, more resources were shifted into coffee production in southeastern Brazil. In the northeast, where the coffee option did not exist, the regional sugar-based economy shrank. Some capital and labor from the northeast migrated to the southeast and helped fuel the coffee expansion in the Paraíba Valley. The expansion was driven by a steadily increasing demand for the commodity in Europe and North America. Nowhere in the world were conditions more favorable for coffee production in the 1820s than in southeastern Brazil. Abundant land, sufficient working capital, and essential infrastructure were all in place; the only element missing was an adequate indigenous supply of labor. By the 1820s the demand for labor on the coffee plantations had far exceeded the supply of workers available from the declining sugar and mining industries. Labor would have to be imported.

Brazil was a huge, sparsely settled country. The abundance of land relative to population guaranteed, from the first days of Portuguese colonization in the sixteenth century, that labor would be in short supply. Unlike Mexico and the Andean countries, Brazil did not have a sizable Indian population or a pre-existing native economy that could be adapted to the requirements of the European colonizers. The Portuguese introduced Old World crops into Brazil—beginning with sugarcane—and raised them for export with slave labor imported from Africa. Commercial food agriculture and ranching developed to support the export sector, and this production also was largely dependent on slave labor. Free persons, regardless of racial or ethnic origin, generally had access to land—despite crown attempts to restrict it to a few *fidalgos*—and could provide their own subsistence. They had few wants and were generally disinclined to sell their labor; planters found it cheaper and more convenient to buy slaves than to hire free workers. The situation did not change appreciably with independence and the accompanying coffee boom. Increased economic activity was reflected in rising slave imports: yearly totals of Africans landed in Rio rose from 26,254 in 1825 to 43,555 in 1828.

While the southeast boomed, the south—Uruguay, Rio Grande do Sul, and Santa Catarina—prospered in furnishing work animals and jerked beef, which was fed to slaves, to the coffee region. The sugar-based economy of the northeast stagnated in the postindependence period, and the north and west—vast regions of forests and grasslands with almost no people—remained undeveloped.

Salvador da Bahia, Brazil's second largest city, was affected by the general weakness of the northeastern economy and additionally suffered the effects of military operations in its sugarcane-growing hinterland during the war for independence, the effects of the decline in shipbuilding, and the effects of the diversion of most of the transatlantic slave traffic from the traditional entrepôt of Bahia to Rio de Janeiro. This last development was caused partly by the shift in slave demand to southeastern Brazil and partly by the British-Portuguese Treaty of 1815 that prohibited the slave trade north of the equator. Bahia's commercial ties were strongest with West Africa north of the line, where consumers had developed a taste for molasses-soaked Bahian tobacco, which was exchanged for slaves. The treaty ban, though indifferently enforced, increased the costs of this business and reduced the returns to Bahian slavers and tobacco producers alike. No such burden was imposed on the slave trade with southern Africa, which remained legal through the 1820s; in this commerce, Rio-based traders had the advantages of traditional ties and geographical proximity.

Transatlantic trade shaped Brazil's economy and society. Most of the country's population of about four million in 1822 lived within one hundred kilometers of the coast. Between major export centers—São Luís, Maranhão, Recife, Salvador da Bahia, and Rio de Janeiro—were numerous smaller ports that fed produce to the larger cities for reexport or local consumption. Sugar production was concentrated on plantations located less than a day's travel by oxcart from the ocean, a bay, or a navigable stream. No river in the sugarcane zone—the coastal strip from Maranhão to São Paulo—was navigable for more than sixty kilometers inland. Coffee plantations extended farther into the southeastern interior along the mule trails established in the eighteenth century to feed gold and diamonds directly to Rio or to intermediate ports like Parati.

Squatters settled in the marginal spaces between royal land grants along the coast and in the undistributed territory of the adjacent backlands, or *sertão*. Mostly subsistence farmers, these *marginais* were the free issue of the mixing of the three races— white, black, and Indian. They accounted for perhaps half of Brazil's population in 1822 and coexisted symbiotically with the big landowners, or *fazendeiros*, and the latters' principal tenants and sharecroppers, the *lavradores*. Members of squatter families were generally available to serve in the militia, to hunt down runaway slaves, and, in times of economic expansion when slave-labor resources were totally committed to export production, to supply food to the plantations, or *fazendas*. In times of economic stability or decline, the fazendas were self-sufficient, and the utility of free subsistence farmers to the export economy was as a reserve labor pool. With little opportunity for regular employment and only occasional demand for its surplus production, the marginal rural population took a large proportion of its income in leisure.

Legal caste distinctions had been eliminated in Portuguese America in the third quarter of the eighteenth century, and the corporatist system that prevailed in much of Spanish America into the postindependence period had no counterpart in Brazil. Corporate rights existed in theory in colonial Brazil, but the institutional framework within which they could be exercised was lacking. Among Brazil's overwhelmingly rural population, high social or ethnic credentials evoked residual respect, but it was those landowners or miners who could field the largest contingents of armed retainers who prevailed in personal and property disputes. Royal judges and clergy—when they acted at all—sanctioned faits accomplis. Exceptions were confined to a few urban areas where priests or royal officials occasionally extended protection to mistreated slaves.

Brazil's black slaves numbered more than one million in 1822, constituting perhaps thirty percent of the country's population. Life was hard and short for these unfortunate individuals; few survived more than seven years of labor on the plantations or in the mines. The purchaser of a slave, however, usually recuperated his investment after only one year. Imported replacements were cheap; there was no economic incentive for owners to expend much on the upkeep of their slaves or to encourage—or even allow—them to reproduce. Brazil's slave population was maintained by the continuing importation of blacks from Africa.

The slave trade was an abomination to Brazilian Emperor Pedro I and his principal collaborators, José Bonifácio de Andrada e Silva and the Marquis of Queluz, all three of whom published abolitionist tracts in the 1820s. The suppression of the transatlantic traffic, the Brazilian abolitionists knew, would drive up the cost of slaves and raise the price of free labor. However, given the free population's habits of underconsumption, the abolitionists had reason to doubt that many ex-slaves would be attracted into the labor market even at substantially increased wages. If the prohibition of African imports were followed by the liberation of slaves already in Brazil—the abolitionists' ultimate objective—most of the ex-slaves could be expected to establish themselves as subsistence farmers on vacant land, to conform to the low consumption levels of the free population, and virtually to remove themselves from the labor force. Brazilian planters, given the physical impossibility of their controlling access to all the land in Brazil, professed to see no alternative to the continuation of the slave-labor system.

The abolitionists' answer to the labor problem was European immigration. Accustomed to levels of consumption above those of Brazil's rural poor, European peasants settling on farms in Brazil could be expected to seek supplemental employment at monetary wages, or at least to produce marketable surpluses on their homesteads, in order to maintain their higher standard of living. Coming from land-scarce societies, they would be predisposed to extract maximum utility from Brazil's most abundant resource. They would bring with them needs for tools and consumer goods, which soon would become necessities also for Brazilian neighbors attracted to their life-style. The appearance of the new goods would induce rural Brazilians to forgo some of their leisure and accept remunerative employment—to acquire the means to satisfy their new needs. The example of the immigrants as producers and consumers would lure other free persons into the labor force and make slavery unnecessary. Or so thought Brazilian abolitionists at the time of their country's separation from Portugal.

The Constitution of 1824

In May 1821, a few days after the departure from Rio of Portuguese King John VI, his son, Dom Pedro, issued a series of decrees cutting taxes and guaranteeing civil liberties and property rights in Brazil. The young regent eliminated the royal salt tax, a move designed to stimulate the production of hides and jerked beef, and he removed the two-percent cabotage tax, lifting a burden from domestic commerce. He declared private property secure from arbitrary seizure. No free person, Dom Pedro decreed, could be arrested without a written warrant from a judge, except when apprehended in flagrante delicto. No citizen could be held for more than forty-eight hours without formal charges and without knowing the identity of his accuser; secret trials were prohibited, and defendants were to be guaranteed the means to conduct their defense. Torture and the pretrial use of chains, manacles, and shackles were forbidden by order of the new prince regent, an avowed liberal and constitutionalist who was committed to sweeping away vestiges of three centuries of arbitrary rule in Brazil. The outbreak of war with Portugal, however, led him to suspend some of the liberal guarantees during the hostilities.

Dom Pedro had hoped to continue Brazil's association with Portugal, but when the Portuguese *Cortes* (parliament) tried to suppress his autonomous government in Rio, the prince decided on formal independence. He was supported by the dominant interests of southeastern Brazil: coffee, sugar, and cotton planters; ranchers; non-Portuguese merchants; and royal judges and other officeholders. He was assisted in governing the country by a group of Brazilian-born, European-trained lawyers, engineers, and scientists, of whom José Bonifácio de Andrada e Silva, a noted mineralogist, was most prominent. With José Bonifácio as head of his council of ministers, Dom Pedro declared Brazil's independence from Portugal in September 1822 and had himself crowned emperor of Brazil in December. Four months later a Constituent Assembly met in Rio to begin drawing up a constitution for the Empire of Brazil.

The debates in the Constituent Assembly began as the war for independence was drawing to a close. The war was financed largely by the confiscation of Portuguese property in Brazil, and the advent of peace was not a welcome prospect to those whose interests were served by a continuation of the confiscations and by flexible criteria for assigning property owners to the vulnerable category of enemy alien. Those who coveted Portuguese property—including the emperor's piratical first admiral, the British adventurer Lord Cochrane who had previously served in the navy of Chile—or who wanted to eliminate Portuguese-born competitors in business or public service sought to maintain the war fever. So did some members of the emperor's government who wanted to retain the emergency powers that allowed them to punish their personal enemies in disregard of Dom Pedro's earlier liberal decrees. Dom Pedro, however, was eager for peace and reconciliation. In July 1823, shortly after learning of the liberation of Bahia, he revoked the emergency war measures, without consulting José Bonifácio, and ordered an end to the imprisonment and persecution of the cabinet chief's personal enemies. José Bonifácio reacted by resigning from the cabinet, together with his brother, Finance Minister Martim Francisco, the architect of the confiscation policy. The two ex-ministers took their seats in the Constituent Assembly, where they joined a third Andrada brother, Antônio Carlos, who was the leading figure in that body, the chairman of the committee that was preparing a draft constitution for the consideration of the full assembly.

The conflict between Dom Pedro and the Andrada brothers was less a matter of ideology than it was a contest of wills. The emperor was impatient for the full implementation of the liberal state, a goal shared by the Andradas but one they intended to postpone until they had meted out exemplary punishment to their enemies, whom they sincerely regarded as threats to the new regime. Their judgment was impaired by their vindictiveness, a fault that Dom Pedro, for all his other vices, did not share. The Andradas were grandsons of a Portuguese merchant who had established himself in the Paulista port of Santos. They had few ties to the Brazilian landed aristocracy and had spent much of their lives abroad; all were graduates of Coimbra University in Portugal, and José Bonifácio, the mineralogist, had studied also at various other prestigious European institutions. Martim Francisco was a mathematician and ethnologist as well as an economist; Antônio Carlos was a lawyer and career magistrate. The intellectual arrogance of the Andrada brothers and the ruthlessness with which they pushed their programs offended many of their government colleagues and accounted for some of the enmity they aroused.

The Andrada brothers wanted the proposed constitution that was formulated by Antônio Carlos's committee to be accepted by the full Constituent Assembly without debate and immediately promulgated by the emperor. Dom Pedro, however, insisted that the committee proposal be scrutinized by the entire assembly, with the delegates having the opportunity to accept, reject, or amend each of the draft's two hundred seventy-two articles. The refusal of the emperor to cooperate in the immediate-adoption scheme added to the tensions between him and the Andrada brothers, which reached the crisis stage as the latter took the lead in whipping up popular hysteria about Portuguese subversion in Rio.

Dom Pedro ordered that Portuguese prisoners taken in Bahia be brought to Rio and given the choice of repatriation or enlistment in the Brazilian army. Portuguese-born merchants in Rio hoped that an ethnically mixed Brazilian army would protect them from nativist pogroms. Native Brazilians, even when they did not covet the property of Portuguese immigrants, were apt to disapprove of the inclusion in the national armed forces of large numbers of foreign-born officers and men likely to have a natural distaste for Brazilian institutions like slavery. Though opposed to slavery, the Andrada brothers, in their contest of wills with Dom Pedro, sought to prevent the incorporation into the military of elements likely to identify personally with the emperor, who, after all, was himself a native of Portugal. In the Constituent Assembly and in the Rio press, the Andradas regularly denounced the Portuguese presence in the Brazilian army.

In November 1823, after particularly virulent speeches by Antônio Carlos and Martim Francisco—in which Portuguese-born officers were likened to wild beasts who should be exterminated—and after the Andradas had invited the nativist mob onto the convention floor, the Constituent Assembly was dissolved on orders of the emperor and Assembly President João Severiano Maciel da Costa, later Marquis of Queluz. That Dom Pedro had been prepared to use force to dissolve the assembly was unsettling to some, but to members of the Portuguese community it meant that the army stood with the emperor and would safeguard their lives and property. The Andrada brothers were arrested and shipped to exile in France.

The dissolution of the Constituent Assembly and the banishment of its leaders was not a blow against constitutional government, the emperor tried to explain to his subjects. He would give the people a constitution "twice as liberal" as the one that had been taking shape in the assembly. In fact, the work of the assembly was far from complete when that body was dissolved: the delegates had finished consideration of only twenty-four of the two hundred seventy-two articles in the Antônio Carlos committee draft. At that rate it would have taken them two more years to produce a constitution. Dom Pedro, wanting faster action, appointed a committee of ten Brazilian-born citizens—including the future Marquis of Queluz and six other former assembly delegates—to meet with him and formulate a constitution for the empire. With the active participation of the emperor the committee got the job done within a month. Early in 1824, the committee document was submitted for ratification to the city and town councils of Brazil and, after a majority had approved it, was proclaimed the constitution of the empire in April. The Brazilian Constitution of 1824, which would remain in effect for sixty-five years, was a gift from the throne; it was not a charter imposed upon the monarch by an elected assembly.

Dom Pedro's constitution was more liberal than the Constituent Assembly proposal in some areas, such as religion, where it permitted congregations of Jews and other non-Catholics to maintain houses of worship, which the assembly would have forbidden. Both documents, however, called for the establishment of Roman Catholicism as the religion of the empire, with the emperor as patron of the church in Brazil. The emperor and his committee were more specific in defining "inviolable" personal and property rights, listing thirty-four as opposed to only six in the assembly proposal. But Dom Pedro's constitution was less liberal in its concentration of power in the hands of a hereditary chief of state.

The Brazilian Constitution of 1824 created a centralized national government of four branches, or powers—legislative, executive, judicial, and moderating. The legislative power was wielded by a General Assembly, or parliament, consisting of a Chamber of Deputies elected for a four-year term, and a Senate whose members served for life. Suffrage was extended to free adult males with an annual income of at least one hundred dollars, but elections were indirect. Local voters chose electors who cast ballots on the provincial level for deputies and senators; in the case of the latter, three nominees were named for each vacancy, with the final choice being the emperor's. Representation in both houses was based on population, including slaves; for every two deputies there was one senator. Provincial governors were appointed by the national executive in the imperial capital; they were advised by elected provincial councils. Constitutional amendments were fairly easy to effect, requiring the approval of two successive parliaments.

The emperor was the "chief of the executive power," which was delegated to a cabinet, or Council of Ministers. The ministers were appointed by the emperor and served at his pleasure; they were not responsible to the legislature, as in systems of parliamentary supremacy. The executive branch enforced the laws enacted by the General Assembly, ran the administrative departments and the armed forces, and conducted the foreign relations of the empire; treaties were sanctioned by the emperor and did not require ratification by the legislative branch. To allay fears that the emperor might sign away the country's independence, the constitution specifically prohibited the union of Brazil with any other nation.

The judicial branch was to consist of a Supreme Court and such lower courts as established by law. The option of trial by jury in both criminal and civil cases was to be offered as soon as practicable—Brazil had no experience with the jury system—but was immediately available in cases involving freedom of the press, which the constitution guaranteed, although citizens could be held accountable for "abuses" as defined by law. Press freedom and personal security rights could be temporarily suspended in cases of rebellion formally declared by the emperor with the approval of the General Assembly. All special jurisdictions were abolished; a single national court system and one body of laws were to apply to all persons in Brazil.

Slaves were not citizens and had no rights under the Brazilian Constitution of 1824. Dom Pedro, in hopes of winning quick acceptance of the charter, sacrificed his strong feelings on this matter. In May 1823, he had declared in a pseudonymous article in a Rio newspaper that people had no "right at all to enslave one another" and that slavery was a "cancer" that was "gnawing away at Brazil."[1] The cancer had to be eradicated by deliberate action, beginning with the total prohibition of the transatlantic slave trade within two years, he had written. In his 1824 constitution he provided himself with treaty-making powers that he could use to try to stop the traffic.

The fourth branch of government, the moderating power, was introduced in the Brazilian constitution as "the key to all political organization." As the moderator or arbiter of the political process, the emperor was allocated certain clearly defined powers, to enable him to break deadlocks and to ensure the functioning of the government in accordance with the constitution and in the permanent interests of the nation. Some of these powers could be found in other Latin American constitutions, usually allotted to the executive—for example, the authority to pardon convicts and reduce sentences and to veto legislation. Most importantly, the monarch could dissolve the Chamber of Deputies at his discretion, before its four-year term was up, and convoke elections for a new parliament. To advise the emperor in exercising the moderating power, the constitution established a Council of State composed of ten members appointed for life, whom the emperor was required to consult on a regular basis and prior to any exercise of the moderating power. The ten-man council that had helped Dom Pedro frame the constitution became, with the same personnel, the constitutional Council of State.

The charter was most readily accepted in booming southeastern Brazil, where coffee planters and merchants perceived a need for political order to preserve and extend their prosperity. The constitution's reception was least favorable in the depressed sugar and cotton country of the northeast. Low export prices and high slave prices were blamed on the government in Rio—on its preoccupation with the coffee economy, its obsession with protecting the solvency of the Bank of Brazil, and its failure to provide the northeast with an adequate medium of exchange. Since 1821, when the departure of the Portuguese court set off a run on deposits, the convertibility of Bank of Brazil notes had been suspended; these, however, rarely circulated outside the southeast. To cover its extraordinary expenses from the war for independence, the government in Rio borrowed from the Bank of Brazil only as a last resort, and new issues of bank notes were kept at a minimum. Much of the specie income of the imperial government was applied to its Bank of Brazil debt and ultimately was used to redeem bank notes, thereby constricting the money supply. But at the same time, rising export earnings from coffee infused more specie into the southeast—and drained it from the northeast, where productivity was lower. By 1824 practically the only currency circulating in the northeast was counterfeit copper coins. Many northeasterners came to the conclusion that union with the southeast was doing their region more harm than good. The promulgation of the centralized 1824 constitution, designed to strengthen that union, was taken as the signal to revolt. Five northeastern provinces, led by Pernambuco and Ceará, declared their independence in mid-1824 and formed a new nation, the Confederation of the Equator. The confederation was short-lived, crushed before the end of 1824 by the imperial navy and army. Constitutional guarantees were suspended in the region, and sixteen ringleaders of the insurrection were executed. The swift and overwhelming reaction of the central government served to deter future revolts in the northeast, although the empire lost its formidable first admiral, Lord Cochrane, who deserted after the campaign and sailed to Europe with the provincial treasury of Maranhão.

The expenses incurred by the imperial government in suppressing the Confederation of the Equator were largely met by an eighteen-million-dollar loan extended to Brazil by British banks in 1824. Some of this money was spent in the northeast, and, generally, the central government paid more attention to the region after the revolt. The imperial treasury in 1826 issued a great quantity of copper coins stamped at four times their intrinsic value, which drove the older counterfeit coins out of circulation while increasing the official money supply in the northeast and elsewhere. But the devaluation of the copper coinage did nothing to stem the flow of gold and silver from the northeast to the more productive southeast. The value of the empire's currency—treasury copper and Bank of Brazil notes—was largely determined by coffee exports, which would stay high for the remainder of the nineteenth century. Sugar and cotton exporters of the northeast were saddled with an overvalued currency that reduced their returns from foreign sales and increased the difficulty of their competing in world markets with producers from Cuba and the southern United States. Once they recognized the impossibility of secession from the empire, the planters of the northeast were more willing to accept the loss of international markets and resign themselves to producing for Brazil's national market.

Evolution of the Parliamentary System under Dom Pedro I, 1824–1831

Portugal recognized Brazilian independence in 1825. That development was facilitated by the dissolution of the Portuguese Cortes in 1824 and the return of the royal prerogative to King John VI, and by British pressure on the Portuguese restorationist government to settle with the ex-colony. The 1825 treaty of recognition provided for a joint commission of Brazilian, Portuguese, and "neutral" British members to determine Brazil's liability for its confiscation of Portuguese property, but the matter was settled in a secret codicil, revealed the next year, whereby Portugal agreed to drop all claims against Brazil in return for the latter's payment of 2.9 million dollars to the Portuguese treasury and its assumption of a debt of 6.7 million dollars that Portugal owed to Britain. By faithfully discharging this obligation, and making regular payments on the 1824 British loan when all other Latin American governments were defaulting on their foreign debts, Brazil impressed its creditors and continued to attract British capital in the second quarter of the nineteenth century.

The growing British stake in Brazil underscored Britain's need for a commercial agreement with Dom Pedro's empire, to replace the expired treaty of 1810 that had been made between London and the Portuguese court in Rio. The first attempt to negotiate a British-Brazilian treaty failed in 1826 because Dom Pedro refused to renew the extraterritorial rights that British subjects had enjoyed in Brazil under the 1810 treaty. The emperor contended that special courts for British residents of Brazil, presided over by British judges, violated the Brazilian constitution, which abolished all special jurisdictions. In the end, however, Dom Pedro compromised: the commercial treaty that was ratified in 1827 allowed British residents to retain their special courts until such time as Brazilian legislation established the national judicial system provided for in the 1824 constitution.

The commercial treaty with Britain also limited the duty on British goods imported into Brazil to fifteen percent ad valorem. The Brazilian parliament reacted to this provision by reducing the tariff on the goods of other countries to the fifteen percent rate. Dominated by export agricultural interests, the Brazilian parliament, which met for the first time in 1826, did not object to low import duties. What the legislators found most offensive in the British-Brazilian commercial treaty were the extraterritoriality provisions, which they denounced as an affront to Brazil's sovereignty. More distasteful than the commercial treaty to the General Assembly was a British-Brazilian treaty on the slave trade that Dom Pedro signed late in 1826. This provided for the complete cessation of the traffic in slaves between Africa and Brazil within three years of final ratification of the treaty, which took place in London in March 1827. Beginning in 1830 the British navy would have the right of high-seas search and seizure of any Brazilian-flag vessels suspected of slaving. Accused slavers would be tried before mixed British-Brazilian commissions and, if convicted, suffer the penalties established for piracy.

Although the Brazilian parliament had no constitutional role in making or ratifying treaties, members of the Chamber of Deputies were especially adamant in registering their displeasure with the slave-trade treaty. They objected to the search-and-seizure provisions as infringements of Brazilian sovereignty and warned that the termination of the slave trade would ruin Brazil economically. The traffic was defended as necessary and humane, because in consigning blacks to slavery in Brazil it "rescued" them from a worse existence in Africa. The cabinet officer designated to answer these complaints, Foreign Minister Marquis of Queluz, made the lame excuse that the treaty had been forced on the Brazilian government by the British. This infuriated the proslavery deputies because Queluz—a Mineiro of uncertain parentage, a university graduate and career civil servant—was a known opponent of the slave trade, the author of a book on the subject published in 1821. The only member of the Chamber of Deputies who took a stand against the slave trade in the 1827 "debate" was Romualdo Antônio de Seixas, a priest from an Amazon river town whom Dom Pedro had named to be archbishop of Bahia.

Like Dom Pedro, Dom Romualdo and the Marquis of Queluz believed that the termination of the African slave trade should be accompanied by the promotion of European immigration into Brazil. They called for a liberal land-grant policy for potential colonists, while most members of the Brazilian parliament, if they were willing even to consider alternatives to black slavery, insisted on rigorous labor contracts that would leave the immigrants little better off than slaves. The emperor developed the idea of using immigrants to fill Brazil's military needs. During the war for independence and the Confederation of the Equator revolt, the imperial government paid the passage to Brazil of immigrant families whose adult male members were immediately inducted into the imperial armed forces. Brazilian recruiting agents in Europe were sometimes remiss in explaining the military obligations to the immigrants they signed up. Nevertheless, several thousand Europeans, mostly Germans and Irish, served voluntarily in the Brazilian armed forces and received land grants at the conclusion of periods of service of eight years or less. While in Brazilian military service these foreigners were organized into elite units and were paid more than their native comrades. They played an important role in the Uruguayan war of 1825–28.

The war to retain Uruguay as a province of the empire was unpopular with the plantation-slaveholding interests that predominated in the Brazilian parliament. Uruguay was unsuitable for the cultivation of plantation crops like coffee or sugarcane and had few slaves; its economy and society promised to develop along lines that, if the province remained in the empire, could pose political problems for the slavocrats of tropical Brazil. When Uruguay's Spanish-speaking majority in 1825 undertook to separate the province from Brazil and join it to the United Provinces of the Río de la Plata, Brazilian slavocrats were inclined to let them go in peace. Even the entry of Argentine troops into Uruguay to support the rebels did not raise much patriotic fervor in Brazil. Parliament undermined the war effort in various ways, by refusing to appropriate funds and by obstructing the recruitment of Brazilian troops. The emperor circumvented the opposition by borrowing from the Bank of Brazil and by employing foreign mercenaries in the fighting.

By the beginning of 1828 the antiwar movement in Rio was concentrating on harassing the foreign troops stationed in the imperial capital. The newspaper *Aurora Fluminense*, published by Evaristo da Veiga, an avowed liberal who was allied with the parliamentary slavocrats, specialized in baiting the Irish, who were portrayed as congenital alcoholics. The native population was incited to acts of violence against the German and Irish soldiers and their families, and the foreigners replied in kind. A full-scale mutiny erupted in July 1828; hundreds of Germans and Irish went on a rampage in Rio, assaulting and killing scores of their tormentors, looting and destroying their property. After three days of bloody fighting, Brazilian troops finally subdued the mutineers. Dom Pedro's immigrant-soldier program lay in ruins, and all the emperor's hopes of winning the war in Uruguay evaporated. The Brazilian government had no choice but to accept a settlement recommended by Great Britain: Uruguay was established as a buffer state, its independence guaranteed by both Brazil and the United Provinces.

With his failure in Uruguay, it became evident that Dom Pedro had lost the upper hand in the political system he had created. The real power lay with the majority in parliament, led by the brilliant—though sometimes erratic—Bernardo Pereira de Vasconcelos, a syphilitic lawyer from Minas Gerais, an unashamed defender of the institution of slavery. In the late 1820s Vasconcelos, representative of the coffee-planting interests of his own southeast region, emerged as the leader of a parliamentary coalition that included northeastern autonomists and nativists and crypto-republicans from various parts of the country. They were united in their distaste for the person and policies of the Portuguese-born monarch. This coalition led by Vasconcelos was really the government in Brazil, an English observer noted; the emperor and his ministers comprised the opposition. The dominant coalition enjoyed the support of most of the country's newspapers, including the *Aurora Fluminense*, whose editor, Evaristo da Veiga, a lifelong resident of Rio, was rewarded with a parliamentary seat in Vasconcelos's Minas Gerais delegation in the 1829 elections.

Dom Pedro recognized the weakness of his position and did not attempt to exercise his constitutional right to veto legislation passed by the General Assembly, even when the laws were designed to fortify the institution of slavery which he abhorred. Under the judicial system adopted by parliament, cases of mistreatment of slaves would be heard by judges elected locally— that is, by the local slaveholders—and not by crown-appointed magistrates. A criminal code drawn up by Vasconcelos provided the death penalty for slave rebellion while virtually exempting nonslaves from capital punishment (a measure that comforted some of the secessionists and other would-be revolutionists tactically allied with the coffee slavocracy). Brazil henceforth would train its own judges and attorneys in law schools established in Pernambuco and São Paulo by act of parliament.

After the mercenary mutiny, Dom Pedro accepted legislation to remove most foreigners from the Brazilian armed forces. Parliament also placed the army and navy, along with other executive departments, under budgetary restraints; funds could not be spent unless appropriated by the lawmakers. These measures made it virtually impossible for the imperial navy to enforce the slave-trade prohibition that went into effect in March 1830. Nevertheless, the navy minister announced that his forces would not allow slavers to depart Brazilian ports for Africa after November 1829, and in May 1830 the emperor reported to parliament that the infamous traffic had been terminated. In fact, the slave trade would continue for two more decades as successive parliaments refused to provide the means for stopping it.

Parliament also refused to renew the charter of the Bank of Brazil, which expired in 1829. The planter-exporters represented by Vasconcelos feared the huge accumulation of capital in the monopolistic Bank of Brazil. Aside from being a major supplier of funds to Dom Pedro's treasury, the bank was the country's principal source of business credit. Merely cutting the ties between the bank and the imperial government would not satisfy the slavocrats, for the bank would retain its potential for financing development inimical to the established economic and social order. Rather than reform the Bank of Brazil, as Dom Pedro urged, parliament liquidated it. The bank's outstanding notes almost equaled the government's debt to the bank, and there were sufficient bullion reserves in its vaults to pay off the balance and return to the stockholders ninety percent of their capital.

Thus, virtually all the bank notes were retained in circulation as Imperial Treasury instruments, along with the debased copper coinage, while the bank's accumulated capital—which had served as a magnet drawing private funds to the bank for reinvestment—was dispersed. The liquidation of the bank was regarded as a disaster by Dom Pedro and by other developmentalists, like the Andrada brothers, who returned to Brazil in the late 1820s and gradually became reconciled with the emperor who had banished them. Martim Francisco, elected to the Chamber of Deputies from Rio in 1829, led the losing fight in parliament to reestablish the bank.

While Dom Pedro was forfeiting these parliamentary battles, the ire of nativists in the streets of Rio was raised by the increased size of the Portuguese community in the capital city. Hundreds of Portuguese liberals and their families, refugees from the despotic regime of the usurper Dom Miguel in Lisbon, flocked to Rio where they placed themselves under the protection of the Brazilian emperor, whose daughter they recognized as their constitutional queen. Tensions increased in 1830 as an imaginative young man from the northeast, Antônio Borges da Fonseca, arrived in Rio and began publishing a newspaper, *O Republico*, that viewed the Portuguese buildup in Rio as the prelude to a planned seizure of absolute power by Dom Pedro and the suppression of Brazil's constitution and independence. Borges organized gangs of nativist street fighters and accompanied them on forays into Portuguese commercial and residential neighborhoods. The Portuguese defended their turf, and as the violence reached a peak in March 1831, the *Aurora Fluminense* demanded that the emperor take steps to end the disorder. Evaristo's newspaper, speaking for the majority in parliament—then in recess— blamed the violence on its victims, the Portuguese.

Dom Pedro rearranged his cabinet on March 19, 1831, and appointed new army and justice ministers who had Evaristo's blessing but, as it turned out, were unable or unwilling to stop the street fighting. In disgust, the emperor dismissed the entire cabinet on April 5 and appointed a new one drawn from among his most dedicated supporters. Evaristo and his colleagues joined forces with Borges and his followers on April 6 to mount public demonstrations and demand that the emperor reinstate the dismissed cabinet. Brazilian army officers and enlisted men—some still resenting Dom Pedro's favoritism for the foreign mercenaries, now gone—were swept up in the nativist fervor and participated in the demonstrations for the restoration of the dismissed cabinet. But the emperor would not surrender his constitutional right to choose his ministers. In a message that was read to the assembled demonstrators on the evening of April 6, Dom Pedro declared that he would "do everything for the people, but nothing by the people."[2]

In the absence of significant popular or military support for his position, Dom Pedro had no choice but to abdicate the throne, which he did before dawn on April 7, in favor of his five-year-old son, Dom Pedro II. The emperor's abdication, which few had expected and only Borges and his followers had actively sought, stunned the Rio populace. Evaristo, his parliamentary colleagues who happened to be in Rio during the recess, and the ranking officers of the army moved quickly to acclaim Dom Pedro II as titular Emperor of Brazil and to head off a republican revolution, the objective of Borges and the *exaltados* (radicals). A temporary regency was proclaimed to serve until the full parliament could meet and appoint a permanent one in accordance with the constitution. The young Dom Pedro II was entrusted to the care of José Bonifácio, his tutor, in compliance with the wishes of his father. The ex-emperor boarded a British warship and sailed a few days later for Europe. Other British and French warships remained in Rio harbor to protect the Portuguese community in case of a revolutionary attack.

Borges and the exaltados, however, were not prepared to launch their revolution in April. They retired from the streets as the new *moderado* government effectively guaranteed the safety of Rio's Portuguese-born residents. Parliament convened in May and elected a permanent three-man regency which, in turn, appointed a cabinet headed by Vasconcelos, who took the post of finance minister. It was this cabinet, not the three-man regency, that was to rule the empire, because the moderating power, as parliament interpreted the constitution, did not pertain to the regency; it could be wielded only by a reigning monarch. Thus, Brazil came under a regime of formal parliamentary supremacy in June 1831. But it was still a centralized monarchy, and the exaltados were determined to overthrow it and establish a federal republic. That idea did not appeal much to the upper classes of the capital city, but audacious northeasterners like Borges da Fonseca did attract significant numbers of Rio's urban poor to the exaltado cause.

The Empire Survives—at a High Cost—1831-1842

The exaltados managed to subvert most of the troops of the Rio garrison. Most of the officers, however, remained loyal to the monarchy and took up arms against the enlisted men when the latter joined a revolt that broke out in Rio in July 1831. The uprising was put down by a battalion of officers and by units of armed civilians organized by Justice Minister Diogo Antônio Feijó. A priest from São Paulo province, the illegitimate son of a priest, Feijó replaced Vasconcelos as the driving force in the moderado government following the suppression of the exaltado revolt. Vasconcelos's capacity for executive leadership was diminished by his physical afflictions; Feijó eagerly shouldered the burden that the great parliamentarian was unable to bear. But Feijó, unlike the conservative Vasconcelos, was a dedicated liberal and an enemy of the slave trade, which had continued despite the treaty ban that had gone into effect in March 1830.

Great Britain put pressure on the Brazilian government to live up to its treaty obligations and do something to halt the illicit traffic. Vasconcelos and the slavocrats wanted the trade to continue and would not countenance the taking of any meaningful steps to stop it. But most of them were willing to vote for an anti-slave-trade law, which they did not intend to enforce, in hopes of pacifying the British. The law of November 7, 1831, passed at the urging of Justice Minister Feijó, declared free all persons entering Brazil after that date. Feijó's genuine enthusiasm for the measure caused some concern among the slavocrats, but the justice minister seemed to be the strongest leader available to protect the southeastern export economy in a time of great turmoil. Feijó was well regarded by the British and had the support of Evaristo—also a British favorite in the 1830s, after he had given up Irish bashing and taken up promoting European immigration.

The removal of the exaltado threat in July 1831 gave rise to a new danger to the moderado government: the possibility of the restoration of Dom Pedro I. Support for the ex-emperor was strong among Rio's urban property owners—natives as well as Portuguese-born—who no longer were compelled to support the moderados out of fear of exaltado mobs. The restorationist movement was led by the formidable Andrada brothers, the eldest of whom was official tutor to the young emperor, Dom Pedro II. Feijó pushed a bill through the Chamber of Deputies to remove José Bonifácio from that position, but the measure was voted down in the Senate, whose members owed their appointments to the ex-monarch. The senators were inclined to respect their former patron's wishes in this matter and also to carry on his resistance to federalism—which Feijó and Evaristo were promoting as a cure for mounting unrest in the provinces.

Disturbances spread through the north and northeast in the aftermath of the abdication as provincial leaders questioned the legitimacy of the government of southeasterners that was trying to rule the empire from Rio. Feijó, Vasconcelos, and Evaristo proposed to create a federative monarchy, to grant the provinces a measure of self-determination in hopes of preempting possible secessionist movements of the type of the Confederation of the Equator, which, given the sorry state of the imperial armed forces, they would be hard-pressed to subdue. The Senate, however, disagreed with this strategy and rejected a federalist reform bill in 1832, which led the moderado cabinet to conspire to abolish the Senate. The plan, devised by Feijó and Evaristo, would have the Chamber of Deputies declare itself the national assembly and immediately adopt a new constitution that would set up a federative monarchy with a one-house federal parliament. Vasconcelos had misgivings about the plan, which would strengthen the hand of Feijó, whose loyalty to the slavocracy was suspect. Honório Hermeto Carneiro Leão, a bright young deputy from Minas Gerais, persuaded Vasconcelos to withdraw his support for the coup d'etat, which was thwarted by a majority vote in the Chamber of Deputies in July 1832. The vote was one of no confidence in Feijó, who promptly resigned from the cabinet.

Vasconcelos and Honório Hermeto, in partnership with Pedro de Araújo Lima, a slavocrat from Pernambuco, ran the central government of Brazil for most of the remainder of the 1830s. They were the founding fathers of the Brazilian Conservative party, which emerged as a formal organization along with the Liberal party in the middle of the decade. The conservatives succeeded where the liberal Feijó had failed, in firing the anti-slavery José Bonifácio as tutor to the young emperor in 1833. José Bonifácio's brother, Antônio Carlos, traveled to Lisbon that year to try to persuade the ex-emperor to return to Brazil. The elder Dom Pedro, on the verge of final victory in a bloody war to restore constitutionalism to Portugal, told Antônio Carlos that his abdication as emperor was irrevocable and that he would return as regent for his son only if the Brazilian parliament elected him to that position. The dim prospects of this occurring seemed to brighten somewhat in the parliamentary elections of 1833, when the restorationists carried every parish in Rio except one. But the more numerous slaveholder-dominated constituencies of rural Brazil voted differently; instead of recalling the ex-emperor, the new Chamber of Deputies passed a bill in 1834 to banish him forever. The effort was unnecessary, for Dom Pedro I died of tuberculosis in Portugal in September 1834. With restoration no longer possible, the late Dom Pedro's principal advocates, the Andrada brothers, joined Feijó and Evaristo in the Brazilian Liberal party.

Brazil's system of government during the minority of Dom Pedro II changed significantly with the adoption of the Additional Act of 1834. This was a set of constitutional amendments that abolished the Council of State (which had been inoperative in the absence of a reigning advisee since 1831), established provincial legislatures, and replaced the figurehead three-man regency with a single regent chosen by electors in a nationwide vote. The single regent was given independent executive power, and presumably he also would have the backing of a majority in the Chamber of Deputies, since he would be chosen by the same electors who had selected the deputies. Vasconcelos, the principal author of the Additional Act, believed that such a concentration of power was necessary to "stop the carriage of revolution," to control the disintegrative forces at work in the provinces.

Vasconcelos did not foresee the election of Feijó as single regent. Evaristo, who owed his seat in parliament to Vasconcelos, deserted his patron in 1834 and plugged relentlessly in the pages of the *Aurora Fluminense* for the election of Feijó. Evaristo's Rio newspaper had enormous influence in the provinces, where local periodicals regularly reprinted its columns—to which provincial intellectuals habitually referred for orientation on national matters. Evaristo's endorsement carried Feijó to victory, and he was sworn in for a four-year term as regent in 1835. Feijó wanted to attract foreign immigrants and capital to Brazil, to expand education, to diversify the economy, to enforce the slave-trade ban, and to reform the Brazilian Roman Catholic church by eliminating the clerical celibacy requirement—which, because it was regularly violated, reduced the moral standing of the priesthood. But he accomplished little as regent; the problems he faced overwhelmed him and forced him out of office after only two years. His unorthodox religious views helped provoke a rebellion in the Amazonian province of Pará. In Bahia, slaves revolted when he did not proclaim their emancipation. Disappointed federalists in Rio Grande do Sul rose in arms when the regent refused to go beyond the halfway measures of the Additional Act and establish a federative monarchy; the southern rebels, called *Farroupilhas* (ragamuffins) declared the independence of the Republic of Rio Grande do Sul in 1836 and successfully defended it against the forces of the Brazilian government. The Conservative majority in parliament was outraged by Feijó's attempted crackdown on the illegal slave trade in 1837. The regent's hopes for Liberal victory in the parliamentary elections of 1837 were dashed when Evaristo died on a visit to his unlikely constituency in Minas Gerais. Feijó resigned in September 1837 and was replaced as regent by the Conservative Araújo Lima.

Regent Araújo Lima enjoyed the support of a renewed Conservative majority in parliament led by Vasconcelos and Honório Hermeto. With the death of Evaristo and the retirement of Feijó, the Liberal opposition in Rio came under the leadership of deputies Antônio Carlos and Martim Francisco (the oldest Andrada brother, José Bonifácio, died in 1838). In the provinces the *Farroupilha* revolt raged on in Rio Grande do Sul, and another major rebellion broke out in Maranhão, but the Conservative central government managed to pacify Pará and Bahia. Peace also reigned in the southeastern coffee country, where production rose with new infusions of slave labor from Africa, introduced behind the turned backs of imperial officials. The implications for the Liberal party were not good. Increasing numbers of planters and merchants were willing to trade liberal principles for slave-generated prosperity and align themselves with the Conservatives, the party unequivocally dedicated to the preservation of Brazilian slavery. The liberal voice of the *Aurora Fluminense* was stilled with the death of Evaristo, and southeastern slavocrats had more money at their disposal to influence opinion in poorer regions of the country. The imperial army had recovered from the trauma of 1828-31 and, under Conservative direction, was destined to crush the rebellions in Maranhão and Rio Grande do Sul. The centralized state was gathering strength under the Conservatives, who, the Liberal Andrada brothers realized, intended to use all the advantages of incumbency to increase their majority in the next parliament. The electoral process would begin with the choosing of electors in October 1840. Antônio Carlos and Martim Francisco devised a scheme that would remove the Conservatives from control of the executive branch before that time.

On December 2, 1839, the young Emperor Pedro II became fourteen years old, the age at which the fabled Portuguese King Sebastian was entrusted with the powers of government in the sixteenth century. There was ample precedent for ending the regency and declaring Dom Pedro II reigning sovereign early in 1840, as Antônio Carlos and Martim Francisco proposed, but the constitution specified the age of eighteen as the minimum for a ruling emperor. The Andrada brothers, with the approval of Dom Pedro II—a mature and serious youth—formed the Society for the Promotion of the Majority to agitate for a parliamentary declaration ending the emperor's minority and making him reigning monarch immediately; the constitution could be amended later to sanction the move. The Andradas, pointing to the revolts in the north and south, justified the extraconstitutional action as necessary to prevent the disintegration of the empire. The regional rebels, according to the Liberal leaders, had taken up arms against the regency, not against the young emperor, whom they were bound to respect once he was properly seated on the throne. The Andradas invited Conservatives as well as

Liberals to join the Society for the Promotion of the Majority and to take part in the crusade to save the country. Individual Conservatives faced a difficult choice. If they joined the Majority Society agitation, they would be assisting the rise to power of the Liberal Andrada brothers, with whom the young emperor obviously had struck a deal. But if they joined their Conservative party leaders in trying to delay the enthronement of Dom Pedro II, they risked incurring his displeasure— which could cost them favors in the future, because sooner or later he was going to become reigning emperor. Many decided that it was more practical to defy Vasconcelos and Araújo Lima than to annoy the emperor. A bandwagon effect was created as Conservatives began defecting to the Majority Society. In July 1840, Araújo Lima stepped down as regent, and parliament hailed Dom Pedro II as reigning emperor of Brazil at the age of fourteen and a half.

As expected, the Conservative cabinet headed by Vasconcelos resigned, and Dom Pedro appointed a new one that included some Conservatives but was dominated by the Liberal Andrada brothers. Antônio Carlos, as minister of justice, used the power available to him to ensure a Liberal victory in the voting for provincial electors late in 1840. The electors were to meet the next year in the provincial capitals to select the members of the Chamber of Deputies scheduled to convene in Rio in May 1842. In the meantime, the old parliament, controlled by the Conservatives, would meet for one more session in 1841.

Before the 1841 session, Dom Pedro II dismissed the Andrada brothers, who had little support in the parliament as then constituted. Also, the boy emperor was angered by reports submitted by municipal and parish judges indicating that the Liberals had rigged the 1840 voting for provincial electors. More significantly, the dismissal of Antônio Carlos and Martim Francisco in March 1841 came after they had ordered a crackdown on the illegal slave trade, the first since Feijó's regency—which confirmed that the Andradas, for all their reaching out to Conservatives during the Majority Society campaign, had not abandoned the principles that made them anathema to the slavocracy. Now that the Andradas had left the government, the Conservatives had to take measures to prevent them from returning to power with a Liberal parliament in 1842. Vasconcelos, Araújo Lima, and Honório Hermeto set out to beef up the power of the central government and use it to convince the provincial electors that they should reconsider their earlier commitments and choose Conservatives rather than Liberals as their representatives in parliament. In addition to the civil apparatus of government, the Conservatives had at their disposal a rejuvenated imperial army under the leadership of General Luís Alves de Lima e Silva, recently returned to Rio from his successful pacification campaign in Maranhão, where, applying Vasconcelos's dual-purpose criminal code, he had sent to the gallows black slaves caught fighting for their freedom and had paroled white rebels. The emperor conferred on Lima e Silva the title of Baron of Caxias, which commemorated the general's famous victory at a place by that name in Maranhão.

The young monarch in 1841 showed himself to be amenable to Conservative advice. To make sure that this would always be available to him, the Conservative parliament that year reestablished the Council of State, which had been abolished by the Additional Act of 1834. This advisory group, which the emperor was required to consult on all important matters, was staffed with lifetime appointees recommended by the Conservative party leadership. Other important legislation enacted in 1841 gave the central government a free hand in appointing municipal judges throughout the country and removed police power from the hands of elected parish judges. A centralized police system, reaching from the Ministry of Justice in Rio down to delegates and subdelegates on the municipal and parish levels, was created to ensure that the imperial cabinet would control the course of political events in the provinces. But the new system was not yet in place at the end of 1841, when the electors met and generally honored their pledges to select Liberal deputies for the new parliament.

As the elected deputies converged on Rio in April 1842, the Andrada brothers waited for the emperor to appoint a Liberal cabinet compatible with the new parliamentary majority. But instead, Dom Pedro II retained the Conservative government and dismissed the Liberal Chamber of Deputies before it had even met. For the benefit of the Conservatives, Dom Pedro II invoked his right under the 1824 constitution to dissolve parliament before its four-year term was up—a power his father had never used. New electors were selected in voting supervised by judges and police chiefs appointed by the central government; Conservatives were named almost everywhere, ensuring that their party would control the next Chamber of Deputies.

Thus, the pattern of politics for the rest of the empire period was set. The government would determine the elections, rather than vice versa. The emperor, wielding the moderating power, appointed the government; if the Chamber of Deputies was controlled by the opposition party, the government would ask the emperor to dissolve parliament and order new elections; he would comply, and the government would rig the elections to get the legislative majority it needed. It was a cynical system based on electoral fraud, necessitated, according to its apologists, by the low level of education prevalent in Brazil. The excuses were made by people who insisted on bringing unlettered slaves into Brazil, refused to provide them or the native-born poor with schooling, and obstructed the immigration of educated free workers into the country. Indeed, the system adopted in 1842 seemed designed to perpetuate ignorance in Brazil. During the two preceding decades elections were probably as honest in Brazil as they were in Britain or the United States at the same time—which means that they were far from perfect. While evolution toward free political institutions optimally responsive to pressures for social change proceeded apace in some countries, it was set back in Brazil in 1842.

The Conservative coup was not accepted by those who, when they were not fighting one another, had led the struggle to establish a liberal state in Brazil. Feijó came out of retirement to join the Andrada brothers and other Paulista and Mineiro Liberals in raising a citizen army to march on Rio and reinstate the Liberal parliament. Even the mistress of the late Dom Pedro I, the marchioness of Santos, joined the effort, committing her personal fortune to the quixotic Liberal movement of 1842. The ragtag Liberal forces were attacked in São Paulo and Minas Gerais provinces and easily defeated by imperial troops commanded by the reactionary Baron of Caxias. The movement's leaders were captured and forced to retire from public life. They were replaced by a new generation of Liberal politicians who came to terms with the dominant slavocracy.

Consolidation of the Empire of Dom Pedro II, 1842-1850

Dom Pedro II was not like his father, a man of passion and vision. The second emperor of Brazil accepted society as it was and devoted his life to moderating change, to maintaining the status quo as far as possible. When the status quo finally became unsustainable, Dom Pedro II was driven from the throne after a reign of nearly half a century. He was not especially astute, but he could distinguish between forces for change and forces for stability, and he invariably chose the latter. His own early rise to power he saw, correctly, as enhancing the stability of the empire. He perceived early on that the Andrada brothers constituted a threat to the social order; they and their ilk were never again to be entrusted by the emperor with political power. In the 1840s Brazil's constitutional monarchy was set on a conservative path that ultimately led to its destruction.

The expanding coffee economy of the southeast generated little demand for change in the early 1840s. Financing coffee production and exportation was simple, worked out among planters, brokers, buyers, and shippers. There was only one bank in Brazil, the Banco do Comércio of Rio, chartered in 1838. Conservative planters still feared banks as potential sources of funding for development that would undermine the social order and resisted their establishment. Other innovations were similarly regarded as dangerous. Vasconcelos vociferously opposed the construction of railroads in Brazil in the 1840s. The southeastern network of mule trails adequately met the transportation requirements of the coffee planters. What they needed were more slaves. On the expiration in 1845 of the search-and-seizure powers granted to Britain under the Slave-Trade Treaty, Vasconcelos proposed that Brazil relegalize the importation of slaves from Africa.

The emperor and more moderate Conservatives, such as Araújo Lima and Honório Hermeto, did not regard relegalization of the slave trade as either necessary or desirable; such an affront to world opinion could galvanize Britain and other powers to effective action to put an end to the traffic, which, on an illicit basis, might continue and even flourish indefinitely. With the British navy scheduled to lose its search-and-seizure authority in 1845, slavers looked forward to reduced risks and lower costs in their transatlantic business. Other business opportunities beckoned with the impending expiration of the British-Brazilian Commercial Treaty in 1844; the possibility arose of establishing a textile industry in Brazil behind a wall of tariff protection.

This last idea was not attractive to philosophical liberals or to conservative southeastern coffee planters, whose production would have to subsidize the national industry, but it did appeal to other slavocrats, especially cotton planters of the northeast, whose product was virtually priced out of world markets. The artificial creation of a domestic market for raw cotton would serve to stabilize slavery as a national institution and thus return some political benefits to the coffee producers bearing its costs. As a nationalist program, subsidized textile manufacturing was advocated by the new leaders of the Liberal party, including Manuel Alves Branco of Bahia. The idea appealed to Dom Pedro II, who wanted to strengthen the bonds of the northeast to his empire.

The young emperor also was concerned with securing the southernmost province of his realm by ending the Farroupilha revolt, which sputtered on in Rio Grande do Sul. After two years of alternately fighting and negotiating with the rebels, the Conservative Baron of Caxias, imperial military commander in the south, had not persuaded the Farroupilhas to lay down their arms. A sticking point was the fate of runaway slaves who had joined the rebel army in response to promises of freedom. Given Caxias's reputation for hanging rebel slaves, black Farroupilhas were understandably reluctant to surrender to him. Concern for their safety was expressed by their white comrades, who indicated that they would be willing to call off their struggle and swear allegiance to the empire if they were offered a general amnesty guaranteed by a Liberal government in Rio. The emperor facilitated the peace process in 1844 by appointing a Liberal cabinet headed by Alves Branco. The next year, the Farroupilha leaders signed a surrender document that granted freedom to slave veterans on both sides in the Rio Grande do Sul war. The white Farroupilhas were integrated into the imperial political system as members of the Liberal party. They did not keep the faith with their black comrades, many of whom were illegally reenslaved.

Manuel Alves Branco was Brazil's first prime minister, a post that was officially created in 1847. The modernization of the cabinet system was one of a number of innovations made under the Liberal administration of 1844–48. With the expiration of the British-Brazilian Commercial Treaty in 1844, import tariffs were raised from an across-the-board fifteen percent to rates varying from twenty to sixty percent ad valorem. Subsequent legislation in 1846 eliminated all duties on industrial machinery. These measures were sufficient to persuade export merchants and sugar planters in Alves Branco's province of Bahia to invest substantial sums in cotton textile manufacturing. English merchants belonging to the Bahian Commercial Association, of which the prime minister also was a member, arranged for the importation of capital goods from Britain and were themselves major investors in Bahia's textile mills. To meet new demands for financing, Brazil's second private bank, the Commercial Bank of Bahia, was chartered in 1845. Farther north, banks were chartered in Maranhão and Pará in 1846, and in 1848 another bank was established in Bahia.

While new financial and industrial entities were appearing in the depressed north and northeast, the southeastern coffee industry—which would have to sustain them—continued to prosper. During the Alves Branco administration, rising coffee exports were accompanied, as usual, by rising slave imports. The African slave trade to Brazil reached its peak under this Liberal government; from nineteen thousand slaves landed in 1845, the estimated annual total rose to fifty thousand the next year, fifty-six thousand in 1847, and to sixty thousand in 1848. The increase occurred despite unilateral British attempts to suppress the trade. When the enforcement powers of the British-Brazilian Slave-Trade Treaty expired in 1845, despite London's pleas to Rio for renewal, the British parliament passed the Aberdeen Act, which sanctioned the search, seizure, and condemnation of Brazilian-flag slavers on the high seas by British authorities without Brazilian government approval. The treaty technically remained in force, and the slave trade was still against Brazilian domestic law (Feijó's act of November 7, 1831), but under Alves Branco the Brazilian government went from ignoring the law to actively aiding the lawbreakers. Imperial military and naval forces protected slavers by firing on their British pursuers as they entered Brazilian territorial waters.

Alves Branco's administration hardly posed a threat to the Brazilian slavocracy, but in 1848 many Conservatives were troubled by news of the revolutions in Europe, fearing that they might inspire Brazil's ruling party to revert to its traditional liberal principles. Dom Pedro II shared their concern and decided to take no chances. He dismissed the Liberal government in September 1848 and summoned Araújo Lima to form a Conservative one.

Pedro de Araújo Lima, Marquis of Olinda, ex-regent of the empire, was the quintessential moderate Conservative. A native of Pernambuco, Araújo Lima had not opposed Alves Branco's scheme to transfer assets to the northeast from the southeast, where regional prosperity was buttressed by the national commitment to the institution of slavery. By the time Araújo Lima became prime minister in 1848, slaves comprised nearly half the population in the coffee-producing provinces of the southeast, while less than a quarter of the people of his native Pernambuco were slaves. The decline in the proportion of slaves in Pernambuco's population accompanied the decline in the provincial economy, which many Pernambucans had hoped the Alves Branco government would reverse. They were not reassured when the Liberal cabinet was replaced by a Conservative one headed by Araújo Lima, who had spent most of his life in Rio and was accused of selling out to the southeasterners. Late in 1848, Pernambucan Liberals—called *Praieiros*, from the beach road where their newspaper was published—rose in revolt against the Conservative government. They failed to capture the provincial capital of Recife, and by early 1849 the Praieira Revolt was crushed. Its leaders were amnestied a year later, closing the books on the last major rebellion the empire would face until half a century later.

Conservative Prime Minister Araújo Lima presided over the enactment of some important reforms formulated under the previous Liberal administration. In 1849 a law was passed permitting the organization of limited-liability companies in Brazil, and the next year a commercial code was enacted. Another law of 1850 provided for the registration of squatter claims and the issuance of marketable land titles. That same year, an equally portentous measure was passed by the Brazilian parliament under the guns of the British navy.

In 1850, British warships in the South Atlantic received orders from London to enter Brazilian waters whenever necessay to capture slavers and to reduce any resistance to their apprehension from any quarter. The Empire of Brazil was left with the choice of going to war with Great Britain or enforcing its own law against the slave trade. It chose to do the latter: enabling legislation passed in 1850, the Queiroz Law, committed the police power of the Brazilian state to the suppression of slave importation, which was effectively accomplished within a year or two.

Thus, in 1850, Brazil adopted measures that would curtail the growth of the slave-labor force, secure private property in land and ensure its marketability, expand credit, and generally facilitate business activity. This legislation provided the framework for modest economic development as the empire entered a long period of internal peace. Brazil embarked on this undisturbed development at a time when much of the rest of Latin America was entering a period of civil strife, precipitated by attempts to promulgate reforms that were in many ways comparable to, but more far-reaching than, the Brazilian legislation.

8

Latin America at Midcentury: A Quickening Pace of Change

As the preceding chapters make clear in dealing with particular Latin American countries, the first quarter-century of independent life brought numerous changes to Latin America, but not many that altered the fundamental structures of society and the economy. There had been an increase in political turbulence, though with important variations among countries, and an increase in the extent of political participation as compared to the colonial era, yet for the great majority of Latin Americans national politics had little meaning. They usually did not take part either in the elections or in the "revolutions." They were still illiterate, still more susceptible to the influence of clergy and rural gentry than to that of partisan ideologues, and still subsisting at a very low level of material comfort, though seldom exposed to actual hunger. There had been, of course, some Latin Americans who hoped independence would usher in more rapid transformations. Rivadavia and his circle at Buenos Aires are perhaps the most clear-cut example, but Santander at the head of the government of Gran Colombia, O'Higgins in Chile, the Andrada brothers in Brazil, and the men who founded the Mexican republic at the departure of Iturbide shared many of the same ambitions. The decade of the 1820s did in fact see a flurry of reform activity almost everywhere. However, some of the "reforms" had only superficial effect, some were quickly repealed,

180

and, with a few partial exceptions such as Venezuela and Guatemala, the next two decades saw an obvious waning of the
impulse to change things. The 1830s and 1840s were typified
instead by a preoccupation with the attainment of order and a
generally moderate approach to questions of religious, social, or
economic policy.

This retreat from the reformist activism of the immediate
postindependence years was in part a result of the resistance
stirred up, most evidently among the clergy, by that first round
of liberal legislation. It was also caused by a spreading conviction
that, until political order was more firmly established, even the
most inherently desirable reform measures were premature.
Equally or more important, however, was the fact that Latin
America's economic outlook had suddenly turned dark. For a
few years, the new nations appeared to have a substantial quantity of resources at their disposal, thanks to the foreign loans
recklessly offered and taken in the European money markets and
also to the buoyant condition of foreign trade, stimulated both by
the availability of foreign exchange from those loans and by the
removal of the last official barriers to trade with non-Latin American ports. But, as pointed out above, these proved to be highly
ephemeral circumstances. Most of the loans were soon in default,
and the sources of credit dried up. Likewise, the volume of trade
necessarily fell off until a precarious balance was reached between imports and what Latin America could pay for with its
exports. It then became harder to conceive ambitious schemes
for rapidly modernizing the new nations in the image of northern
Europe or the United States, and Latin Americans scaled down
their expectations in a mood of greater realism.

The Resumption of Export Growth

The mood of Latin America, or at least of the middle and upper
sectors of the population, changed again about midcentury, as
most countries entered a period of around twenty-five to thirty
years in which economic growth provided a renewed basis for
optimism and liberal reformers generally seized the political
initiative. To the extent that economic growth was in fact the key
variable—and it was by no means the only influence at work—it

was centered in the external sector, where some spectacular increases in the quantity and value of Latin American exports took place. Statistical records for the period are incomplete and often unreliable, but the figures in Appendix 2 can be taken as a rough indication of what was happening in a select group of countries. Not surprisingly, there were conspicuous differences in the rate and timing of the increases. In Mexico, there would be no real surge of export-led growth until after about 1880, whereas in Colombia, say, exports quadrupled from the 1830s to 1880 and then performed erratically for the rest of the century. Nor was the growth in Latin American trade truly impressive by worldwide standards: general international trade increased five times from 1840 to 1870, and U.S. exports almost eight times from 1845 to 1880. Nevertheless, in strictly Latin American terms, the expansion of trade was substantial.

The fact that Latin America's economy grew no faster than it did reflected the existence of both resource limitations and structural constraints, on whose relative importance scholars disagree. There is also disagreement about the relative importance of external and internal stimuli for such growth as occurred, but it is generally accepted that the former were most decisive. Indeed, the North Atlantic capitalist economy about 1850 was entering a phase of sustained expansion that is one of the clearest of the upward movements identified by Russian economist Nikolai Kondratieff in his study of long-term business cycles. This phase lasted until roughly the mid-1870s, but it was merely superimposed upon, or reinforced by, a number of trends favoring ever closer integration of Latin America into the world market. The Industrial Revolution itself, initially concentrated in Britain, northern France, and Belgium, was spreading out to other parts of Europe and the United States and in the process creating new demands for industrial raw materials as well as for imported foodstuffs to be consumed by a population that was becoming steadily more urban. Industry, however, was not only spreading geographically. The efficiency of steel-making processes, steam engines, and other basic elements of the emerging industrial civilization underwent sharp improvement during the second half of the century, creating still more demands in the industrial countries for commodity imports while leading to the production of more, cheaper, and better manufactured goods to sell in exchange. In Great Britain, the repeal in 1846 of the last of the so-called Corn Laws signaled the abandonment of all tariff protectionism in favor of a trade free both of duties and of other artificial restrictions. British publicists urged other countries, including Latin America, to embrace liberal economic principles in foreign trade with equal resolution, which not many did; but the power of the British example as well as increased ease of access to Britain's own market were favorable circumstances for trade expansion in Latin America as elsewhere.

The United States, which was both rising industrial power and major commodity exporter, was actually in a better position than Latin America to meet the growing world demand for foodstuffs and raw materials. Yet there were tropical commodities such as sugar and coffee that North America did not offer, and there were other products—Argentine hides and Chilean minerals, for example—that Latin America could supply competitively thanks to low production costs. The continuing drop in ocean-freight rates, with technological advances in the shipping industry, likewise favored Latin American trade. And shipping advances did more than lead to lower freight rates. The increasing speed and reliability of steam navigation would make it possible to ship some perishable commodities or other kinds of merchandise for which sailing ships and the earliest steamships had not been suited, creating totally new export industries. An example is the exporting of live cattle from the Río de la Plata to Europe, first accomplished in the 1860s; only then was it possible to transport animals quickly and efficiently enough, in conditions that would permit them to be sold and eaten after arrival.

In the case of live cattle exports, it was soon apparent that shipping technology had actually outdistanced the palatability of Argentine beef. Though technically feasible, the operation did not become a commercial success until a few years later, by which time needed improvements in breeding and care of livestock (including care en route) had also been carried out. This, in turn, underscores the fact that external factors tending to promote closer ties to the world market could not operate in isolation from internal developments in Latin America. However, internal factors did increasingly support an expansion of trade, and not merely in the sense that local producers, such as the Argentine estancieros, proved capable of taking steps needed to respond to external stimuli. There had also been in some countries a decline in political turbulence, which was a circumstance favorable to economic growth though not in itself capable of creating it. In this respect, Argentina was better prepared for trade expansion when Rosas fell than when he first rose to power, and the same could be said even more truly of Chile after Portales—though not, alas, of Mexico. On another front, even the rather limited liberal economic measures so far adopted in Latin America had tended to remove obstacles to the movement and investment of goods and capital. The abolition of the tobacco monopoly in one country, of restrictions on interest rates in another, of compulsory tithe payments even more widely, were all straws in the wind. Such moves would be multiplied and carried much farther in Latin America in the years after 1850, the better to let private entrepreneurs take advantage of favorable market conditions.

The expansion of export trade necessarily had an impact on other activities within Latin America. It provided business for brokers, insurers, shippers, and other commercial middlemen, of whom many were foreigners established in Latin American ports. It stimulated the development of transportation systems to move the export commodities to harbor, providing both potential cargo and freight payments with which to cover the cost of improvements. Railway construction is here the most obvious case, as more and more Latin American countries sought to follow the example of Spanish-held Cuba, where the first railroad of Latin America had been completed as early as 1838. The lines were not built solely for the convenience of international commerce—except perhaps the Panama Railroad (1855)—but without them its increase would have been measurably less. And, whether built by foreign companies or by Latin American governments with the proceeds from overseas borrowing, railroads were mainly financed by a revival of foreign investment in Latin America, which gathered momentum from essentially the 1860s to World War I.

The fact that part of the income accruing to the export sector was spent on a variety of domestically produced goods and services represented one more way in which the expansion of trade was felt more widely, although it is no less true that a substantial share of the proceeds went right back overseas in payment for imported manufactures. These included both luxuries for the well-to-do and factory mass-produced textiles for the workers. Domestic artisans, in any case, did not receive much benefit; if anything, their situation continued to worsen. There was little they could do about it, for the economic developments of the period strengthened the hand of precisely those groups that felt the prosperity of Latin America depended on a course of specialization in primary commodities for whose production the region had comparative advantage, while importing finished industrial goods that could be obtained for less abroad than it would have cost to make them at home. To the extent that liberalism was identified with the cause of freer trade, export-led growth thus clearly favored the adoption of liberal economic policies.

André Gunder Frank, who as one of the founders of "dependency theory" has emphasized the overriding importance of external factors in Latin America, expressed the relationship between trade and liberal reformism in particularly sweeping terms when he proposed the hypothesis that

> the Liberal reform in any particular country did not occur simply when Liberal ideas arrived there, but when the new mono-export production of coffee, sugar, meat, wheat, cotton, or tin had expanded sufficiently to account for, say, over 50% of total national exports. Although some people may have long wanted the Liberal reform, for ideological reasons, it is this metropolis-stimulated expansion of Latin American export production that in each country gave certain sectors of the bourgeoisie the economic and political leverage to undertake the Liberal reform.[1]

Frank's argument obviously assumes that in Latin American economies a pronounced export orientation has involved specialization in just one leading commodity, which is true in broad-brush terms but hardly an essential condition for the existence of a link between export growth and the success of liberalism. It would be enough to frame the hypothesis in terms of a percentage of gross domestic product (GDP) represented by exports generally, except for the fact that reliable GDP estimates are harder to come by than export statistics.

Neither does it matter whether the "bourgeois" label can be properly applied to all those sectors in Latin America that in Frank's words gained "the economic and political leverage" to carry out liberal reforms. What is clear is that the landowners and mine owners who produced export commodities and the merchants who handled them (and handled the return cargo of imports financed with the proceeds) had good reason to support liberal economic programs. A primary-producing export economy was one in which not just protective tariffs but most other forms of government economic regulation, from fiscal monopolies to traditional limitations on the sale and alienation of landed property, appeared simply counterproductive. Such an economy required, in principle, freedom of operation for private businessmen so that they could quickly respond to market forces, and that is exactly what nineteenth-century liberalism stood for in the economic sphere. The creed of political liberalism, with its emphasis on individual rights and curbing of arbitrary power, nicely complemented this very approach.

Then, too, there is the fact that the upturn in export trade provided Latin American countries with a higher level of resources than they had been accustomed to in recent years. It was thus possible to recapture some of the optimism that lay behind the earlier round of liberal reforms adopted in the immediate aftermath of independence. And the governments themselves, which continued to derive the bulk of their revenue directly or indirectly from foreign trade, enjoyed an increase in the funds at their disposal. This did not mean that they now felt free to spend large sums of money on programs of social welfare, for that is not what liberalism stood for in the last century. Especially in Argentina, however, a beginning could be made toward the expansion of public education. And certain highly illiberal traditional imposts—such as the Indian tribute in Peru—could be finally abolished because the money they produced was no longer so necessary. In Peru and a number of other countries, a fuller treasury likewise made it easier to liquidate the last vestiges of black slavery, because the government could now credibly offer to compensate the dispossessed slaveowners.

The greater solvency of Latin American governments even made it possible in many cases to resume service on defaulted foreign debts, which in turn made it possible to obtain new loans from abroad and created a climate attractive to other forms of outside investment. This was something liberals had long favored, although in a strict sense foreign capital was ideologically neutral and went simply to those places where a satisfactory return seemed likely; in the latter eventuality, it did not necessarily wait even for the resumption of public debt service. The fact remains that the growth of trade served to multiply channels for all sorts of contacts with the outside world, bringing Latin America, for better or worse, into closer touch with economic developments in Europe and the United States, not to mention with the intellectual and cultural currents of the mid-nineteenth century, which were running mostly in a liberal direction.

A New Generation, New Ideas

Whether or not the role of the external economy was as critical in the flowering of post-1850 Latin American liberalism as Frank contends, a generational shift within Latin America clearly helped prepare the way. Up to this point, the dominant figures in most countries were men like Páez and Santa Anna who had been participants in the independence wars or at least could have been had they so desired. (Such men as Rosas and Portales did not desire.) The harsh realities which so often frustrated their projects contributed to the mood of relative moderation if not conservative reaction that prevailed generally through the 1830s and 1840s. But by midcentury these men were giving way to a new generation whose members attended exclusively postcolonial schools, had been directly exposed to notions and ideas that circulated only in limited form before, and had not yet had time to become disillusioned. In New Granada, they had imbibed the utilitarianism of English philosopher Jeremy Bentham under the auspices of Santander's Plan of Studies and continued to read Bentham and other authors of doubtful orthodoxy even when they fell into official disfavor, among other reasons because nobody bothered to remove them from library shelves. In the case of Argentina, many spent their formative years in exile from the Rosas dictatorship, for which reason they were all the more dissatisfied with the performance of the previous generation, including both Rosas and his henchmen and the Unitario leaders who had proved incapable of getting rid of him. In Mexico, there was even greater reason to be dissatisfied with the performance of those who lost (or allowed to be lost) half the nation's territory. Young Chileans had less cause for angry repudiation of the work of their predecessors, but the post-Portalian stability had been somewhat unexciting, and even boredom can at times be a revolutionary spark.

The new leaders coming of age at midcentury, confident that they could do better than those they replaced, were in one sense intent on completing the work of independence itself by clearing away what still remained—which was quite a lot—of outdated colonial institutions. Paradoxically, however, they were even more beholden to foreign models and ideas as they set about to renovate their respective countries. Attention was centered now above all on France, whose cultural and intellectual primacy had survived the defeat of Napoleon I. As a model of economic development, France was overshadowed by Britain, and as a political beacon by the United States, although France did experience substantial industrial growth, and under the "bourgeois monarchy" of King Louis-Philippe (who had come to power in 1830) it was for the most part a respectable example of moderate liberal constitutionalism. Mainly, France was to educated Latin Americans a fount of thought and culture, including political thought often far in advance of what the well-meaning but uninspiring Louis-Philippe stood for. When that monarch was finally overthrown by the Revolution of 1848, Latin America's fervor for things French reached new heights. Indeed, the revolution itself made almost as intense an impression in Latin America as in the rest of Europe. In far-off Bogotá none other than Mariano Ospina Rodríguez, cofounder of the Conservative party and sponsor of the Jesuits' return to New Granada, rang church bells in celebration on hearing the news that a second French Revolution had taken place. One can easily imagine the ecstasy that the news must have caused among those more radically inclined than Ospina.

The Revolution of 1848 could excite both public-spirited conservatives and every variety of liberal because it not only returned France (for a time) to the right path of republican government but also awakened vague hopes of indefinite human progress that anyone could interpret to suit himself. Nevertheless, the predominant ideological influence now emanating from France to Latin America was a romantic liberalism rhetorically tinged with utopian socialism. The former strain was exemplified by the work of poet-historian Alphonse de Lamartine, whose *Histoire des Girondins* exalting republican ideals in the epoch of the first French Revolution is conventionally credited with helping to bring on the second, including its New World repercussions. The socialist strain was derived chiefly from the writings of Saint-Simon and his followers, whose prescriptions for social betterment were fuzzy enough to have quite broad appeal. Indeed, the term *socialist*, which came to be widely used in the Latin America of the period, was taken so loosely as to be almost meaningless. The concept of a society consciously planned by the state or by associations of producers, as found in Saint-Simon and others of the "utopian" school in Europe, was often overlooked by self-styled socialists in Latin America who were as much committed as any doctrinaire economic liberal to allowing individuals full freedom to act in accord with natural socioeconomic laws; they were socialists only in rhetoric and in a sincere if sometimes misguided concern for social welfare. (As yet, only a handful of Latin Americans had heard the name of Marx, whose Communist Manifesto also appeared in 1848.)

The romantic liberalism and muddled socialism of the midcentury generation would meet their principal ideological challenge in the form of positivism, whose creed of "Order and Progress," standing for a more tough-minded approach to Latin American problems, began to be preached in Mexico by Gabino Barreda in the 1860s and in other countries about the same time or a little later. To French sociologist Auguste Comte, the founder of positivism as a social philosophy, that creed was to be converted into reality by distinctly authoritarian means under the leadership of a scientific elite, whereas most Latin American positivists, mixing

Comte's teachings with the social Darwinism of Englishman Herbert Spencer, made room for economic free enterprise as leading through competition and natural selection to the more perfect society. But Spencerians in Latin America as well as strict Comtians were ready to accept some sacrifice of *political* liberty. They were prepared to do so in large part because they, in turn, had come to feel some disillusionment with the results of doctrinaire liberalism as feverishly practiced above all in the 1850s and early 1860s.

The Reformist Pattern

Whatever may have been the precise causes—economic, generational, intellectual, and other—the fact is that in roughly the third quarter of the nineteenth century Latin America experienced a concerted effort to implement liberal measures of every kind. The result still was not to be radical transformation in the life of the people, because nineteenth-century liberalism was essentially a movement by and for the more progressive members of the middle and upper social strata, and the typical liberal reforms, like freedom of worship and abolition of the fuero, were mostly meaningless to the average man or woman. They seldom had to do with wages or working conditions and in some cases would even affect working-class groups adversely. Nevertheless, liberal reformers now largely completed the job of clearing away the legal structure of individual and corporate special privileges inherited from the colonial regime and abolishing the most glaring restrictions—political, religious, and economic—on individual liberty.

All this happened with a remarkable degree of synchronization from country to country. To cite one example, no less than six sovereign South American republics carried out the final abolition of slavery in the same four-year period from 1851 through 1854. These were Venezuela, New Granada, Ecuador, Peru, Argentina, and Uruguay, all countries that during or just after the war of independence had begun the process by adopting laws of free birth and now, at the stroke of a pen and almost simultaneously, set free the slaves who had been born too soon to benefit from the free-birth principle. The church entered its darkest period almost everywhere, at least from the standpoint of its institutional interests, and the rush to reexpel the same Jesuits who had been widely permitted to return during the preceding years offers one more excellent example of synchronization: Venezuela, 1848; New Granada, 1850 and again 1861; Ecuador, 1852; Mexico, 1856; Uruguay, 1859. In this case, unlike abolition of slavery, the near simultaneity of actions taken did not result merely from the spontaneous operation of similar causes. For Ecuador was pressured by the government in Bogotá to do something about these archenemies of human progress, or at least of liberal governments, after the ones expelled from New Granada initially took up residence just south of the border.

In political matters, it is sometimes held, the period was marked by systematic weakening of the state, carried out in the name of individual initiative and private enterprise. To such commentators as the Chilean Claudio Véliz, this was the "liberal pause," an aberrant departure from the enduring traditions of Iberian and Ibero-American society which happily reasserted themselves with the revival of strong central government in the present century.[2] Some leftist critics have denounced a conscious conspiracy of merchants, agro-exporters, and dominant minorities generally to do away with legal and institutional obstacles to the selfish pursuit of their material interests, including their exploitation of the popular masses. These interpretations are not wholly unfounded, as a certain flowering of federalist constitutions and sweeping legal guarantees of individual rights went hand in hand with express deregulation of various kinds of economic activities. The picture, though, is more complex than those who bemoan the weakening of the state have usually recognized. For one thing, the simultaneous weakening of the church by liberal anticlericalism redounded intentionally or not to the *strengthening* of the state, and the upturn in foreign trade, whether cause or effect of liberal measures, provided the state with additional resources. Neither did liberal governments necessarily renounce the state's prerogative, if not obligation, to give positive assistance to private enterprise for the creation of transportation infrastructure and the like.

There are also a number of countries that depart from the overall pattern. One of these is Brazil, not so much because of the existence of monarchy—Dom Pedro II was a more liberal ruler than some liberal presidents—as because Brazil both moved earlier than most to adopt certain liberal measures (such as religious toleration) and was conspicuously later in adopting others (such as abolition of slavery). A more clear-cut exception is Guatemala, where the conservative dictatorship of Rafael Carrera continued past midcentury into the 1860s; only in the following decade did Guatemala undergo the full onslaught of liberal reformism. An even more striking exception in some ways is Ecuador. In the early 1850s it both freed slaves and expelled Jesuits, and in 1857 it permanently abolished Indian tribute. But from 1860 to 1875, it slipped under the control of Gabriel García Moreno, who not only brought back the Jesuits but made Roman Catholicism an express condition for citizenship and had the nation formally dedicated, in a grand public ceremony, to the Sacred Heart of Jesus. García Moreno promoted public works and primary education, but his single-minded devotion to maintaining the sway of the Roman Catholic religion set him definitely apart from other rulers of his day and made him a symbol of repressive obscurantism to liberals throughout Latin America. Ecuador, too, would have its heyday of liberalism, but not until the very end of the century, following the revolution that brought Eloy Alfaro to power in 1895. Perhaps one should also classify as somewhat exceptional, though at the opposite extreme, the cases of Mexico and Colombia, two countries that during the 1850s and the beginning of the next decade enacted just about every measure that the liberal imagination had managed to conceive up to that point. Yet not only were they rather more important countries than Guatemala and Ecuador to begin with, but they can fairly be regarded as models of what Latin America as a whole was tending toward but nowhere else so fully attained.

9

The Heyday of
Liberal Reform in
Spanish America (1850–1880) I:
Mexico and Colombia

Mexico: La Reforma, 1855–1861

The revolution that launched Mexico on the course of thorough-going liberal reform began in the state of Guerrero. That entity, formerly the Pacific coastal zone of the state of Mexico, had been created in 1849 during the moderate federalist administration of José Joaquín Herrera and was named for Vicente Guerrero, the puro martyr betrayed in Acapulco and executed in 1831, presumably on orders of the archconservative Lucas Alamán. The first governor of the state of Guerrero was a comrade of the fallen hero, another insurgent veteran of the struggle for independence, General Juan Álvarez, a hispanicized Indian with perhaps a trace of African blood. Guerrilla commander, regional strongman, caudillo, Álvarez was an ardent federalist, a defender of states' rights. Governor Álvarez was a puro, but his liberal principles were sufficiently elastic to allow him to tolerate the conservative dictatorship of Santa Anna for nearly a year, until the central government in Mexico City directly threatened the autonomy of Guerrero. Then, in February 1854, he met in the town of Ayutla, Guerrero, with Ignacio Comonfort—a white moderado, recently dismissed from his job as customs collector at Acapulco by Santa Anna—and together they issued a call to arms against the regime in Mexico City.

Álvarez and Comonfort were unsuited to lead the drastic reform movement that their revolution became once their forces had occupied Mexico City in November 1855. The direction of the new regime was set not by the partners of Ayutla but by puro exiles who had returned to Mexico during the struggle against Santa Anna and were appointed to head the major departments of the Álvarez-Comonfort government. Rather than mirror the federalism of Álvarez or the gradualism of Comonfort, the movement that became known as *La Reforma* would reflect the aggressive and uncompromising liberalism of the puro exiles. The former exiles eschewed moderation and, although they paid lip service to federalism, regarded states' rights as an obstacle to the full implementation of individual freedom, which they were sworn to effect. They would use all the power available to the central government to eradicate the corporatist system, so that liberty might at last flourish in Mexico.

Among the returned exiles was the new Mexican foreign minister, Melchor Ocampo, illegitimate son of a Michoacán hacendado, visionary advocate of the disentailment of landed property, true believer in the social benefits of yeoman agriculture. More economics-minded was the minister of development, Miguel Lerdo de Tejada, of Jalapa, Veracruz. Lerdo's family background was remarkably similar to that of his fellow Veracruzano, the deposed dictator Santa Anna; both sprang from the preindependence middle class of merchants and bureaucrats. Lerdo, in fact, had served Santa Anna in 1853 as subminister of development and had been instrumental in promoting Mexico's first railroad, which received its charter in 1849 and by 1854 stretched nineteen kilometers inland from Veracruz. By then, however, Lerdo had broken with Santa Anna over the latter's suppression of civil liberties. Lerdo fled to New Orleans, where he joined Ocampo and another puro exile, the ex-governor of Oaxaca, Benito Juárez. Juárez was destined to become minister of justice in the Álvarez-Comonfort government and, eventually, to take over as supreme leader of La Reforma.

Benito Juárez was a full-blooded Zapotec Indian who spoke no

Spanish until, at the age twelve, he left his native village and became the house servant of a Franciscan lay brother in the provincial capital of Oaxaca in 1818. Juárez's employer and benefactor provided for the youth's early education and sought to steer him into the priesthood. But Juárez chose instead a secular career in law, married the adopted daughter of an Italian immigrant merchant in Oaxaca, and entered local politics as a pure federalist. A supporter of Gómez Farías on the national level, Juárez was governor of Oaxaca during and after the war with the United States. Although his administration in Oaxaca was noted for its moderation, Juárez was nonetheless driven into exile by Santa Anna. Associating with Melchor Ocampo in New Orleans, Juárez became convinced of the futility of halfway measures. In a matter of days after taking over the justice ministry in Mexico City, Juárez secured the assent of President Álvarez, War Minister Comonfort, and his puro cabinet colleagues for the promulgation of the *Ley Juárez*.

The Juárez law of November 1855 abolished the ecclesiastical and military fueros, the exemption of the clergy and the military from ordinary civil and criminal jurisdiction. It withdrew the basic privilege of priests and army officers to be judged on all matters exclusively by their own corporate courts; henceforth the jurisdiction of church tribunals and courts-martial would be limited to members of the clergy or armed forces in cases of infraction of canon law or military regulations. The reaction of the military to the Juárez law was muted, for most of those who had fought for the revolution understood that their struggle was against corporate privilege, and those who had resisted them had been defeated and were conscious of their weakness within the reorganized federal army. And the cause of military privilege was unlikely to attract much support from the general public. But the ecclesiastical fuero was another matter: the idea of subjecting the agents of God to the laws of man was distasteful to many of the faithful. In Mexico City they filled the streets, shouting for "religión y fueros" and demanding repeal of the Juárez law. In Puebla an organized revolt was threatened.

President Juan Álvarez was unprepared to handle the situation. He resigned and was succeeded by the moderado Comonfort, who had the backing of the military. The outmaneuvered civilian puros left the provisional government in December 1855, although Development Minister Lerdo soon returned as finance minister. Juárez went home to Oaxaca, but the law bearing his name stayed on the books, and the conservative mobs in Mexico City were not quieted. Comonfort made a military show of force in Puebla that temporarily averted a civil war but exacerbated the underlying tensions in that conservative city. The president tried to mollify the church while pursuing basic reform. Special efforts were made to cast decree laws in language that would not offend the clerics. This was the case with *Ley Lerdo*, promulgated in June 1856.

The Lerdo law prohibited the corporate ownership of rural and urban real estate. There were some exceptions: ecclesiastical corporations could own church buildings and monasteries, municipal corporations could keep their town halls and jails, and Indian village corporations or *ejidos* could retain communal possession of certain pastures and woodlands. Other corporate-owned lands and structures were to become the property of the people who occupied them, or, if unoccupied, they were to be sold at public auction with the proceeds, less a ten percent sales tax, going to the former corporate owners. In the case of occupied properties, rents were to be converted to mortgage payments and paid, in the same amounts as before, to the former corporate owners; each parcel was to be appraised at a value that would allow its amortization over a period of years. However, if the occupant failed to claim the property and execute a mortgage within ninety days of publication of the law, the property could be declared vacant and sold at auction. This situation was common in rural areas, where priests denounced the law and urged the faithful—including tenants of the church and ejido members—to ignore it. The law was applied nonetheless. By the end of 1856, the government had reassigned ownership of more than twenty-three million dollars in real estate, of which about twenty million had belonged to the church.

Comonfort and Lerdo tried to convince the Mexican hierarchy that divestiture was in the best interests of the church, that the conversion of its entailed estates into liquid assets would expand its capacity for carrying out its spiritual mission in Mexico. But the corporatist spirit proved stronger than the evangelical impulse, and much of the cash that flowed into church coffers from Lerdo law transactions went into a war chest to finance the overthrow of the government. Chances for an accommodation between church and state diminished as the Lerdo law was followed by decrees secularizing cemeteries, limiting the fees that priests could charge for administering the sacraments, and requiring civil registration of births, marriages, adoptions, and deaths; and they all but disappeared with the promulgation of the Constitution of 1857.

The new constitution was produced by a national convention that met in Mexico City early in 1857. The delegates were mostly lawyers and mostly puros. The document they drew up was labeled federalist, but it allotted far more power to the central government than had the Constitution of 1824. The federal Congress could impeach state governors, and the federal Supreme Court could invalidate state elections. Universal male suffrage was formally introduced, but elections for federal officials were indirect, with voters in congressional districts choosing electors who selected the members of the unicameral Congress and, in a nationwide ballot, named the president and the Supreme Court justices. There was no vice-president of the republic; in case of the death or resignation of the president, the chief justice was to assume the presidency provisionally, pending the selection of a new president by special election. A bill of rights provided for freedom of speech and the press, equal justice under the law, prohibition of involuntary servitude, and the right to bear arms. The constitution was silent on religion; it did not grant religious freedom or toleration, but neither did it recognize Roman Catholicism as the national religion.

The Mexican hierarchy reacted angrily to the constitution's failure to establish Roman Catholicism or to prohibit the practice of other religions in Mexico. Moreover, the clergy tended to view the constitutional guarantees of freedom of expression as an invitation to blasphemy and heretical proselytization. The ban on involuntary servitude opened the door for monks and nuns to renounce their vows, a disturbing prospect to those concerned with clerical discipline. There was no relief for the church from the Juárez law, which was enshrined in the constitution, nor from the Lerdo law, which likewise was given constitutional status but without its exemptions for communal pastures and woodlands. The Mexican hierarchy, with the support of the pope, anathematized the constitution and declared excommunicated anyone who swore allegiance to it—which all government employees were required to do. The winners of the first elections under the constitution were automatically excommunicated as they took the oath of office. These included Ignacio Comonfort, elected constitutional president, and Benito Juárez, elected chief justice. Comonfort was far more disturbed by the situation than was Juárez; the president clung to the hope of a reconciliation with the church and indicated that he favored amending the constitution to make it more palatable to the clergy. His attitude encouraged conservative army officers who staged a coup in Mexico City in December 1857.

The military in the federal capital closed down the puro-dominated Congress, arrested Benito Juárez, and offered their support to President Comonfort—if he would forswear the constitution, rule by decree, and make peace with the church. Comonfort accepted the military offer but later had second thoughts. In January 1858, he freed Chief Justice Juárez, resigned the presidency, and departed for exile in the United States. Juárez went to Querétaro, where he was proclaimed president of the republic in accordance with the constitution, and, after hostilities got underway, he moved his government to Veracruz. The Conservatives held Mexico City and, before the end of 1858, acclaimed as their president Miguel Miramón, a brilliant young militarist, one of the surviving boy heroes of Chapultepec in the war with the United States.

In the Mexican civil war of 1858–1861, the War of the Reform, the Conservatives had the advantages of church support and a preponderance of the country's military talent. Conservative troops were led personally by their president and by Leonardo Márquez—another white professional soldier, crafty and ruthless—and Tomás Mejía, a resolute and resourceful Indian caudillo. The Liberals had the advantage of control of Mexico's principal port, Veracruz, and its revenue-producing customs house. And with Juárez as president, Melchor Ocampo as foreign minister, and Miguel Lerdo as minister of justice, the Liberals in Veracruz possessed political leadership far superior to that of the Conservatives in Mexico City. Popular support for the Conservatives was strongest in the central heartland, among the hacendados of the Valley of Mexico, the mercantilist industrialists and urban masses of Puebla and Mexico City, and village Indians devoted to the communal way of life. The Liberals found favor among free-trade-oriented businessmen and workers of the port of Veracruz, among traditionally federalist hacendados and unincorporated Indians and mestizos of the peripheral states, and among enterprising individuals throughout the country who saw profit opportunities for themselves in the forced sale of church and ejido property. The seizure of church property accelerated in areas under Liberal control. And with the church at war with the constitutional government, proceeds from the sale of church lands would not be handed over to the enemy hierarchy; they were appropriated for the Liberal cause. In 1859, President Juárez signed a law nationalizing without compensation the property of the Roman Catholic church in Mexico. Other decrees emanating from Veracruz formally proclaimed the separation of church and state, outlawed monasteries, ordered the suppression of all nunneries upon the death of the present occupants, and forbade the wearing of clerical clothing in public. These measures infuriated the faithful, who tended to rally more firmly than ever to the Conservatives, the professed defenders of Catholic civilization. The depravity of the Liberals—in the view of Conservatives—was confirmed in 1859 when Foreign Minister Ocampo negotiated an agreement with U.S. envoy Robert M. McLane to sell to the United States a transit zone across the Isthmus of Tehuantepec for two million dollars. Although the U.S. Senate ultimately rejected the McLane-Ocampo treaty, the Liberals remained vulnerable to charges that, after looting the church, they planned to sell the country to Protestant foreigners.

The Conservatives, however, also made financial deals with foreigners, with European bankers, who purchased their government bonds at hefty discounts. Both sides in the civil war levied forced loans on foreign residents of Mexico. In the end, the Liberals, with the friendship of the United States and the customs revenue from Veracruz, prevailed. Miramón was defeated and slipped away to Europe on a French warship, while Mejía and Márquez took to the hills to wage guerrilla warfare against the Liberal government that was installed in Mexico City in January 1861.

Miguel Lerdo decided to make a bid for the presidency in the elections that were scheduled for March 1861, but he died before all the votes were cast, and acting President Juárez was elected for a regular four-year term. Another collaborator-turned rival of the president, Melchor Ocampo, returned to his home state of Michoacán, where he was promptly captured and executed by Márquez's Conservative guerrillas. Juárez's control over the Liberal movement was strengthened by these developments, but his government was beset by seemingly insoluble foreign and domestic problems. The federal treasury was empty, Mexico's European creditors were demanding payment, and Juárez's Yankee friends were embroiled in their own civil war. The Mexican president declared a two-year moratorium on all government payments to foreigners, a move that Britain, Spain, and France found totally unacceptable. Those three nations agreed to jointly occupy Veracruz and collect their debts by attaching Mexico's customs revenues. Spanish troops seized the port in December 1861 and were joined there the next month by British and French expeditionaries.

Mexico: Imperial Interregnum, 1862–1867

The British and Spanish in Veracruz were serious about collecting debts, but the French were there to revive the Mexican Conservatives, to help them oust the Liberals and restore monarchy to Mexico. Exiled followers of the late Lucas Alamán had convinced French Emperor Napoleon III that this was a feasible project. Spain and Britain pulled out of the tripartite intervention when France's intentions became clear, and French soldiers were sent marching on Mexico City. Defeated by Mexican Liberals near Puebla in May 1862, they returned to Veracruz and tried again the next year with a much larger force. In 1863, French troops won a series of victories and entered Puebla and Mexico City to the cheers of the people of those Conservative cities. President Juárez and his government withdrew toward the north, under the uncertain protection of a dispirited Liberal army, pursued by French and Mexican Conservative forces.

Napoleon III regarded the Mexican venture as a way of satisfying France's imperialist urge, as a means of currying favor with the pope and European Catholics, as an opportunity for the profitable introduction of European capital and technology into a backward country—to transform that country and burnish the French emperor's image as an agent of progress. He and his countrymen had no intention of restoring clerical power and archaic corporatist institutions to Mexico. The Mexican Conservatives were misled—or, rather, they deceived themselves—on that score. They accepted Napoleon III's nominee for the Mexican throne, Archduke Maximilian of Austria, and happily went about arranging a plebiscite in Mexico to ratify the return of their country to Hapsburg rule and, presumably, to the glory of the sixteenth and seventeenth centuries. Before sailing to Mexico to accept his crown in 1864, Maximilian extracted a promise from Napoleon III to keep the French army in Mexico for at least three more years; in return, Maximilian committed his government to pay the cost of the occupying forces, and he recognized and guaranteed payment on virtually all the claims Europeans made against the Mexican government. Before setting foot in Mexico, Maximilian tripled its foreign debt.

But Emperor Maximilian I also brought new infusions of capital to Mexico. French investment revitalized the textile industry of Puebla. British capital undertook the resumption of work on the Veracruz–Mexico City railroad. The Mexican imperial government, which by 1865 effectively controlled the country except for a few Liberal enclaves along the U.S. border, promoted European immigration, encouraged foreign investment, chartered the country's first commercial bank (a branch of the London Bank of Mexico and South America), and generally improved the environment for enterprise by issuing Mexico's first commercial code and guaranteeing individual property rights, including those of purchasers of church property. To the great disgust of Mexican Conservatives, Maximilian gave his imperial sanction to the Lerdo and Juárez laws.

Conservative disillusionment with his regime was one of Emperor Maximilian's major problems. Others included continued

U.S. recognition of the Juárez government (ultimately relocated on the Rio Grande across from El Paso, Texas) and Prussian aggressiveness in Europe, which was creating pressure for the recall of French troops from Mexico for the defense of France. Late in 1865, French and imperial forces began a major sweep of the northern border area, to complete the pacification of the country while the Mexican empire still had the services of foreign troops. Believing that Juárez had disbanded his government and crossed into the United States, Maximilian declared the belligerency ended and signed an order in October 1865 prescribing the death penalty for anyone taken thereafter in arms against the empire. But the war was not over, President Juárez was still in Mexico, and the Mexican Liberals who were captured and executed by Maximilian's troops were not simply bandits.

Supplied from the United States, Mexican Liberal forces launched a successful counteroffensive in 1866. About the same time, Prussia defeated Austria in the Seven Weeks War and Napoleon III called his troops home from Mexico. The businesslike French emperor had decided to cut his losses and write off the Mexican venture, and he urged Maximilian to follow suit, to abdicate his throne and return to Europe. But Maximilian, encouraged by his native marshals—Miramón, Márquez, and Mejía—decided to stay and fight. He concluded that he could win with the unqualified support of the Mexican Conservatives; his mistakes had been to rely on the French army and to endorse the Liberal reform. What his subjects wanted, his marshals assured him, was a genuinely Hispanic, Catholic, and corporatist Mexico. But the departure of the French and Maximilian's conversion to corporatism did not save the Mexican empire. The Conservatives fought gallantly, but Liberal arms prevailed, and Miramón and Mejía were captured and executed with Maximilian in June 1867. Márquez managed to escape to Cuba.

Mexico: From Reforma to Porfiriato, 1867-1884

Benito Juárez returned to power in Mexico City in July 1867. Elections were scheduled late that year, and Juárez was challenged for the presidency by the popular Liberal General Porfirio Díaz, a mestizo from Oaxaca. The president was declared reelected after the federal Supreme Court had invalidated pro-Díaz results in some states. By manipulating the federal electoral machinery, Juárez was able to stay in office until his death in 1872. Juárez, the civilian liberal lawyer, felt that strongman methods were sometimes necessary to extirpate the bad habits of the past, such as the tendency of Mexicans to flock to charismatic military men. Although the president was committed to using the power at his disposal to remove the last obstacles to the establishment of a regime of individual liberty in Mexico, he nevertheless made some compromises with the past; in the interests of social peace in the countryside, he suspended the disentailment of certain categories of ejido property.

The distribution of church lands had already been accomplished, creating a new class of landowners inclined to back the Liberal establishment, headed by Juárez, against upstarts like Díaz. Foreign capitalists attracted to Mexico by Maximilian had no choice but to rally to Juárez if they hoped to recoup anything from their investments. They were understandably concerned when the restored republic repudiated the empire's bonded debt along with Maximilian's commercial code. But Juárez's government promised to revamp the republic's legal system and in 1870 produced a modern civil code. British investors in the Mexican Imperial Railroad were sufficiently encouraged to form a new company and negotiate a contract with the Liberal government to complete the Veracruz–Mexico City line. The first train rolled into the Mexican capital from the Gulf coast in 1873, the year after Juárez died.

It was during Juárez's last years that the pseudoscientific doctrine of positivism, with its lack of concern for individual liberty and contempt for the democratic process, achieved a secure foothold in Mexico. Juárez's minister of education was Gabino Barreda, an avowed disciple of Auguste Comte, the French positivist philosopher who had welcomed Napoleon III to power in France. With little prestige in France or any other advanced country after 1870, Comte's turgid formulation of altruistic love, environmental determinism, obedience to authority, and hierarchical organization was adopted as the principal guide to development in much of Latin America by the end of the nineteenth century. Juárez, an old-time liberal, was skeptical of the Comtian doctrine, but he saw the advantages of infusing Mexico's fledgling public school system with a secular sense of order and discipline. Indeed, Juárez in his last administration seemed preoccupied with order and discipline, with the disciplining of regional forces and the imposition of centralized order in Mexico. He created a national rural police to discourage the thousands of demobilized soldiers who roamed the countryside from taking up banditry or political troublemaking, and he did not shrink from intervening in the states with federal army troops when things got out of hand.

Nevertheless, a free press flourished in Mexico City during Juárez's presidency, there was freewheeling debate in the federal Congress, and the Supreme Court vigorously maintained its independence from the executive and legislative branches. The political process was susceptible to manipulation, but the contests were real and their outcomes uncertain. The presidential election of 1871 was decided in Congress, after the electoral college became deadlocked in a three-way race involving Juárez, Porfirio Díaz, and Sebastián Lerdo de Tejada, a civilian lawyer and brother of the late Miguel Lerdo. A deal was struck between Juárez and Lerdo that left the former in the presidency, made the latter chief justice, and left General Díaz out in the cold. Díaz revolted and was driven into the hills of Nayarit by the federal army. The next year, when Juárez died, Lerdo succeeded to the presidency, granted amnesty to the fugitive Díaz, and got himself elected to a full four-year term.

President Lerdo generally continued his predecessor's cautious policy of reconstruction and development. Educational opportunities expanded slowly, and by 1874, sixteen percent of Mexico's school-aged children were said to be attending classes, compared to about five percent in the 1850s. The National Preparatory School, housed in a building confiscated from the Jesuits, continued to turn out teachers imbued with the positivist motto "Order and Progress." Some nationalized Catholic schools were continued in operation by state or municipal authorities, and some schools were built where none had existed before. In view of its meager resources, the Juárez-Lerdo government made significant gains in education. Economic progress was less evident, even in the Mexico City–Puebla–Veracruz corridor served by the country's first railroad. The high freight rates of the railway, almost equal to those charged by mule-train operators, limited the general benefits of the innovation. And the return on capital was so meager as to discourage almost anyone from investing in further railroad construction in Mexico. Although a British-Mexican company received a concession from the Lerdo government to build a railroad from central Mexico to the U.S. border, it did not lay any rails.

Lerdo announced his candidacy for a second four-year term in 1876 and thereby provoked an armed rebellion by General Díaz, who charged that Lerdo planned to rig the voting; even if he did not, Díaz declared, no president should be allowed to serve more than one full term. "Effective suffrage and no reelection" was the Porfirista slogan. After much maneuvering and a little fighting, Díaz seized power in Mexico City, drove Lerdo into exile, and got himself elected constitutional president at the end of 1876. In office, Díaz kept his word and supported and signed a constitutional amendment forbidding the immediate reelection of the president.

Porfirio Díaz came to power at a time of falling silver prices, which had both negative and positive implications for Mexican economic development. Silver was Mexico's principal export and the basis for its currency; declining silver prices, in the absence of rising production, reduced the nation's income and its capacity to import. Silver production had risen since 1821, but the figure for 1877, 24.8 million pesos, still fell short of the total for 1809, the year before the war for independence began. Modest volume gains in the 1870s, the most peaceful decade for Mexico since the century's first, were offset by lower unit value. Until 1873, the Mexican silver peso was equal to the U.S. dollar, but in that year the United States halted the free coinage of silver as domestic and worldwide production soared, upsetting the traditional silver-gold value ratio of about sixteen to one; by 1877, the Mexican silver peso was worth only $.91 U.S., and at the end of the century its value had declined to less than half that of a gold-backed U.S. dollar. The steady devaluation of money had a long-term positive effect in that it caused consumer prices to rise in

Mexico while they were falling in most of the rest of the world, thereby stimulating investment in Mexican production for domestic consumption. But the effect was scarcely felt in the 1870s as Mexico shipped forty-two percent of its exports, mostly silver, to the United States and, in effect, imported the U.S. depression of those years.

President Porfirio Díaz wanted to expand Mexico's railroad system, which in 1877 consisted of six hundred forty kilometers of track, almost all of it lying in the Veracruz–Puebla–Mexico City corridor. But foreign investors had yet to perceive the potential of the Mexican economy, and they were understandably leery of the regime of the mestizo general who had seized power in yet another Mexican revolution. In the absence of foreign capital, Mexican government funds were appropriated to pay for or subsidize railroad construction by Mexican companies, with indifferent results. Gaps were left in the lines as builders defaulted, and some stretches of track were so poorly laid as to be useless. Díaz had more success in stringing telegraph lines, adding significantly to the twenty-five hundred kilometers in use when he took office. His government beefed up the rural police, who apparently received instructions to summarily execute anyone caught cutting telegraph wires. In Mexico City and other urban areas, however, Díaz generally respected civil and political liberties during his first term in office.

Porfirio Díaz was genuinely popular. He was credited with streamlining the government, firing useless bureaucrats, and rooting out corruption in the customs service. Much of the money he saved went into his ill-advised railroad-building program, but that at least gave the country a feeling of moving forward, and it provided some jobs for rural workers. He also gave Mexico a sense of stability. Troops loyal to the president moved rapidly and with unusual ferocity in putting down a Lerdista revolt in Veracruz in 1879—the last political uprising the country would face in the nineteenth century. The newly imposed order did not suffer from Díaz's toleration of a free press and unrestricted debate in the two houses of Congress (the Senate had been restored in 1875), nor from his insistence on stepping down from the presidency after the 1880 elections. In fact, the peaceful transfer of power from Porfirio Díaz to his elected successor—

Manuel González, a Porfirista general—was taken as a sign that Mexico had attained political maturity. Foreigners now were interested in investing in the country.

Shortly before Díaz turned over the presidency to his protégé González, the Mexican government signed a contract with a company organized by North American capitalists to build and operate a railroad between Mexico City and El Paso, Texas. In return for subsidies averaging about seven thousand pesos a kilometer, payable in forty-year bonds at six-percent interest, the Central of Mexico Railway accepted government rate regulation. Similar contracts were let during the González administration (1880–84) for the construction of other lines to the Mexican capital from Laredo, Texas, and Nogales, Arizona. The construction was pushed with great vigor, and before González left office in 1884, a Central of Mexico train rolled into Mexico City from El Paso. During the four years of the González administration, Mexico's rail system grew from about a thousand kilometers of usable track to more than fifty-seven hundred kilometers. The railroads were built by North American companies because they had the construction capacity, were conveniently located, and were attracted by the subsidies and guaranteed returns on capital offered them by the Mexican government. They were not built as part of a Yankee conspiracy to suck silver out of Mexico, as the United States was awash with silver and its mining industry was in a depression.

The new railroads, as Manuel González and Porfirio Díaz had foreseen, greatly reduced production and shipping costs for the mines and, together with the introduction of the cyanide refining process, increased the profitability of silver extraction despite falling prices. And the availability of rail transportation spurred the exploitation of deposits of other metals, such as gold, copper, and lead. The natural market for these metals was in the industrialized nation on Mexico's northern border, which was also the logical source of capital for new mining ventures in Mexico. The government of Manuel González encouraged investment in Mexican business in general with the promulgation of a comprehensive commercial code in 1884, and specifically in mining with a revision of the country's mining laws. While the Spanish principle of exclusive crown (i.e., government) ownership of subsoil metal deposits theoretically was retained, the long-term leasing and trading of mineral rights were facilitated, and hydrocarbons were specifically excluded from the national patrimony: private individuals and companies could buy and sell coal or petroleum deposits just as they bought and sold land.

Land along the railroads became more valuable, and pressures for the disentailment of the remaining communal holdings mounted. There were ejido Indians who wanted to sell their birthright and hacendados who were eager to buy it. The division of communal lands, which had slowed under Juárez and Lerdo, speeded up under Díaz and González. With railroads greatly extending the supply radii of Mexican cities, the profitability of large-scale food and fiber agriculture spread over the country, and a trend toward larger landholdings got underway.

Financing for new agricultural and business enterprises was more readily available with the establishment of the country's second commercial bank, the National Bank of Mexico, in 1881. Despite the name, the bank was a private one, controlled by French capitalists; it accepted demand deposits and, like the London Bank of Mexico and South America, was authorized to issue banknotes. Though Mexico still had no central bank, by the early 1880s it was able to generate the money supply required to sustain steady economic growth.

With all their spending for railroads and other infrastructure, the administrations of Díaz and González had little left for investment in human capital. There were modest increases in the numbers of schools, teachers, and pupils in the 1880s, but the Mexican population remained overwhelmingly illiterate and short on marketable skills. Rather than educate Mexican peons, it seemed easier and cheaper to attract European immigrants to Mexico with offers of land. The Mexican government hoped to tap into the flow of skilled and highly motivated people from Europe to North and South America. To find land to offer prospective immigrants, a law was enacted in 1883 to entice private companies to survey the country's unoccupied and unclaimed real estate; the companies could keep one-third of the land they surveyed and marked off in twenty-five-hundred-hectare parcels. The other two-thirds were to go to the government, to be sold or granted to immigrants or to people who sponsored immigrants. The plan did not work; few immigrants were attracted to Mexico—fewer than the three thousand native Mexicans who migrated to the United States yearly in the 1880s—and only a handful settled on the twenty-five-hundred-hectare tracts. Most of these lands were eventually incorporated without restriction into the big haciendas.

The Mexican liberal reform, as it culminated in the administration of Manuel González, invited abuse. Lands occupied by poor people could be declared vacant by larcenous surveyors and sold out from under them. Illiterate Indians who received deeds to ejido property could be deprived of them by theft or trickery. The church, their corporate defender since the Spanish Conquest, no longer had the strength to stand up for them. The deprived and the dispossessed were now at the mercy of the liberal state. An independent judiciary, a free press, and political democracy might have responded to their concerns, as occurred in some other rapidly developing countries. But these essential institutions of liberalism were suppressed soon after Porfirio Díaz returned to power in 1884 and set up a dictatorship, ending seventeen years of relative freedom in Mexico. The national debate on social policy was stifled before it began, information was suppressed, and the unfortunate republic wound up with a crippled society and an economy as distorted as its political system.

The Liberal "Reform" in New Granada/Colombia: The First Phase, 1849–1854

Though the Mexican Reforma is the most familiar example of midcentury liberalism at work, the achievements of Colombian liberals of the same period closely paralleled and in some respects went beyond those of the Mexicans. The Colombian equivalent of the Reforma got underway a few years earlier, and it was not ushered in by the overthrow of an irresponsible dictatorship such as that of Santa Anna; its origin was an electoral victory won by the opposition Liberal party against the ruling but divided Conservatives. General Tomás C. Mosquera, who served as president from 1845 to 1849, had been an ardent supporter of Bolívar even during the latter's final dictatorship and was marked as a Conservative by past actions as well as associa-

tions, but he was a highly personalist and unpredictable statesman who on several key issues adopted policies virtually indistin-
guishable from those of most Liberals. Both his personalism and
his lack of doctrinal consistency made trouble for Mosquera
within the Conservative party, with the result that pro- and anti-
Mosquera factions supported different Conservative candidates
for the presidential succession. Under these circumstances, the
Liberals were able to impose their own choice, the veteran of
independence and well-to-do landowner, General José Hilario
López.

López's party was divided also, although the division did not
reach a critical stage until after the election. On one side were the
better-educated young Liberals, drawn from the middle and
upper sectors of society, who felt that at last the time had come
to take all the theoretical ideals of liberalism and put them into
effect without more delay. Theirs was a somewhat romantic,
doctrinaire brand of liberalism, whose adherents came in due
course to be dubbed *Gólgotas* from the references they made to
the "Martyr of Golgotha," Jesus Christ. This did not mean that
they were in the least proclerical. Their perspective was one of
secular reformism, and they accordingly looked on Jesus as a
prototype of nineteenth-century liberal, who, if he had been born
eighteen hundred years later, would have ardently opposed the
ecclesiastical fuero and compulsory tithes and all manner of
outdated privileges. Their own solution to all problems of the
day was simply to free individual initiative and enterprise from
the bonds imposed either by the state or by such private corporations as the church.

Another current among the Liberals was a working-class, popular faction, drawn not from the Liberal peasantry (whose
members, exactly like Conservative peasants, were usually pas-
sive followers of local party chieftains) but from the urban artisans, the one working-class element that showed any tendency to
participate in politics on its own and with a consciousness of class
interests. The artisans were not solidly Liberal, for both parties
cut across class lines, but it was the Liberal artisans who played
the most active role, and they interpreted the feelings of artisans
generally in attacking the outgoing Mosquera administration un-

mercifully for its sponsorship of a sharp reduction in tariff rates. This had been one of the "liberal" policies of the "Conservative" Mosquera, and it angered the artisans regardless of party affiliation. To be sure, they were being hurt not just by lower tariffs on competing foreign manufactures but by the final establishment, also under Mosquera's auspices, of permanent steam navigation on the Magdalena River, which appreciably diminished the isolation from the outside world that had been even more important as a form of protection to the artisans of the interior. In any case, the anger of the artisans was channeled into political action by the network of Democratic Societies, political clubs that began springing up in Bogotá and larger towns in the late 1840s, enlisting lower-class support for Liberals against Conservatives and calling loudly for higher tariffs.

There was a third element of Liberals which fell somewhere in between. These were the *Draconianos*, led by military men who had taken their stand with the Liberals for any number of personal reasons but whose belief in strong government and distrust of ideological abstractions would eventually align them predominantly with the artisans against the Gólgotas. However, to repeat, intraparty differences did not matter as long as the Liberals were out of power, working together to get into power. In much the same way, middle- and upper-class French liberals started the French Revolution of 1848 by appealing successfully to the urban workers for support and got along very well with them until they attained their immediate objective. Before it was all over, those same middle- and upper-class liberals found themselves shooting down the workers in the streets of Paris. Exactly the same would happen in the streets of Bogotá, although there the crisis took a little longer to mature, and before the shooting began a large first installment of the Colombian Reforma was already enacted.

In effect, the four-year term of President López (1849–53) plus the first year of the next four-year term, to which his fellow Liberal General José María Obando was elected, saw a veritable frenzy of reform activity. Liberals abolished such terms of address as "Excellency" and "Honorable" as contrary to ideal republicanism and went around calling each other "Citizen" in imitation of French revolutionary custom. In political affairs generally, their intent was to introduce the untrammeled reign of liberty, so that there was even a law adopted giving absolute freedom of the press with no limitations even in the case of libel. (Slander by the spoken word was still punishable for a few more years.) The Liberals further introduced universal male suffrage as part of a new national constitution they adopted in 1853 and, exactly as would be the case in Mexico four years later, with serious misgivings on the part of some who doubted the common man would know how to use this right; but democratization of electoral practices was now in the air in Europe and North America, and Colombia followed suit. Moreover, once Colombian Liberals agreed to give all men the right to vote, they proceeded to arrange for all kinds of offices—including Supreme Court justice—to be filled by direct popular election. In a single province, that of Vélez, Liberal zealots even enacted woman suffrage, apparently for the first time in the hemisphere.

The women of Vélez lost the vote, when the provincial ordinance was struck down by the national Supreme Court, before they ever had a chance to exercise it. Neither did the votes of newly enfranchised male voters always get counted, but at least the principle of a democratic suffrage was established. The 1853 constitution likewise went partway toward introducing federalism as a system of government, through such concessions to provincial autonomy as allowing the people of each province to elect their governor rather than having him appointed as before from Bogotá. But the distribution of power was still weighted in favor of the central government, thanks in part to the strong opposition of the Draconianos to the erosion of national authority.

In economic matters the watchword was laissez-faire, reflecting above all the influence of the Gólgotas. The most significant single measure in this connection was the final extinction of the state tobacco monopoly. Though ordered by a law passed (with strong Liberal support) under the Mosquera administration, it took effect only in 1850, during the presidency of López. Believers in the economic principles of orthodox liberalism then found vindication for their beliefs in the rapid expansion of tobacco production, especially in the upper Magdalena River valley. This expansion had other causes too: the establishment of steam navigation on the river and favorable conditions in the European tobacco market. The result, in any case, was a fundamental change in the pattern of foreign trade, with gold permanently losing the hold on first place among Colombian exports that it had occupied since the colonial period. The growth of tobacco exports was accompanied by—and helped pay for—a sharp growth of imports, particularly as the Liberal regime continued the low-tariff policies of Mosquera rather than acceding to the protectionist demands of the artisans.

The output of gold was falling in absolute as well as merely relative importance, and one reason was another Liberal reform of the period—the complete abolition of slavery. This was accomplished in 1851 and affected those slaves born too soon to benefit from the Gran Colombian free-birth law of 1821, plus younger children born to slave mothers since 1821, whose freedom had not yet become fully effective. Altogether, about twenty-five thousand persons were set free, mainly concentrated in plantation and mining districts of the western provinces or the Caribbean coast. The impact was most severe on mining because it had been more dependent than agriculture on slave labor, and many of the freedmen drifted off to subsistence farming rather than staying on the job for pay.

The abolition of slavery—especially with compensation offered to the dispossessed slaveowners—was fully in line with the Liberal objective of ending artificial restrictions on the free play of natural economic laws, in this case that of supply and demand in the labor market. Similar thinking was reflected in the Liberal approach to the nation's other large, depressed racial minority— the Indians. Here the key issue was division of the communal village lands, which had been ordered before but never fully implemented. A concerted effort to carry out the law in this matter was now launched, with a simplification of procedures and removal of any limitation on an Indian's right to dispose as he wished of his individual share of the former common lands once they were divided up. Indians still managed to avoid liquidation of their communal system in some areas, mainly southwestern Colombia, but elsewhere communal property was converted into individual plots, and if more powerful neighbors cast a covetous glance at those plots, they sometimes—not invariably—

found a way to ease the Indians off them. The latter would then be converted into a landless subgroup, available to work on creole estates at nominal wages. To that extent, the transformation of communal into individual property helped enlarge the scope of supply and demand in the labor market as well as in the real estate market itself.

Last but far from least of the Liberal reforms were those in the field of religion. Among them was the expulsion, or rather reexpulsion, of the Jesuits, who had been let back in during the 1840s by the Conservatives and were sent into exile again in 1850. The Jesuits had many sympathizers among the population at large, so the government did not tackle the problem directly but casually discovered that the Spanish decree of 1767 expelling Jesuits from the Spanish Empire had never been formally repealed in Colombian legislation and was therefore technically still in force. Other religious reforms included the abolition of the fuero and of compulsory tithe collections, the final establishment of religious toleration (except for Jesuits), and the formal separation of church and state. The last two reforms came as part of the new constitution of 1853, and the separation of church and state represented an obvious departure from what had been the previous Liberal position. However, Liberals had formerly insisted on maintaining the patronato in large part in the hope of using the control it gave the state over church affairs for overcoming potential clerical resistance to the reforms they sought to enact. With a significant portion of those reforms now enacted, they could afford, as in Mexico a few years later, to be more true to their own principles and turn the church loose to manage itself. To be sure, there were still two key demands of nineteenth-century anticlericalism which had not been attained: outlawing of all religious orders, not just the Jesuits, and the general confiscation of church property. These would also come but would have to wait a little longer.

The clergy, on its part, was glad to get out from under state control, although it regretted the loss of moral and other support it had traditionally derived from its association with the state. It objected also to such corollaries of separation as the introduction of civil marriage and, worse yet, as a corollary of that particular corollary, legalized divorce. However, divorce was not destined to last long this time around, so that anyone anxious to get rid of a spouse had to move quickly. One who made it in time, with ironical consequences in due season, was Rafael Núñez, the doctrinaire Liberal of the 1850s who as president three decades later would restore the church to a position of influence comparable to that from which he and his fellow partisans had removed it at midcentury. In so doing, Núñez would annul the second marriage he entered into after gaining divorce and thereby strip his own first lady of the respectability conferred by legal matrimony.

Not surprisingly, the pace of reform aroused strong opposition in many quarters, and an abortive Conservative revolt occurred in 1851. It was premature and easily suppressed. More serious was the factional squabbling within the Liberal camp, which increasingly pitted both the artisans and the Draconianos against the Gólgotas. The artisans were angered above all by the failure to satisfy their demand for tariff protection, while the Draconianos viewed their factional opponents as effete intellectuals and/or grasping merchants who were engaged in undermining the state itself. Differences of policy were reinforced by latent social antagonisms, which caused both the low-born artisans and the somewhat nondescript Liberal military men who formed the backbone of the Draconianos to resent the elitist aura of the Gólgotas. Things came to a head in April 1854, when a group of Draconiano officers overthrew President Obando—who in most respects belonged to their wing of the party but refused to undo the innovations of the Gólgotas by unconstitutional means—and inaugurated a brief military dictatorship under José María Melo. They received strong support from the artisans, who formed worker battalions to defend the revolution and terrorize merchants and intellectuals. But the movement was finally suppressed, and several hundred artisans were sent off to penal colonies in Panama and other unwholesome places to teach them a lesson.

The Liberal "Reform" in Colombia: Pause and Apogee

In suppressing the Draconianos and artisans, members of the Gólgota faction joined hands with loyalist Liberal generals such as ex-President López and with the Conservatives, who were glad to lend a hand in Liberal disputes. The leading figures of the Conservative party differed sharply with the Gólgotas on some issues (e.g., church policy) but had roughly similar views on others (e.g., the tariff) and generally shared an upper-class background. Moreover, the Conservatives promoted their interests so successfully that they emerged as senior partners in the new provisional government set up after the suppression of the revolt and then elected one of themselves, Mariano Ospina Rodríguez, as president in 1857. The Conservatives did not stay in power long, but they brought the Jesuits briefly back again, and they presided over the adoption of another new constitution in 1858, which differed from the preceding one mainly in that it was overtly federalist in nature. It was odd at first glance that such a constitution should be promulgated under Conservative auspices, but the fact was that federalism had already been making strong inroads before it was issued. The process gained momentum in 1854 when the previous constitution was amended to authorize establishment of the so-called State of Panama as a self-governing entity except for defense, foreign relations, and certain other details that were still reserved to the central authorities. Other regions immediately demanded and obtained similar privileges for themselves, so that creating a uniform federalist system for the entire country did at least tidy things up. For that matter, even some Conservatives were becoming attracted to the principle of federalism, while still others saw a strategic advantage in that no matter who might occupy the presidency or control the Congress at Bogotá, federalism would presumably assure them of solid control in those individual states where they happened to be strongest.

Conservatives were soon to have the chance to test the strategic advantages of federalism for opposition parties, since in 1860 a civil war broke out which removed them again from national office. One reason for this new outbreak was the feeling of many Liberals that the Conservative Ospina administration was not loyally observing the federalist spirit of the new constitution. But there were other causes, including sheer personal antipathy between Ospina and ex-President Tomás Mosquera, who had suddenly turned Liberal and led the revolt. As Mosquera had never been a very orthodox Conservative, the change in affiliation was not wholly surprising. Furthermore, the revolution succeeded. Thus, the Liberals were back in, and as one of their very first measures, the Jesuits were back out. This time, too, all religious orders suffered the same fate: just as in Mexico during the same years, convents and monasteries were officially suppressed. The latter step was taken in 1861, in the first flush of Liberal victory. Indeed, all church property was now confiscated by the government and put up for sale—again as in Mexico in the same period.

The victorious Liberals capped off their handiwork by adopting still another national constitution in 1863, which, however, lasted a good twenty-two years. One of its less controversial features was the formal restoration of the name Colombia to what since the breakup of Gran Colombia in 1830 had been officially calling itself New Granada. To be exact, the new title was United States of Colombia, for the federalism enshrined in the 1858 constitution was retained and in fact carried to even greater extremes, just as in almost every respect the Colombian Constitution of 1863 represents the most advanced form of liberalism that any Latin American nation achieved (or was afflicted with) in the past century. The states not only received extensive powers in running their own affairs but were treated virtually as independent nations; they kept their own armed forces, and most came to issue their own postage stamps. The national government, on its part, was made as weak as possible, lest it be in a position to violate either state or individual rights. Thus, the president was limited to a two-year term, and he could serve again only after a two-year wait. He was to be elected on a basis of one state, one vote, with each state free to decide for itself which inhabitants should enjoy the suffrage. This in turn marked the end of Colombia's first experiment with universal male suffrage, since roughly half the states proceeded to reinstate literacy requirements that disenfranchised the great majority. (Liberals had observed the Conservatives winning too many elections once all men were given the vote, with the result that on this issue they clearly began to have second thoughts.)

The new constitution was further equipped with a bill of rights that reaffirmed absolute freedom of the press, with automatic immunity for writers and editors from libel suits as before, and gave unrestricted freedom now to the spoken word as well.

From four-letter words (or Spanish equivalent) to calls for subversion, anything one said was constitutional. The same bill of
rights recognized the absolute inviolability of human life, which
served to end capital punishment, and at the same time—incon-
sistently perhaps—recognized every citizen as having the inalienable right to use and deal in arms and ammunition.

Colombian Liberals had in fact overdone things. With both
individual and states' rights carried to such extremes, the national
authorities could not effectively maintain order; state governments were made or unmade by local revolutions, and there was
little the Colombian president could do about it. Likewise, by
their attacks on the church the Liberals had offended a majority
of Colombians, so that they were able to stay in power only by
rigging the elections—and they did so all the way to the 1880s,
when they finally lost power as the result of a new split in their
own ranks. But the right to vote was the one political freedom
consistently tampered with. Speech and press were free according to the constitution, and the only attempt by a Liberal president of the period to seize dictatorial powers (Mosquera himself,
in a final term in 1867) was thwarted by his fellow Liberals,
though with Conservative support. The rulers of the period also
showed commendable interest in education, enacting in 1870 the
principle of free, obligatory primary instruction and importing
professors of education from Germany to set up normal schools
for the training of teachers. This noble effort failed to produce
the desired results, both for lack of resources and because the
extension of state schools under Liberal auspices (and with Luth-
eran heretics included in the German normal school mission) was
equivalent in the eyes of many Conservatives to a concerted
attack on religion. The resulting agitation was a principal reason
for the outbreak of a major, though unsuccessful, civil war in
1876.

The tightening of relations with the world market that began
with the tobacco boom of the 1850s meanwhile continued. Exports per capita, which had been declining before 1850, increased one hundred twenty percent from 1850 to 1882. Sales of
tobacco eventually fell off, but a succession of other commodities—cotton, quinine, coffee—offset the decline. In each case
except coffee, of which Colombia was just beginning to be a

serious exporter, the pattern was one of a brief speculative frenzy followed by loss of markets as Colombian producers proved unable to match the prices or quality of other exporting countries. Yet any given export boom, while it lasted, brought benefits not just to merchants and landowners but also to workers and suppliers. With perhaps some exaggeration, it was claimed that peasants attracted by high wages to the tobacco fields were eating meat for the first time in their lives.

Unfortunately, not everyone benefited. Commodity booms often led to higher internal prices even for people who were not sharing in the proceeds, while domestic artisans steadily lost ground in the face of the increased imports that ultimately increased exports had made possible. Even with the growth of trade, moreover, Colombia's economy remained the least developed of all the major Latin American countries. The nation's first commercial bank was founded only in 1870, a year in which per capita income may have come to about forty dollars (admittedly worth more then than now). With many people living still on the margin of the money economy, such a figure did not mean quite what it would in Europe or North America, but for Colombia it reveals that secular stagnation still had not truly been overcome. Nor would it be, until the definitive takeoff of the Colombian coffee industry early in the next century. Liberal reforms had created some of the preconditions for that development by clearing away structural obstacles—but they probably also delayed its advent by unleashing further civil strife at both national and state levels.

The Liberal era drew to an end in the 1880s, at a time when a temporary downturn in the export economy tended to weaken the Liberal cause. The reaction was led by Rafael Núñez, a former doctrinaire Liberal himself who had become disillusioned with the results of Liberal policy and who formed an alliance, at first mainly tactical but ultimately programmatic, with the Conservatives. As president (for a second time) in 1885, Núñez seized upon a hare-brained Radical Liberal uprising, which he easily crushed with Conservative help, as pretext to declare that the 1863 constitution had "ceased to exist." The next year, he replaced it with the constitution that is still in effect, though much amended, today. By the Colombian Constitution of 1886 and other related measures, including a concordat with the Vatican in 1887, Núñez both restored an ultra-centralist political organization, whereby the national president named all the governors in the country and the governors in turn named all the mayors, and returned the church to a position of power and privilege. In both respects, the reaction against liberal doctrine had gone considerably farther in Colombia than in the Mexico of Porfirio Díaz. But then Núñez's Conservative allies, unlike the Mexican Conservatives, had not entered into a treasonable compact with any foreign power. Núñez never formally joined their ranks—trying instead to launch a new third party, called National—but in practice they became the political beneficiaries of his handiwork, constructing a Conservative hegemony in Colombia that was to last almost a half-century, until 1930.

10

The Heyday of Liberal Reform in Spanish America (1850–1880) II: Argentina, Chile, and Some Other Cases

Argentina: Post-Rosas National Organization

Just as Colombia was experimenting with an extreme form of doctrinaire liberalism under the auspices of the Gólgotas and Mexico was entering the age of La Reforma, Argentina after the fall of Rosas in 1852 almost inevitably embraced liberalism too, but a somewhat more moderate brand of it. Justo José de Urquiza, who headed the coalition of foreign and domestic enemies that finally defeated the Rosas dictatorship, was himself the longtime federalist chieftain of the province of Entre Ríos and as such had been for many years the collaborator of Rosas, but in turning against the latter he gave notice of his conviction that it was time for the country to receive a definitive constitutional organization and to use the resources available to the nation's government for something more than just the maintenance of internal and external security and the protection of the economic interests of Buenos Aires estancieros. Urquiza thus moved to turn Argentine federalism into a liberal and progressive force as distinct from the largely negative and reactionary force that it had been under Rosas. At the same time, in the final battle against Rosas, he had joined hands with the dictator's archenemies, the Unitarios, who except for their centralist stand on political organization had always been close to the mainstream of Latin American liberalism.

Though conditions were presumably favorable for the emergence of a broad liberal consensus, the situation was complicated by a number of confusing side issues. A protracted feud was soon underway between Urquiza and the Unitarios, who after the defeat of Rosas came out of hiding and forced retirement or streamed back from their places of exile abroad. As they included in their ranks a high proportion of the country's ablest and best-educated leaders—the greater part of Argentina's intellectual elite—they assumed that it was somehow their right to rule. Moreover, Urquiza had spent so many years as ally of Rosas and thus a hated enemy that it was hard to get used to being on the same side with him. There was also a revival of the old jealousy between Buenos Aires and the other provinces; and this regional struggle closely parallels the personal and factional difficulties between Urquiza and the former Unitarios since the latter again obtained control of the city and province of Buenos Aires, just as in the days of Rivadavia, while Urquiza controlled the rest of the country. For about ten years, there was almost continual squabbling between Buenos Aires and the interior, most of the time without literally coming to blows.

The first skirmishes with Buenos Aires did not deter Urquiza from going ahead with plans for national organization. Under his auspices, a constituent convention meeting at Santa Fe produced the Argentine Constitution of 1853, which was the first really effective constitution Argentina had. Though amended numerous times, temporarily replaced by the Peronista constitution of 1949, and often suspended in whole or in part, the 1853 constitution is again today in force, giving it one of the best survival records among constitutions of Latin America. It was a federalist document, frankly modeled in key respects after that of the United States; it therefore gave the separate provinces a real measure of control in management of their own affairs. But it also set up a complete national administration—such as Rosas never wanted—with president, central bureaucracy, Congress, and Supreme Court. And it embodied a generally sensible, moderate brand of federalism, quite unlike that of the Colombian 1863 constitution, with specific safeguards designed to prevent a recurrence of the near anarchy that had plagued Argentina intermittently before the imposition of Rosas's version of law and order. There was, for example, the provision that no Argentine province should have the right to declare war on another province and also the provision that the national government could "intervene" in the affairs of a province, by force if need be, in order to uphold the republican and federal form of government. That is, should republican and federal institutions be threatened, the president could depose the provincial governor or other provincial officials and take whatever steps were necessary to correct the situation.

As things eventually turned out, almost any governor who made trouble for the president was in danger of being called a menace to republican and federal institutions and being put out of office, although with elections usually manipulated by the party in power, it was not easy for an outright oppositionist to get elected in the first place. By the end of the century, though Argentina was still operating under an ostensibly federal constitution, the political system was more nearly centralist, thanks in considerable part to the intervention clause that served to keep the provinces—particularly the smaller and weaker ones—under the continual threat of a takeover by the national authorities. In the beginning, however, with Urquiza serving inevitably as first president under the constitution, this was not true to quite the same extent. Now that Rosas was gone, the assorted local caudillos who in practice ran the Argentine provinces were not easy to push around, and they could have turned on Urquiza if he had gone too far in asserting the power of the national administration.

In addition to providing for an outwardly federalist political structure, the new constitution provided Argentina with other benefits of liberal republicanism: separation of powers, individual rights, and so forth. The separation of powers, like provincial autonomy, was destined to be less real in practice than on paper, with the executive gaining definite ascendancy over the other two branches as time went on. But as far as individual liberties were concerned, Argentina from the Constitution of 1853 until well into the twentieth century built up a quite passable record. Elections might be crooked and provincial governors arbitrarily deposed, but one could come right out and say it was a terrible government without imminent danger of going to jail or facing a firing squad. It is also of interest that the electoral system was at least in principle democratic, on the basis of universal male suffrage. The constitution did not deal with the question directly, but certain of its provisions were interpreted as excluding, by implication, the imposition of property or other restrictions on the right to vote. Argentina attained this democratic conquest in the same year, 1853, as Colombia, and four years ahead of the Mexican Constitution of 1857; it would merely take more than half a century to make the right meaningful in actual practice.

In the same progressive spirit, the Argentine constitution finally abolished the fuero, decreed freedom of religion throughout the nation, and declared the immediate emancipation of all remaining slaves. The latter were not numerous, since no one had been born a slave in Argentina since 1813 and slavery had suffered further attrition through voluntary manumission, self-purchase, and the taking of slaves for military service (with freedom as reward if they survived). Indeed, the Afro-Argentine population, which at independence made up roughly a quarter of the population in the city of Buenos Aires, was itself disappearing, because of a complex of factors that included ethnic-cultural assimilation and simple reclassification into other racial categories—processes that the ending of slavery could only accelerate. Then, too, the constitution incorporated a good number of other legal and institutional reforms of the sort conventionally promoted by liberals throughout Latin America. But as far as the church was concerned, these did not include any further moves against church property or against the integrity of the religious orders, and in Argentina the patronato was retained. This relative moderation in the area of religious reform contrasts not only with the frantic anticlericalism of Mexico and Colombia during the same period but also with the blows struck against the church by Rivadavia in the 1820s. One reason, no doubt, is the mere fact that what remained of church property and influence in Argentina was not great enough to be perceived as a serious threat to the progress of the century. Another reason is that the constitution was essentially the work of Urquiza's supporters and advisers from the Argentine interior, where traditional Catholic orthodoxy was stronger than in Buenos Aires.

The sponsorship of the new constitution by the provincial caudillo Urquiza was in fact sufficient reason for the province of Buenos Aires, whose government was now dominated by the former Unitarios, to refuse to ratify it and remain outside the Argentine Confederation as a sovereign and independent state. This meant, among other things, that the final abolition of slavery was delayed in liberal, enlightened Buenos Aires until the porteños could bring themselves to accept Urquiza's constitution. But Urquiza as president put the constitution into effect in all the rest of Argentina. For the present, the national capital was established at the humble river town of Paraná (population about five thousand), which happened to be the capital of Urquiza's home province of Entre Ríos.

In addition to resolving the problem of national organization, even if it had to be done without Buenos Aires, Urquiza settled one other long-standing problem—again without Buenos Aires. This was the problem of free navigation on the Paraná River, which Rosas had been determined to keep closed to foreign commerce in order to protect the trade monopoly of Buenos Aires. On this issue he had simply continued the policy of all previous porteño rulers, and he thereby sacrificed the interests of his allies, the Federalists of the provinces upstream. Urquiza, however, came from one of the very provinces that had been hurt by the Buenos Aires monopoly. At the earliest opportunity, he therefore opened the river to foreign shipping, and as president of the confederation, he negotiated treaties with foreign powers that in effect gave international recognition to the opening. All this paved the way for the rapid rise of Rosario as the confederation's chief port. Even after the river was opened, most Argentine trade continued to flow through Buenos Aires, which had the best facilities for handling and distribution of goods and, in the whole province of Buenos Aires, the richest internal market. The separatist Buenos Aires government, moreover, launched a campaign of virtual economic warfare to discourage foreign ships from going on up the Paraná; and the porteños' success in holding onto the lion's share of foreign trade left the government of Urquiza in dire financial straits, because the customs duties derived from trade continued to be the most reliable source of tax revenue. But at least the principle of open navigation was established, never to be lost again.

One other accomplishment of the Urquiza regime was the active encouragement given to immigration, which had been first encouraged without much success by Rivadavia in the 1820s and then languished during the Rosas years. The new policy is summed up in the repeatedly quoted slogan of Urquiza's adviser Juan Bautista Alberdi: "To govern is to populate" (*Gobernar es poblar*). Alberdi himself was one of the select number of returning Unitarios who attached himself to the fortunes of Urquiza and through his writing was the man who chiefly inspired the Constitution of 1853. He was of provincial origin and on most issues a moderate; but he was essentially a moderate liberal, and he shared the enthusiasm of other Latin American liberals for the impetus to economic and other forms of progress that could be gained by importing new blood, new ideas, and new attitudes, particularly from the enlightened peoples of northern Europe. Hence, the constitution he inspired contained a number of articles expressly designed to stimulate immigration, whose encouragement was included among the official duties of the national president and Congress.

One way in which immigration was promoted consisted of group colonization schemes, in which a promoter would arrange to bring over families from Europe, settle them on public land, and obtain reimbursement for his expenses in installment payments by the immigrants themselves. The first permanent colony of this sort was established in the province of Santa Fe, at a site appropriately named La Esperanza—"Hope"—and under the auspices of the provincial government. When the settlers proved unable to meet the terms agreed upon for paying the costs incurred by both the promoter and the province itself, the national administration came to the rescue and provided a needed extension of time. Other colonies followed, and not just in Santa Fe, but Santa Fe long held a place of leadership. Precisely because it had been one of the poorest and least developed provinces before the fall of Rosas, it had ample land for agricultural settlement still available for distribution, whereas the better part of Buenos Aires had already been parceled out to private owners. It became—relatively speaking—an oasis of small immigrant farmers in a country dominated by large estates. Thus, too, immigration to Santa Fe came to fulfill the ideal of fostering a more democratic social structure, to a degree seldom matched elsewhere in Latin America. Needless to say, many newcomers came out individually rather than in organized group settlements, and they went to the city and province of Buenos Aires as well as to the other provinces. Whatever form or direction it took, the tide of immigrants reached its full extent in the later nineteenth century. But it had its beginning in the 1850s.

Buenos Aires, on its part, not only shared in the process of immigration but in other respects was undergoing much more rapid growth than the provinces of the confederation. The wool boom, in particular, which had begun during the latter part of the Rosas era, gained further momentum. Hence, Buenos Aires did not need to offer special inducements to attract new settlers; the rate of economic growth, combined with greater ease of access, gave inducement enough. Buenos Aires obtained the country's first railroad, stretching some ten kilometers west from the city into the pampa in 1857. That first stretch of track was partly financed by the provincial government itself, but such incipient state socialism was not typical of the period. For the most part, Buenos Aires was content to embrace a fairly untrammeled form of laissez-faire capitalism, which agreed with liberal economic dogma and was well suited to the expansionary tendencies of the period.

The job of bringing Buenos Aires back into union with the rest of the country was finally accomplished in 1859–61, though it took two brief civil wars, each pitting the government of Buenos Aires against the confederation. The first was won by the confederation, the second (in 1861) by Buenos Aires—which thereupon reentered the fold, led by its governor, Bartolomé Mitre. A porteño by birth who had spent much of his life as one of the Unitario exiles from the regime of Rosas, Mitre promoted himself from governor to provisional president of the nation (at the expense of Urquiza's immediate successor rather than of Urquiza personally) and then stayed on for a regular six-year term (1862–

68). As a condition for joining the union, Buenos Aires did demand certain changes in the Constitution of 1853, but they were generally minor. The constitution retained its essentially federalist character, which the erstwhile Unitarios were now prepared to accept, particularly as their man, Mitre, was going to be president. The capital was, of course, moved back to Buenos Aires, and Mitre set out to bring the benefits of progress, as understood by the Buenos Aires liberal elite, to the previously benighted interior.

As first ruler of a truly unified Argentina, Mitre maintained control by at least some of the same methods used by Rosas, though placed now at the service of a full-fledged constitutional government. There were subsidies from the national treasury to the more amenable provincial caudillos, various kinds of meddling and intrigue—now under sanction of the federal constitution's "intervention" clause—to remove those not cooperating, and the use of superior military force to crush overt armed resistance. A high point of uprisings in the interior provinces came during the War of the Triple Alliance of 1865–70, which Mitre entered on the Brazilian side in opposition to Francisco Solano López of Paraguay (see chapter 11). That alignment was far from popular in Argentina to begin with, and it became less so as the war dragged on with heavy losses and often arbitrary impressment of recruits, some of whom were marched off to Paraguay in chains lest they desert. But Mitre skillfully used the was as a pretext to crack down on internal troublemakers and in the midst of it passed on the presidency to the greatest of all Argentina's nineteenth-century liberals, Domingo F. Sarmiento.

Argentina: On the Eve of the Golden Age

Mitre had not wanted Sarmiento as successor, although the differences between them were not so much of ideology as of temperament and regional origin. Whereas Mitre was sometimes willing to compromise, Sarmiento was far too aware of his own absolute rightness in all things to have much patience with those who disagreed with him. He once advised Mitre not to worry overmuch about shedding the blood of rebellious gauchos: it was the best possible fertilizer for Argentine soil. As president himself, Sarmiento thus went about repressing untutored caudillos with a gleeful enthusiasm that Mitre never quite mustered. And though both men were ex-Unitarios, Sarmiento was originally from the western province of San Juan and Mitre a porteño who tended to equate the good of Buenos Aires with that of Argentina as a whole. Sarmiento had also traveled in the United States, most recently as Mitre's minister to Washington during the U.S. Civil War, and he unabashedly took the United States as model for what he would like to see happen in Argentina.

Above all, Sarmiento had been impressed by the U.S. system of free public education, which he considered the key to the rapid success of the North American republic. Schools were essential for the attainment of meaningful political democracy, because, as Sarmiento once observed, "an ignorant people will always elect a Rosas." They would aid economic development, because basic literacy equipped people both to perform more complex tasks and to absorb the commercial advertising that (as he shrewdly noted) was so integral a part of U.S. capitalist society. Not least, public education would serve to inculcate the values of Argentine patriotism among the immigrants (and their descendants) whose contribution to creating a modern, progressive Argentina appeared just as critical to Sarmiento as to Alberdi. As director of schools in the secessionist government of Buenos Aires in the 1850s, Sarmiento had a first chance to promote the cause of education, and as national president from 1868 to 1874, he had his great chance. Like the Colombian liberals of the period, he imported normal school teachers from abroad, but his were from the United States, not Germany—a mission of sixty-five women educationists to be exact. He greatly increased educational spending, and though it took until the eve of World War I even to cut in half the illiteracy rate of roughly two-thirds that existed when he took office, he left Argentina with clearly the best school system in Latin America and an official commitment to education that might fluctuate in intensity but was never abandoned. To make certain that the momentum continued, Sarmiento engineered the election of his education minister, Nicolás Avellaneda, as his successor.

Avellaneda's opponent had been ex-President Mitre, who insisted that victory was stolen from him and organized a rebellion.

Whether fraud truly made the difference in this one case (probably it did not), the phenomenon was prevalent enough throughout the electoral process, and it lay behind much of the continuing political turbulence at both national and provincial levels, of which Mitre's refusal to accept defeat peacefully is just one example. But it is also symptomatic of larger developments that Mitre lost the civil war as well as the election. The effectiveness of armed resistance was steadily diminishing, thanks both to the growing expertise of the national army, duly seasoned now in battle against Paraguay, and to the equally steady improvement of transportation and communications infrastructure that allowed the authorities to deploy forces ever more quickly to the site of trouble. It should merely be emphasized that peaceful protest was at the same time generally respected: speech and press were free, even if elections were not.

Among those vanquished by the nation's armed forces were the Indians of the southern pampa and adjoining Patagonia. With their seminomadic ways, they took up a substantial portion of total Argentine territory whose resources they did not even attempt to exploit intensively, while still denying them to other occupants. This situation could not be allowed to continue, and Avellaneda's minister of war, General Julio A. Roca, brought the ancient battle between creoles and Indians to its foreordained conclusion by waging what Argentines call the "Conquest of the Desert" during 1879–80. Those Indians who survived were reduced to reservations, much as was happening in the same years in the United States, while their former lands were incorporated at last into the effective national economy.

Roca went on to be elected president in the very year his Indian campaign ended. Before he could take office, however, it was necessary to suppress one more rebellion, this one launched by leaders of Buenos Aires province seeking to head off a move to convert the city of Buenos Aires into a federal district vaguely comparable to the U.S. District of Columbia. When the revolt was defeated, federalization of the capital was easily accomplished. The province then built itself a new capital downstream at La Plata. But the separation of the national capital from what had been far and away the most powerful of all the provinces tended to lessen the fears of people in the interior that they would always be unfairly pushed around on behalf of Buenos Aires interests; successful resolution of the "capital question" thus really marked the final step in the nation's political unification. Over the following years, Roca and his successors—one of whom was Roca himself, who returned for a second presidential term in 1898–1904—presided over a steady further consolidation of domestic order, maintained more by peaceful political manipulation than by use of force.

A complementary kind of unification was proceeding apace with the construction of a major national railroad network. Though the first railroad dated from the 1850s, expansion began in earnest during the following decade with a line connecting Rosario on the Paraná with Córdoba in the nation's center and additional track stretching out both south and west from Buenos Aires. By 1876, rail had penetrated to Tucumán in the northwest, and by 1880 Argentina already had a system roughly three thousand kilometers in length, easily Latin America's largest. With its mostly flat terrain, Argentina was a relatively easy country to build railroads in; it further had a dynamic economy, capable of generating freight traffic to make them profitable.

Railroad construction both tied the nation together economically and facilitated its insertion into world markets. The former effect could be seen when the railroad to Tucumán set off a major expansion of sugar production in that province, which with improved transportation (and the help of a protective tariff) now displaced Brazil as supplier to the Buenos Aires market. Yet railroads also facilitated getting primary commodities to the ports for export and carrying imported manufactures back to the interior in return. The growth of foreign trade was in any case spectacular. Wool was now the principal export, and with the introduction of improved stock, the quality improved as well as the quantity. Cattle did not disappear, however, and though sales of dried, salted beef—the output of the traditional saladero— were in decline, improvements in breeding and in transportation and processing were laying the basis for the initiation of fresh meat exports to Europe. Live cattle led the way, but more significant as a sign of things to come was the first transatlantic shipment of refrigerated beef, which occurred in 1876. It went from France to Argentina, and obviously not because Argentina needed the meat; the purpose was to demonstrate feasibility of the technique. When the meat that arrived was served up as a banquet dish, it received mixed reviews; some of the diners felt there was still work to be done on the system. But all acknowledged the tremendous economic potential of the new technology, and that potential was soon realized.

The leading role of animal products in export trade was nothing new, even if the relative importance of different items was changing. Something entirely new was the beginning, again in the 1870s, of Argentina's modern career as an exporter of farm products. Until the start of that decade, the country was importing wheat and flour from Chile and the United States. By 1880, it was a net exporter of wheat, although the major expansion of grain exporting was yet to come. Railroads as a more efficient means of getting farm produce to port were one reason for this development, but the critical obstacle previously holding back crop farming in Argentina had been sheer insufficiency of labor. Farming, after all, is more labor-intensive than ranching, and immigration, as it gradually gained momentum—for a net addition in the 1870s of almost a quarter-million to a population that stood at less than two million at the start of the decade—now made the difference. Thereby Argentina was able to import its farm laboring population ready-made from overseas—something it really had to do, because no self-respecting gaucho was going to earn his living trudging behind a plow.

In reality, free-living gauchos of the old school were being pushed aside not just by the expansion of crop farming but also by sheep, to say nothing of the intrusion of state control (made increasingly effective by railroad and telegraph and other conquests of the modern age) into hitherto peripheral regions. Their plight thus became the theme of one of the classics of Argentine literature, *Martín Fierro* by José Hernández, which portrayed the gauchos as innocent victims of all the self-appointed agents of modernization, including the military who impressed them into service and then—as crowning indignity—put them to work tilling the commanding officer's fields. The book sold roughly forty thousand copies in five years, a phenomenal number for Latin America at the time and a tribute not just to its literary merit but also to the author's ability to articulate widely felt grievances. It was, however, a hymn to a lost cause. The winning cause was that of another Argentine classic, *Facundo*, by Sarmiento himself. First published in exile as an anti-Rosas tract, it equated the gaucho subculture with "barbarism" and looked for "civilization" to be brought to Argentina through a wholesome influx of foreign customs, ideas, and naturally also blood.[1]

A keen disappointment to Sarmiento was the fact that arriving immigrants, except in the area of the earliest agricultural colonies, seldom had the chance to become small independent landowners in the manner of the U.S. pioneers he so admired. They ended up as hired hands or tenants instead, or they drifted into the cities; but then an even smaller percentage of native-born rural workers came to own land. Uneven distribution of landed property continued to be the rule. Nevertheless, Argentina attracted immigrants precisely because it was perceived, on balance, to offer greater opportunities than the countries from which they came. It attracted investment capital, too, above all from Great Britain and for railroad construction. Lines going through the choicest farm and livestock areas tended to be built by foreign companies, whereas in outlying districts where potential profits were less obvious, the Argentine state was often reduced to building railroads itself. Likely as not, however, it would do so with the help of government loans raised in London, so foreign capital again played a role. There was additional foreign investment in commercial and financial services. But the principal factor of production—land—remained predominantly in Argentine hands, and if the economy was increasingly geared to foreign markets, it was therefore because Argentine producers found greater opportunities in selling abroad than at home.

Frank acceptance of an international division of labor seemingly ordained by nature was one facet of a largely unquestioned national commitment to laissez-faire. There were a few exceptions, of which two have been mentioned: the fact that the government itself undertook to build certain railroads that were deemed of national interest but failed to offer sufficient incentives to private enterprise, and the granting of tariff protection to the sugar producers of Tucumán. The sugar producers, of course, included some politically important large landowners, which helps explain their success in influencing policy. No similar protection was afforded as a rule to infant manufacturing industries, and that is just one of the ways in which the development course on which Argentina had embarked was unbalanced. Nevertheless, the approach chosen by the liberal ruling class—of minimally regulated, outward-directed economic growth—was about to be vindicated many times over, in at least the short run. From 1880 to World War I, the economy would grow at an annual rate of around five percent and increasingly set Argentina apart from the rest of Latin America in terms of material progress. The value of per capita exports came to be three and one-half times the Latin American average, and per capita product slightly over half the figure for the United States. This privileged situation was not going to be permanent, but it was good while it lasted.

Chile: Liberalizing the Portalian State

Argentina's economic and political development in the third quarter of the century was already beginning to overshadow Chile as a model of exemplary achievement in Spanish America, but Chile's ruling groups still had reason for self-satisfaction. Brief and unsuccessful civil wars in 1851 and 1859 failed to break the continuity of constitutional government, as presidents took one another's place by electoral means and the rule of law represented just that—a rule and not exception. The output of copper and silver continued to increase, and by 1860 Chile was the world's leading copper exporter. Agricultural production was also increasing. A boom in wheat sales to California and Australia in the 1850s proved short-lived, but rising exports to the British market compensated for that loss. Until the 1890s, Chilean wheat production was still larger than that of Argentina.

Infrastructural development was likewise impressive. Chile was the first country of Latin America to develop an integrated national telegraph network, and railroads (starting in 1849 or several years earlier than in Argentina) along with coastal steamships further tied the nation together for purposes of both trade and political unification. There was even a beginning of industrial activity, though as yet concentrated in food and beverage processing, notably brewing and flour milling.

These developments naturally enhanced the private fortunes of the interlocking network of aristocratic families who owned the large estates, mines, and those commercial enterprises not controlled by foreigners, as well as dominating the nation's political life. The working masses, still overwhelmingly engaged in agriculture, gained less. The long-term tendency was for size of estates to diminish through subdivision, but there was no real change in the pattern of land concentration and owners preferred to use large amounts of poorly paid labor rather than experiment with capital improvements. Since there was ample rural labor available, production could increase without a comparable increase in productivity per worker. And while organized colonization schemes brought some German settlers to the southern provinces, the central agricultural zone was a net exporter of hands to the mining districts, the cities, California, and even Peru, where Chilean laborers were preferred to native Indians for railroad building. By draining off potentially more dissatisfied elements of the peasant population, such migration helped prolong the traditional calm of the countryside. In mining, despite much higher wages than on the land, the harsh conditions and irregularity of employment contributed to the early appearance of labor militancy, with sporadic protests, sometimes violent, against employers or government. However, this did not yet pose a true threat to stability.

The workers of the northern copper and silver mines took part in the two civil wars of the 1850s, but they were scarcely the originators of either conflict. Mainly, this resurgence of political strife reflected fissures within the ruling class itself, which some scholars have tried to associate with conflicts of interest between different economic sectors but which reflected even more clearly the existence of regional rivalries and the strength of new intellectual trends. Precisely because in Chile—as elsewhere in nineteenth-century Latin America—the upper class was not highly differentiated occupationally, it is not easy to distinguish one faction from another on the basis of economic interests, but in both 1851 and 1859 the main centers of rebellion were in the north and the south, where resentment of Santiago was widespread. At the same time, intellectually, the main impetus came from an increasingly assertive liberalism that sought both to limit the power of the Chilean executive and to take up the business of social and religious reform left unfinished by the liberals of the 1820s whom Portales had vanquished.

The radical wing of Chilean liberalism was represented by the Society of Equality, founded in 1850. Its most notorious figure was the same Francisco Bilbao who had shocked the Chilean establishment with his "blasphemous" writings in 1844. The Society of Equality in 1850, with an appeal combining elements of doctrinaire liberalism and utopian socialism, organized antigovernment demonstrations and attracted intellectuals and artisans in sufficient numbers for the authorities to see fit to dissolve it by the end of the year. President Manuel Bulnes then went on to arrange the election of his chosen successor, Manuel Montt, in 1851 and to suppress the rebellion that broke out in protest against the election result. Nevertheless, change of various kinds was in the air. Entailed estates, long a focus of controversy in Chile, were prohibited for good in 1852. And over the following years the Chilean Congress made increasing use of its constitutional prerogative to approve (or disapprove) the national budget as a lever to compel the president to tailor policies and cabinet appointments to the wishes of the congressional majority. Chile was on the way to evolving a system of parliamentary rule that respected the letter of the 1833 constitution but was quite foreign to its original spirit.

The weakening of executive authority was also caused in part by a revival of agitation over religious issues. Liberals, especially those who shared the radically anticlerical views of Francisco Bilbao—though the latter had fled the country during the political agitation of 1851—were eager to introduce full religious toleration, abolish the fuero, and establish both civil marriage and secular control of cemeteries. At the same time, within the clergy and among proclerical laymen, there was an observable stiffening of resistance to liberal innovations as well as to the traditional exercise of state control (under the patronato) over questions of external church administration. Inspiration for this Catholic militancy came ultimately from Rome, where Pope Pius IX was launching a general counterattack on liberal and secular values. The government of President Montt, which favored only gradual change in religious matters, was caught between two fires, with proclerical extremists joining hands with anticlerical liberals when tactical expediency directed.

The outcome, as far as the church was concerned, was some further erosion of its status. Religious toleration, which for Protestant foreigners had long existed de facto, was formally enacted in 1865, and the fuero was ended in 1875. Most other anticlerical demands would take longer to enact, but meanwhile religious controversy had a major formative influence on the political party system, as proclerical forces in 1857 split the ruling Conservative party and took the greater part of it into opposition to Montt. (The latter's supporters reconstituted themselves as National party.) Antigovernment Conservatives were quite prepared to cooperate with Liberals in weakening the state, as a means of lessening pressure on the church and because in this matter they faithfully interpreted the instincts of the Chilean upper class. As pointed out years ago by the Chilean publicist Alberto Edwards Vives in his insightful *La fronda aristocrática en Chile*,[2] the natural inclination of both Liberal and Conservative aristocrats was to favor a weak national executive, since they would then have more room to cut a fancy figure on the political stage themselves, through parliamentary service or otherwise. The alarm generated by the turmoil of the 1820s had for a time counterbalanced this tendency, causing the Chilean aristocracy as a whole to accept the Portalian settlement. By the third quarter of the century, however, its members were less fearful of anarchy and more prepared to do what came naturally. Interestingly, when in 1874 property (though not literacy) qualifications for voting were abolished, the Conservatives were prime movers, confident that an enlarged electorate could be more easily manipulated by the landed gentry than controlled by the national executive. The Portalian state continued, insofar as it meant a stable legal and constitutional order. The unquestioned primacy of presidential power was at an end.

Those set on undermining presidential supremacy were not content with building up the powers of Congress as a counterpoise but also campaigned to limit the president himself to a single term. Adopted in 1871, this reform broke the tradition of always giving the chief executive a second five-year term, which had been in effect from the 1830s, when Portales's ally Joaquín

Prieto was first to be reelected, to the 1861–71 period of the moderate José Joaquín Pérez. The same tendency to impose constitutional limits on presidential reelection had been seen even earlier in other countries of Spanish America, where the need for such measures was perhaps more obvious than in Chile but their effectiveness was still open to question. In any case, by the time President José María Balmaceda (1886–91) tried to reverse the erosion of executive leadership in hopes of using the presidency to promote (among other things) a more active economic development policy, it was already too late. Balmaceda was overthrown by the supporters of Congress, which as a result gained even greater influence.

Ultimately more important than the evolution of executive-legislative relations were developments in the nitrate fields of the Atacama Desert. Chilean laborers, capital, and entrepreneurs began moving into this area at a time when the greatest part of it belonged still to Bolivia and Peru. In collaboration with British investors, and in response to world demand for nitrates as both fertilizer and a material for explosives, Chileans built up a major new export industry. By so doing, they were also laying the basis for the War of the Pacific of 1879 to 1883, in which Chile would again fight against and defeat its two neighbors to the north and would annex the entire nitrate-producing region.

Further Variation on the Liberal Pattern: Venezuela, Peru

In Venezuela, where the regime of José Antonio Páez had borne at least a distant structural resemblance to the Chilean system, the years following midcentury witnessed an ever greater divergence from the Chilean model that culminated in final emergence of a positivist-oriented dictatorship. As noted in chapter 5, a fissure between agricultural and commercial interests among the original supporters of the so-called Conservative Oligarchy— the party of Páez—helped lead to its collapse in 1848. In traditional Venezuelan historiography, the next ten years came to be known as the "Liberal Oligarchy," and the term is apt enough in that a military clique allied with elements of Venezuela's Liberal party kept control of government. Generals José Tadeo and José

Gregorio Monagas, who happened to be brothers, took turns in the presidency, and though their initial alliance with the Liberals had been strictly tactical, they did carry out such typically liberal measures as expelling the Jesuits and ending the last vestiges of slavery. The Monagas regime likewise put through one measure that was diametrically opposed to doctrinaire liberal economic thinking but had been a demand of the Liberal party in its effort to woo debt-burdened agriculturalists: repeal of the "Law of the 10th of April" of 1834, which had removed limitations on the rate of interest.

For the rest, the Liberal Oligarchy was characterized by some loss of efficiency and honesty of administration as compared to its Conservative predecessor, and by a frequently unsettled state of public order. Quite apart from Conservative attempts to stage a comeback, there were intra-Liberal and personalistic feuds. More serious still was a climate of social unrest in much of the country, made evident through an incease in banditry, among other phenomena. At the root of such unrest lay class and racial antagonisms that flared up during the war of independence itself and had since remained never very far from the surface. The continuing difficulties of the coffee industry, as well as the disruption of the Páez system and the disorderly style of the Monagas regime, were aggravating circumstances.

Matters came to a head in 1858, though only after that regime had been finally deposed by an alliance of Conservatives and disgruntled Liberals. It proved easier to unite against the common enemy than to work in harmony afterward, with the result that Liberals launched another revolution to claim power entirely for themselves. The struggle became known as the Federal War (1858–63), but the term is a bit misleading, as the founder and still preeminent civilian leader of the Liberal party, Antonio Leocadio Guzmán, admitted later on. He cynically observed that the Liberals had needed a "banner" for their cause, and though a national convention had just enacted a federalist constitution for Venezuela, it had neglected to put that label on the document; hence, the Liberals decided to proclaim federalism as their objective, ignoring the fact that for most purposes it had already been achieved. If the political platform of the Liberal revolutionists was thus somewhat bogus, their struggle did eventually subsume much of the country's existing social unrest, as Liberals curried popular support by posing as champions of the common people against haughty aristocratic Conservatives. There was much exaggeration in this, too, but the tactic was widely successful. Nor did Liberal spokesmen bother to counteract (if they did not actually propagate) rumors that freedmen would be returned to slavery if the Conservatives won.

The Federal War dragged on for five years, with few pitched battles but much nasty guerrilla fighting. When the Liberals finally won, they gave Venezuela still another constitution, in 1864, that was resolutely federalist and democratic, assuring the states of a large measure of internal autonomy and individual citizens of equal rights of every kind, including universal male suffrage (which had technically been first introduced in 1857 as a Monagas ploy). In many respects the constitution bore a close resemblance to the ultraliberal Colombian constitution issued a year earlier; not for nothing had Antonio L. Guzmán spent time in Colombia when the Federal War was going badly for his side and even served as delegate to the Colombian constitutional convention. As in Colombia, moreover, all-out federalism did not prove conducive to public tranquillity. There were state-level and national uprisings, and even an abortive comeback by the Monagas faction.

In 1870, Antonio Guzmán Blanco, son of Antonio L. Guzmán, seized power in a Liberal uprising to inaugurate a new era. He had been a general in the Federal War and afterward was sent to Europe to negotiate a settlement with Venezuela's foreign creditors—something he accomplished at great profit to himself, through both legal and illegal commissions. He was a man of talent without doubt, not overly burdened with scruples but sincerely committed to modernization of all kinds. Guzmán Blanco is remembered for the beautification of Caracas with new public buildings, plazas, and statues (a disproportionate number of these bearing his own name); for promoting the visits of European opera companies; and for trying to indoctrinate his countrymen in the benefits of fine wines and personal bathing. He also promoted the development of transportation infrastructure, including railroads, of which a number of short stretches were built, or at least commenced, to link Caracas and other cities with the coast. These were frankly intended to tighten the link between Venezuela and the world economy, and in similar vein Guzmán Blanco encouraged all forms of foreign trade and investment. Yet he also saw the need for investment in human resources and issued a decree for free, compulsory primary education soon after seizing power. Though he could never make this fully effective, his zeal for education marks him as the Venezuelan counterpart of Argentina's Sarmiento. And when he left office for the last time in 1887, Venezuela had acquired virtually the same number of schools that it would have in 1930.

Guzmán Blanco's recipe for bringing Venezuela into the modern world included a further weakening of the Roman Catholic church, which was forbidden to inherit real estate although it lost only some, not all, of the property it already had. The fuero was finally ended, civil marriage established, and convents closed, in all of which he showed himself an adherent of doctrinaire liberal anticlericalism just when it was beginning to lose much of its appeal elsewhere in Latin America. His economic policies were no less classically liberal. His political style, on the other hand, was distinctly personalistic and autocratic. Guzmán Blanco liked to be referred to as "The Illustrious American," and those who did not flatter him or do his bidding could expect difficulties of various kinds. He never—almost never—shot people, but he did gag and exile, and he did not feel bound to observe mere legal technicalities. He skillfully manipulated regional caudillos, giving them a free hand locally and paying them subventions from the federal treasury as long as they kept order in their own bailiwicks and did not challenge his control at national level. For subsidizing caudillos, as well as for the statues of himself and other forms of infrastructure, Guzmán Blanco took advantage of an upturn in revenue collections that reflected both the relative stability he had given Venezuela and his generally more efficient administration of national affairs. In that last regard, he gave special attention to the development of the central bureaucracy in Caracas on which he relied to keep things going even when every few years he left the presidency for an extended European tour. Unfortunately for him, after going off to Europe in 1887, he received a message from Caracas suggesting that he just stay there. Sensing that his erstwhile friends and supporters had decided they could get along without him, he chose to follow the advice. All through the era of Guzmán Blanco, Venezuela continued to function ostensibly as a democratic and federal republic. His government might better be described as in practice a mild dictatorship, but if so it was an enlightened dictatorship. Guzmán Blanco was one of the larger number of late-nineteenth-century strongmen of Latin America who, coming originally from Liberal ranks, were prepared to sacrifice liberty where necessary to better serve the positivist goal of order and progress. Mexico's Porfirio Díaz is easily the best-known example of the school; Guzmán Blanco, for what it may be worth, is more highly regarded in his country today.

In Peru, meanwhile, the impetus for a modest program of liberal reform and public improvements came from a fortuitous export boom that began slightly before midcentury. It was fortuitous from the Peruvian standpoint in that it did not develop out of any of the traditional sectors of the economy—uniformly depressed since the time of independence—but rather was based on exploitation of a heretofore neglected resource that cost nothing to produce and had a seemingly inexhaustible overseas market. The bonanza was *guano*, or bird droppings, a form of high-quality fertilizer that sea birds had been depositing for centuries without charge along the Peruvian coast; and since it almost never rained in the arid coastal region, the guano had been accumulating in ever higher mounds, just waiting to be shoveled onto ships for Europe. The shoveling was not a very pleasant job, but it required no advanced technology—mainly picks, shovels, and wheelbarrows—and not really many shovelers. The profits were enormous.

The Peruvian state, claiming ownership of the promontories and offshore islands that the birds liked to frequent, contracted with both foreign and native businessmen to load and ship the guano. The treasury thus gathered in the largest share of the proceeds, in the form of commissions, taxes, and fees of different kinds. Total national government income increased five times over in twenty-five years, thanks mainly to guano. On the whole, however, the income was not wisely spent. Some of it went to pay off domestic creditors, who all too often fraudulently inflated their claims just as soon as they glimpsed a possibility of actual repayment. More went for building railroads up into the Andean hinterland, where construction costs were enormous and, because of the impoverished state of the highland economy, the chances of profitable operation minimal. To a great extent, actually, what happened was that Peru raised loans for railroad construction in Europe, assuming that future guano revenues would easily provide for repayment, with the result that by 1875 Peru was the largest single Latin American borrower in the London market. Alas, the guano boom ended much sooner than the debts.

The most positive side effects of the guano boom were no doubt two reforms of the mid-1850s. One was the final elimination of slavery in 1854, made acceptable to the slaveowners by payment of compensation; finding money for the purpose was no longer a problem. The other was final abolition (also in 1854) of the Indian tribute, which was simply no longer necessary as a source of revenue. These measures in turn had still other indirect effects, both positive and negative. Some of the former slaveowners put at least part of their indemnity payments to productive use in the modernization of sugar and other plantations of the irrigated coastal valleys. For replacement of slave labor, however, the planters imported great numbers of Chinese coolies—in the end something like eighty thousand—whose voyage across the Pacific replicated the horrors of the African slave trade and who then labored under semislavery conditions after arrival. (Chinese were used in shoveling guano also.) As for the tribute, Indians were happy to be rid of it, but creole and mestizo landowners were less happy, since the tribute had served not only as a source of government revenue but also as a means of inducing the Indians to do wage labor, to earn money with which to pay the tribute. In the absence of this indirect compulsion, highland landowners began increasing their pressure on Indian lands, so as to gain leverage over the Indians of a different sort. The communal village properties, which Bolívar had ordered divided into small, and more vulnerable, individual holdings in 1824, were mostly still undivided at midcentury, among other reasons because non-Indians had felt no strong incentive to usurp them. Paradoxically, abolition of the tribute provided more of an incentive to implement the division, although the process was still a gradual one.

In political organization, Peru in the third quarter of the nineteenth century debated the merits of decentralization but never embraced a full-fledged federalist system. The religious question generated heated debate among small numbers of liberal and conservative intellectuals but never became a central focus of political struggle, and reforms carried out at the church's expense were distinctly limited; they did not go much beyond the elimination of compulsory tithe collections and of the fuero. In short, Peru maintained a record of moderation in political and religious matters that is well exemplified by the difficulty of assigning an ideological label to the outstanding national leader of the period, General Ramón Castilla. A mestizo of middle-class social background, Castilla proved an able political as well as military leader, whose two presidencies (1845–51 and 1855–62) were noted for the atmosphere of stability attained and for constructive accomplishments in many different fields, among them the completion in 1851 of a railroad linking Lima with its port, Callao. It was Castilla who finally ended slavery and the tribute, though not while actually exercising the presidency. Those two measures, along with his general commitment to national modernization, no doubt mark him as more liberal than otherwise. However, he was above all a pragmatist, and, after first seeming to go along with it, he turned back a liberal movement to weaken the presidency in favor of the legislative branch, in what would have been a Peruvian parallel to the latest political trend in Chile.

That former foreign enemy came gallantly to Peru's support when a brief conflict broke out between Peru and Spain in 1864, triggered by allegations of mistreatment of Spanish settlers in Peru. A Spanish fleet seized the guano-rich Chincha Islands, thereby provoking a display of solidarity with Peru by seven Spanish American nations that met in an American Congress at Lima later the same year. Though the treaties of formal alliance adopted by the congress remained a dead letter, exactly as happened with those resulting from the Panama Congress of 1826, it did give diplomatic support to Peru against Spain, and when the quarrel degenerated into declared warfare, Ecuador, Bolivia, and Chile joined on the Peruvian side. For this act of neighborliness, Chile suffered a Spanish bombardment of the port of Valparaíso. Nevertheless, the Spanish naval force did withdraw, and Peru regained the guano islands.

In the immediate aftermath of the war with Spain, Peruvian national politics presented a picture of considerable confusion, but the various crises and disturbances made little difference in the life of the population as a whole. In 1871, for really the first time, an organized political party with a coherent program made its appearance. This was the Civilista party, whose very name proclaimed that the time had come to dispense with the military rulers who had largely dominated the scene since independence and whose record, with the principal exception of Castilla, was thoroughly undistinguished. The party's leader was Manuel Pardo, an enlightened member of the coastal aristocracy who had gained practical experience serving under some of those military presidents himself. Pardo and his associates called for the ending of military and also clerical interference in politics, the adoption of more responsible government fiscal policies, and a major emphasis on education, including efforts to assimilate the highland Indians by teaching them Spanish. Alas, Pardo succeeded in being elected president in 1872 only to reap the consequences of several decades of economic mismanagement. The gradual exhaustion of guano deposits aggravated the financial difficulties of the national government, and Pardo's attempts to save money by cutting the budget of the armed forces aggravated military unrest. His positive accomplishments, as a result, were disappointingly slight.

Precisely to offset the inexorable decline of guano income, Peruvians were showing ever more interest in the export potential of nitrates found in the southern coastal province of Tarapacá. With a view to maximizing the government's benefits from this source, Pardo in 1875 nationalized a major part of the nitrate industry, though at the cost of angering private parties already engaged in their exploitation. The fact that some of these parties were Chilean, or other foreigners who looked to Chile for support, naturally strained Peru's relations with Chile, which was at the same time embroiled in a controversy with Bolivia involving exploitation of nitrates in the stretch of desert coast under Bolivian ownership that separated Peru from Chile. Both within and without the armed forces, tension with Chile not surprisingly led to bitter criticism of Pardo's economizing at the expense of the military. At the end of his term, Pardo judged that times were simply not propitious for another civilian head of state and engineered the choice of a former military president with a confusingly similar last name, Mariano Ignacio Prado. It was the luckless Prado who had to cope with the final crisis with Chile. When war broke out between Chile and Bolivia in 1879, Peru was brought in by virtue of a secret alliance with the Bolivians—and thus also shared in the decisive defeat that Chilean arms once again administered.

The War of the Pacific caused the loss of Peruvian nitrate territories to Chile, not to mention still other human and material losses; and defeat further ushered in a new round of political instability. The war revealed how little true integration had been achieved among the component parts—ethnic, social, geographic—of the Peruvian nation and how superficial the guano-based development of the last few years had been. To be sure, the works of infrastructure and the main legal reforms adopted would remain in place, to be added to at some future date, but the guano-era debts also remained, to burden later generations. Peru's Bolivian ally, which in the war lost not just part but all of its Pacific coast, was at least spared that problem, as its rulers had never enjoyed anything quite like the Peruvian bonanza and therefore had not been caught up in the same degree of speculative folly.

Neither had most of the other Spanish American countries experienced anything quite like Peru's fleeting mid-nineteenth-century "dance of the millions," although Argentina was about to enter on a rather more solid export boom. What all, or almost all, of the countries did share was some combination of increased exposure to the world economy and liberal tinkering with domestic institutions. These parallel tendencies varied in depth and intensity, but they were seldom absent from the picture. They were present in Cuba and Central America, which will be dealt with separately in chapter 12. And they could be seen in Brazil, in sometimes uneasy coexistence with those two distinctive features of the Brazilian scene, slavery and the monarchy.

11

The Flowering and Decline of the Brazilian Empire (1850–1885)

The year 1850, midpoint of the nineteenth century, was an important one in Brazilian history for a number of reasons. In that year, the Empire of Brazil enacted a commercial code that provided for the formation of limited liability companies and generally laid down the rules for economic enterprise in the realm of Dom Pedro II. Agriculture, Brazil's biggest business—a risky one under almost any circumstances—became a little less uncertain and more attractive to entrepreneurs and investors with the Land Law of 1850; at least the law spelled out the legal requirements for establishing possession of landed property. That same year, a nagging question about agricultural labor was answered with the passage of the Queiroz Law which finally put teeth in the abolition of the slave trade. Slavery was doomed in Brazil, and sooner or later the country's planters would have to find replacements, machines or free workers, for the human chattel that no longer could be imported from Africa. Another force for change was the 1850 epidemic of yellow fever, the first in two centuries to hit Santos and Rio, which sent members of the imperial family and other coastal residents scurrying for mountain refuges above the ceiling of the low-flying *aedes aegypti* mosquito—although at the time they did not know that was what they were fleeing from.

The plague boded well for the growth of the salubrious city of São Paulo on the rim of Brazil's central plateau. A modest provincial capital in 1850, São Paulo was the site of one of Brazil's two law schools (the other was in Pernambuco) which for more than two decades had been forging a native class of professionals, bureaucrats, and statesmen: the "Mandarins of Imperial Brazil."[1] The law school graduates tended to be more concerned with matters of geopolitics and national grandeur than were their planter or merchant fathers. Although some law students and graduates had supported the Praieira revolt in Pernambuco, that was over in 1849, and the erstwhile rebels were pardoned in 1850. With the defeat of the Praieiros, nationalism triumphed over regionalism, and the creed of federalism virtually disappeared from the Brazilian political scene for the next two decades. The imperial army that had put down the regional revolts of 1824–49 was, in 1850, available for deployment beyond Brazil's borders. In 1850, imperial Brazil began providing material aid to the government in Montevideo that was resisting the forces allied with Argentine dictator Juan Manuel de Rosas.

Economic Development and Platine Intervention: 1850–1868

The Alves Branco tariff of 1844 (as noted in chapter 7) greatly increased the duties on British manufactured goods imported into Brazil. The managing partner of a British trading firm in Rio, Irineu Evangelista de Sousa, perceived an opportunity and persuaded his associates in England to invest in an iron foundry in Niterói, across the bay from the imperial capital. The foundry was purchased in 1846 and its capacity expanded under the new ownership, with equipment imported duty-free, thanks to a measure enacted that year that exempted industrial machinery from import tariffs. In 1849, after the emperor had dismissed Alves Branco and the Liberals and had replaced them with a Conservative cabinet, Irineu was elected to parliament as a Conservative, and his foundry received an imperial government contract to supply iron pipe for the modernization of the capital city's waterworks. By 1850, Irineu was probably the richest man in Brazil—certainly in terms of liquid assets. He had a huge accumulation of cash that he was eager to reinvest.

Irineu Evangelista de Sousa was a native of Rio Grande do Sul, the son of a poor herdsman who was killed in a dispute over some cattle. At the age of ten, Irineu traveled to Rio, where, through his widowed mother's family connections, he landed a job in a Portuguese immigrant's small tea and candle shop; he moved from there to the dry-goods store of another Portuguese, as a clerk-apprentice; then, when that Portuguese retailer declared bankruptcy, one of his creditors, the importer Carruthers and Company, hired Irineu as a clerk. Irineu soon rose to partner in the firm, and when its founder retired to England in the 1830s, the ex-clerk from Rio Grande do Sul was left in charge of its operations. The firm prospered enormously under the management of Irineu, who established close personal relationships with the leaders of Brazil's Conservative party. When the Conservatives decided to challenge Rosas in the Río de la Plata, Irineu was encouraged to make loans and sell war materiel and other supplies to Brazil's allies in Uruguay. After the liberation of Uruguay in 1851, Irineu received various commercial, agricultural, and industrial concessions from the pro-Brazilian Colorado government in Montevideo, and he was named collector of Uruguayan customs, so that he could collect for himself the money the republic owed him.

In Brazil, Irineu established a bank in the imperial capital in 1851. That same year, the Conservative government awarded him exclusive mining rights in the southern provinces of the empire and a contract to build and operate a gas-lighting system in Rio de Janeiro. In 1852, the imperial government gave Irineu a thirty-year monopoly of steam navigation on the Amazon River with an annual subsidy of more than eighty thousand dollars for the first fifteen years. He also received exclusive rights to operate a steamboat service on Guanabara Bay from Rio to the plain of Mauá, and to build a railroad across the plain to the foot of the Orgãos mountains. This project was of particular interest to the emperor, who had a summer residence and refuge from yellow fever in the mountains at Petrópolis. The proposed railway would connect with an existing stagecoach road from Petrópolis and greatly reduce Dom Pedro's travel time between palaces. Irineu's railroad, fifteen kilometers long, was Brazil's first. Upon its completion in 1854, Irineu received the title of Baron of Mauá. He was forty years old.

The Baron of Mauá's good friend, Honório Hermeto, now the Marquis of Paraná, headed the Brazilian government from 1853 to 1856. This was the beginning of a ten-year period of political "conciliation," of coalition cabinets including Liberals headed by a Conservative prime minister. Under the power-sharing arrangement, Mauá did not get as favorable treatment as when the Conservatives were in complete control. His bank was not given authority to issue bank notes, and in 1853 it was practically forced into a merger with the Banco Comercial, which had the authority but had never used it. The new bank was authorized a total of one hundred fifty thousand shares: eighty thousand shares went to shareholders of the former Mauá and Comercial banks, while seventy thousand were reserved for the Brazilian government, which kept forty thousand and resold the remainder to the public. The operations of this second Bank of Brazil were not confined to the Rio area; unlike its predecessor, it established branches in all provinces, and its notes circulated as legal tender throughout the country. Responsive to government policy, the bank, for as long as the empire lasted, tried to maintain the exchange value of the Brazilian milréis at twenty-seven British pence (fifty-four cents U.S.), the rate prescribed by Brazilian law. At times, however, when the bank was forced to suspend convertibility, its notes traded unofficially at a discount.

Fixed exchange rates were not to the liking of the Baron of Mauá, whose avowed aversion to government regulation was as great as his demonstrated appetite for special privilege. Mauá soon liquidated his holdings in the official bank and established another private bank, the Banco Mauá, which served the credit needs of his myriad enterprises—in manufacturing, food processing, transportation, construction, and land speculation and colonization—in Brazil, Argentina, and Uruguay. In Uruguay, where Mauá was known as "the Brazilian peril," things got sticky in 1854 when the opposition Blanco party rose in arms against the Colorado government that had granted the baron so many concessions. But the Marquis of Paraná (Honório Hermeto) obliged his friend by dispatching four thousand Brazilian troops to Uruguay to put down the rebellion and save Mauá's investments. Mauá's position in Uruguay remained precarious, a fact that the baron was acutely aware of. He began cultivating the goodwill of important members of the Uruguayan opposition, the Blancos—who were, after all, the republic's more popular and somewhat more conservative party. He pursued rapprochement in Uruguay with special vigor after the death of Paraná in 1856, when the political center of the Brazilian conciliation began to shift, the Liberal party gaining strength with the adherence of some important defectors from the Conservatives. Mauá could no longer count on protection from Rio for his enterprises in Uruguay. The baron, however, was prepared when the Blancos took power in Uruguay in 1860; he offered his support to the new government, and it was accepted. For the time being, his holdings in the republic were safe. The Blanco position, however, was far from secure; the unification of Argentina under a longtime Colorado ally, Bartolomé Mitre, in 1861 and, the next year, the inauguration of a Liberal government in Brazil constituted serious threats to the Uruguayan regime.

The new Brazilian prime minister was Zacarias de Góis e Vasconcelos of Bahia, one of a group of younger members of parliament who called themselves progressives and had switched from the Conservative to the Liberal party. Zacarias and his fellow progressives, like José Tomás Nabuco de Araújo of Pernambuco, were disillusioned by the corruption and cynicism of the leadership of the Conservative party, by its manipulation of the electoral system and its failure to press for essential reforms like the abolition of slavery. Sincere converts to liberalism, they were dedicated to the propagation of their new faith within Brazil and beyond its borders. Disinclined to compromise, they had difficulty governing in Rio. Zacarias lasted less than a week as prime minister; he was replaced by the venerable Pedro de Araújo Lima, now Marquis of Olinda, who, while he remained nominally a Conservative, was a patron of the progressives. The Liberals, sparked by the progressives, would have the upper hand in the imperial government until 1868.

The Liberal ascendancy in Brazil coincided with the succession of Francisco Solano López to the dictatorship of Paraguay in

1862 on the death of his father. The change was more of person-
alities than of policies, for the son was firmly committed to the
father's program of state-directed modernization of the country's
economy and the building up of its armed forces, to deter aggression by Paraguay's giant neighbors, Brazil and Argentina, who
had long-standing claims to Paraguayan territory. But the
younger López had a flamboyant style that masked his essentially cautious nature and misled his allies, who placed too much
faith in him. Paraguay's natural ally was Uruguay, whose Blanco
government—now backed by the monopoly capitalist Mauá—
was threatened by the Liberal government of Brazil. López said
that he would come to the rescue of Uruguay with his army if the
Brazilians invaded that republic, and the Blancos believed him.

The stage was set for a Brazilian invasion of Uruguay when the
Colorados rebelled against the Blancos in 1863. The Uruguayan
Colorados had close ties with Brazilian Liberals in the province
of Rio Grande do Sul; the Liberal party there was made up
mostly of ex-Farroupilhas or descendants of those secessionists of
1835–45 who had been supported in their struggle against the
empire by the Colorados of the neighboring republic. Family
and business alliances developed along with the political and
military relationship between Brazilian Liberals and Uruguayan
Colorados in this border area. When the Colorados rose in arms
in Uruguay, their forces included quite a few of their relatives,
employees, and liberal coreligionists from across the border in
Brazil. The Blanco government responded to this unofficial invasion from Brazil by confiscating the Uruguayan property of
Brazilians whom they identified as supporters of the rebels.
Blanco raiders even crossed into Brazil and looted ranch houses,
driving off cattle and horses.

Early in 1864, Zacarias became prime minister of Brazil for the
second time; he was committed to taking a tough stand against
the Uruguayan Blancos. Neither Zacarias nor the emperor feared
another war in Uruguay. Dom Pedro II welcomed the prospect
of war; it would give an "electric shock" to Brazilian nationalism,
he believed. And it would distract attention from the slavery
question, which increasingly was being raised in Brazil in the
months following Lincoln's Emancipation Proclamation and the
abolition of slavery in the Dutch colonies in America. For as long

as the war lasted, a Brazilian decision on what to do about slavery could be postponed. And if Paraguay entered the war on the side of Uruguay, the struggle would be prolonged, and the empire would have a better claim on the sympathy of liberals at home and abroad, for Brazil would be fighting a dictatorial regime that denied freedom of expression and killed or exiled its opponents. The bombastic and murderous Francisco Solano López seemed the ideal foil for the scholarly constitutional monarch—although, in fact, López's intellectual gifts were at least equal to those of Dom Pedro and his scholarship (in linguistics) more impressive than the emperor's dilettantism.

Events in 1864 marched relentlessly toward war. To no avail Mauá pleaded with the emperor for peace. The Blanco government of Uruguay was handed an ultimatum: restore within thirty days the property its partisans had taken from Brazilians or face the consequences. Assured of support from Paraguay, Uruguay rejected the ultimatum. The Brazilian army crossed the Uruguayan border in September, and the Blancos fought back fiercely. The Paraguayans did not march to their aid until it was too late. López made his first belligerent move in November, when his forces seized a munitions-laden Brazilian steamboat on the Paraguay River near Asunción; then they invaded the Brazilian province of Mato Grosso, the destination of the steamboat, where imperial troops were concentrating, presumably for an invasion of Paraguay. Only after the successful conclusion of this preemptive operation early in 1865 did Paraguayan troops strike out across Argentina for Uruguay to relieve the Blancos. When they got there, the Blancos had already surrendered to the Brazilians and the Colorados. And by crossing Argentine territory without permission, the Paraguayans gave the government in Buenos Aires a pretext for declaring war on them. In May 1865, a formal alliance was signed in Montevideo by Brazil, Argentina, and the new Colorado government of Uruguay—the Triple Alliance against Paraguay.

Paraguay inevitably lost its war with the Triple Alliance. It was Latin America's biggest war, in which hundreds of thousands of combatants, including the great majority of the males in Paraguay's population of about half a million, were engaged over a five-year period. Paraguay suffered the most casualties—the number is disputed by historians and demographers—while among the allies Brazil sustained the greatest losses, thirty thousand to fifty thousand combat-related deaths. The slaughter continued despite repeated attempts by López to negotiate an armistice; he was willing to meet all allied demands except those for the liquidation of his government and the allied occupation of his country.

Allied policy was set by Brazil, which bore most of the material and human costs of the common war effort. The Brazilian emperor and his government were determined to mete out exemplary punishment to the Paraguayans for daring to violate the borders of the empire, and they meant to establish Brazil as a nation to be respected among the powers of the world. Before the war began, Brazil had suffered the humiliation of a British blockade of Rio de Janeiro in 1862–63. That confrontation arose over British complaints about Brazilian mistreatment of *emancipados*—Africans liberated from captured slave ships and set free in Brazil—and about some alleged Brazilian transgressions against British persons and property. The anglophile Baron of Mauá helped arrange the lifting of the blockade in January 1863, but the Brazilian government refused to bow to British demands and proceeded to expel Queen Victoria's minister from Rio and break diplomatic relations with London. Relations were reestablished on Brazil's terms during the Paraguayan War in September 1865, when a British envoy journeyed to the battlefield at Uruguaiana, scene of a famous Brazilian victory, and presented his credentials to Dom Pedro.

Mauá had opposed the war, but once it was underway he offered his services to the allies. His bank lent money to the imperial government and marketed Brazilian bonds abroad, and his factories turned out armaments and uniforms for the Brazilian armed forces. Mauá was not a favorite of Brazil's Liberal government, which awarded its contracts to others whenever possible. However, there often was no alternative provider of essential goods and services, especially in southernmost Brazil and Uruguay, in the war zone. And the supreme allied commander in the war was the Conservative Marquis of Caxias, who had no objection to doing business with Mauá.

Annual Brazilian government expenditures tripled during the war years. Long-term effects of the spending included the expansion of Brazil's manufacturing capacity, especially in textiles. Some of the money was appropriated to buy or subsidize infrastructural improvements, such as telegraph lines from Rio to the war zone and military roads in the southern provinces. But the most important project completed during those years, the Santos-Jundiaí railroad, was unrelated to the war effort. The concession had been awarded in 1856 to a British company in which Mauá had an interest; the Brazilian government guaranteed the company an annual return on capital of seven percent for at least thirty years. Completed in 1867, the one-hundred-thirty-nine-kilometer line linked the port of Santos to the city of São Paulo and the agricultural town of Jundiaí. The railroad was immediately profitable and opened up São Paulo's fertile western plateau to coffee cultivation. The construction of a railroad from Rio through the old coffee country, the Paraíba Valley, to São Paulo, was pushed during the war years but would not be completed until ten years after the first train rolled into São Paulo from the port of Santos. The net effect of wartime development favored São Paulo and Santos, and the areas to their west and south, over the rest of Brazil.

In 1868, Brazilian forces overran the last major fortifications before the Paraguayan capital of Asunción. The end of the war was in sight, and the victorious general, the Marquis of Caxias, could look forward to a dukedom and the return of his Conservative party to power in Rio. Caxias and the emperor did not intend for the imperial government to remain in the hands of the Liberal Zacarias in the postwar era. But Zacarias and his reformist Progressive League, which dominated the majority Liberal party, had effective control in parliament; the prime minister was unlikely to face a vote of no confidence. Caxias and Dom Pedro had to find another way to force his resignation. It was Caxias who threatened to resign as supreme commander of the allied forces at the gates of the enemy capital if Dom Pedro followed the prime minister's recommendation and appointed a Liberal to a vacant Senate seat. The emperor deemed Caxias indispensable; he ignored precedent and appointed a Conservative to the Senate seat. Dom Pedro's resort to a dormant royal prerogative provoked the angry resignation of Zacarias and his cabinet. The emperor replaced them with Conservatives, dissolved parliament, and convoked elections which the new ruling party naturally won. He welcomed Caxias back to Rio after the general's triumphant entry into Asunción in January 1869. The war, however, dragged on in the Paraguayan countryside for another year, until Marshal Francisco Solano López was run through by a Brazilian lancer.

The Liberal Empire Strikes Out: 1868–1885

From the conciliation through the Zacarias administrations, 1853–68, parliamentary government in Brazil became more representative, beginning to reflect more faithfully the main currents of opinion abroad in the country. A multiplicity of factions within the two-party system made for some instability—there were eleven cabinets in those fifteen years—but the changes in administration resulted from the free play of parliamentary forces and were not imposed by the crown, as in earlier times. The power-sharing principle, observed during most of the period, discouraged the manipulation of local elections by the central government. Not only was progress being made, it seemed, toward a truly representative system, but by mid-1868 the government appeared to be both stable and effective. Zacarias had been prime minister for nearly two years, his administration had mobilized the country for victory in the Paraguayan war, and his Liberal party and Progressive League of ex-Conservatives had won the struggle for control of parliament and were preparing to lead Brazil into the postwar era under a banner of political and social reform. Then the emperor, his innate fear of change aroused by his Conservative-dominated Council of State, intervened and ousted the Liberals from power in July 1868. The Conservatives got control of the government, defections to the Liberals ceased, and reformers lost heavily in subsequent elections.

Outraged and out of power, the Liberals could not agree on a program for reform, so in 1869 they issued two manifestos. Both called for the direct election of members of parliament, measures to ensure honest elections, decentralization of authority, and the abolition of slavery. One document proposed gradual abolition, while the other demanded immediate emancipation of the slaves; the more radical manifesto also called for suppression of the Council of State, elimination of the moderating power, universal male suffrage, and the establishment of a federal system, with the popular election of provincial governors and police officials. The Liberal manifestos of 1869 set off a heated national debate, in parliament and the press, in the imperial capital and in the provinces. At the end of 1870, a new party joined the debate with the founding of the Brazilian Republican party and its Rio newspaper, *O Pais*. The Republicans, who had no representatives in parliament, issued a manifesto calling for the election of a constitutional convention which, they hoped, would abolish the monarchy and set up a federal republic. The Republican manifesto was silent on the question of slavery.

The signers of the Republican manifesto did not necessarily oppose the abolition of slavery; they simply aimed to exploit divisions among the Liberals and Conservatives on the issue. If the traditional parties managed to get together and enact an abolition law, the Republicans could expect to pick up the support of disgruntled ex-slaveholders. If the traditional parties failed to act, the monarchy would become as anachronistic as the servile institution it protected, and progressive Brazilians would have no choice but to join the Republican movement. Most of the founders of the Republican party shared the political ideals of the Liberal reformers; that is, they favored an open political system, a broadening of the electorate, a government responsive to the will of the people expressed in free elections. What these Republicans and Liberal reformers were working toward, at varying speeds, was representative democracy. But there were others, a small but growing number in the Brazil of the 1870s, whose vision of progress did not include democracy. These were the positivists, followers of the doctrines of Auguste Comte, partisans of authoritarian rule by a "scientific" elite, of state-directed economic and social development. They had a natural constituency in the technical branches of the military, and their influence would spread to the modernizing sectors of civilian society as traditional conservatives, including the emperor, continued to thwart the designs of Brazil's liberal democrats. Dom Pedro II was not unmindful of the dangers he faced; he simply underestimated the extent of accommodation necessary to save his throne. He concluded that the slavery question could be definitely resolved with the enactment of a free-birth law, and in 1871 he named as prime minister a moderate Conservative known to favor such a measure. Other Conservatives resisted it, and Prime Minister Rio Branco had to appeal to the Liberal minority in parliament for the votes necessary to pass the free-birth law. While Zacarias refused to help—not because he opposed freeing the newborn but because he thought the measure did not go far enough, and, in any case, he was not disposed to do the Conservative government any favors—Nabuco de Araújo rounded up enough Liberal votes to pass the bill. The Rio Branco Law of 1871 was supposed to liberate all children born to slave mothers after enactment of the law. The children, however, remained bound in involuntary servitude to their mothers' masters. The latter were not required to free them until they attained the age of twenty-one. Slaveowners had the option of freeing them at the age of eight, each in exchange for a government bond with a face value of about three hundred dollars. Thus, the principle of compensation was enshrined in the Rio Branco Law. Nabuco de Araújo's son, Joaquim Nabuco, noted disapprovingly that the law would preserve slavery in Brazil until the 1930s. Another Liberal democrat, Rui Barbosa, remarked that if the government was to compensate anyone, it should be the slave, not the master.

In parliament, however, Zacarias was one of the few Liberal reformers to vote against the Rio Branco Law. Zacarias also opposed the Conservative government—while Nabuco de Araújo supported it—when Rio Branco became embroiled in a conflict with the established church. The prime minister, like so many slaveowners in the southern United States, was a freemason; in fact, he was the grand master of freemasonry in Brazil. When some Brazilian bishops ordered the expulsion of freemasons from Catholic lay brotherhoods (irmandades), the government—in the name of the emperor, patron of the church in

Brazil—countermanded the orders of the bishops. Two of the bishops proceeded with the purges despite the government injunction and were jailed for their defiance of lawful authority. The emperor, who was not very religious but took great pride in his position as patron of the church, stood behind the prime minister as he met the ecclesiastical challenge to imperial authority. The bishops remained in prison for a year, until they were pardoned in 1875, and the freemasons remained in the irmandades until the fall of the empire.

As demonstrated by the episode of the bishops, the church was not very powerful in Brazil. The church controlled little wealth, and in the 1870s it was fashionable to dispute its doctrines. The established church administered to the spiritual needs of the unfashionably faithful, promoted social intercourse among the population in general by sponsoring festivals and irmandades, and provided ceremonial support for the monarchy. As fewer native Brazilians entered the priesthood, immigrants came in increasing numbers to serve as Catholic clergy in Brazil.

Immigration increased in Brazil after the Paraguayan War as technological advances made ocean passage cheaper and, with the enactment of the Rio Branco Law, the stigma of slavery began to fade from the empire's image in Europe. Nearly two hundred eight thousand foreigners took up residence in Brazil in the 1870s, more than twice the number of the previous decade. A large number of these immigrants came to the province of São Paulo, where local authorities and coffee planters made an agreement with the imperial government in 1871 to jointly subsidize transportation of agricultural workers from Europe. However, the amount appropriated by the imperial government to subsidize immigration was meager during the administration of Rio Branco, who pursued restrictive fiscal and monetary policies. Between 1871 and 1876, the money supply dropped at a rate of two percent a year. This caused a sharp contraction of the Brazilian economy, which, together with the concurrent world depression, ruined Mauá and many lesser entrepreneurs in Brazil. Ironically, the Mauá bank declared bankruptcy just a few months after the baron had been promoted to the noble rank of viscount in recognition of his services to the empire in connecting Brazil to Europe via undersea telegraph cable in 1874.

Rio Branco was willing to do almost anything for his friend Mauá except bail him out financially. The prime minister was obsessed with stabilizing the Brazilian currency, with returning the milréis to its prewar par value of twenty-seven British pence, a goal that was attained in 1875. Over the long run, Brazil's fixed exchange rate tended to lower the prices of imported manufactured goods (which were falling worldwide), yet rising Brazilian import duties tended to increase them; by the end of the 1870s, tariffs averaged fifty percent ad valorem, with textiles at sixty percent. Consumer prices were also pulled up slightly by a modest increase in demand that accompanied the decline of slavery after 1850. In the second half of the nineteenth century, Brazil experienced an average annual rate of inflation of about two percent. Income gains, however, exceeded price rises in all regions of Brazil except the northeast. The fairly wide regional distribution of income gains resulted primarily from the legislated transfer of assets from the southeastern coffee exporters, who, in turn, were subsidized by the unpaid labor of black slaves. By 1875, coffee accounted for half of Brazil's total annual exports of one hundred six million dollars, and the coffee provinces of São Paulo, Rio de Janeiro, and Minas Gerais held half of the country's remaining one and a half million slaves.

Some of the biggest slaveowners in the province of São Paulo were Republicans who resented the empire's redistribution of their export earnings to the other provinces through tariffs protecting inefficient industrial and agricultural production. The Paulista Republicans' newspaper, *A Província de São Paulo*, likened their province to a locomotive pulling twenty empty boxcars. In terms of population as well as wealth, São Paulo was grossly underrepresented in the imperial parliament, and Paulista Republicans, the country's most vocal advocates of provincial self-determination, were shut out of the official political process by the prevailing system of indirect and manipulated elections. In the late 1870s, the decade-old Liberal campaign for electoral reform gathered irresistible momentum, and the Liberals returned to power in 1878. The new prime minister, Viscount Sinimbu, was a slaveholding sugar planter from the northeast who took a moderate approach to electoral reform, favored protection of the Brazilian textile industry to maintain a national market for his region's inefficiently produced cotton, and cared not at all for proposals to abolish slavery.

While Sinimbu and his cabinet were working on electoral reform and tariff matters, Joaquim Nabuco and other Liberal party democrats launched a national campaign against slavery in 1879. They waged their struggle for abolition in parliament, in the press, and in the streets and *praças* of towns and cities throughout the empire. The situation soon was beyond the control of Sinimbu, who was replaced as prime minister in 1880 by another Liberal, José Antônio Saraiva, ex-associate of Joaquim Nabuco's father in the Progressive League, a statesman willing to consider new measures against slavery once legislation on elections and the tariff had been enacted, which occurred in 1881.

The tariff of 1881 raised protection to new levels, while the Saraiva electoral law of the same year provided for the direct election of members of parliament from single-member districts and added some provisions to ensure an honest vote count. However, the Saraiva Law did not satisfy the democratic demand for universal male suffrage; instead, it raised the income qualification for voting. The first parliamentary elections under the law were held in 1884 as the abolition campaign was getting into high gear. In that year, two northern provinces, Ceará and Amazonas, declared themselves free of slavery, and an "underground railroad" to assist fugitive slaves began to take shape. The elections produced an unprecedented balance in parliament: sixty Liberals, fifty-five Conservatives, and, for the first time, a Republican contingent—three deputies, all from São Paulo, including that province's biggest slaveholder.

Joaquim Nabuco and the abolitionists remained a minority in the Chamber of Deputies, but the effectiveness of their public agitation enhanced their parliamentary influence. They gave their support to Liberal Prime Minister Manuel de Sousa Dantas, who introduced a bill to free all slaves over the age of sixty. The Dantas bill, however, was defeated in a vote of no confidence which forced the prime minister's resignation. Opponents of the bill were not distressed by the prospect of losing their sexagenarian property; what they objected to was the bill's failure to reaffirm the principle of compensation. José Antônio Saraiva returned as prime minister and proposed a bill providing token compensation to the owners of emancipated sexagenarians. But the proslavery majority, emboldened by their earlier victory, now insisted on a fugitive slave provision as well. Saraiva capitulated to the slavocrats and formulated his bill under the guidance of the Conservative Baron of Cotegipe. The bill passed in the Chamber of Deputies, although most of the members of Saraiva's Liberal party voted against it, prompting the prime minister to resign. The emperor replaced him with Cotegipe, who formed a Conservative government. Cotegipe was thus prime minister when the sexagenarian bill passed the Senate and was signed into law by the monarch. The Saraiva-Cotegipe Law provided conditional freedom for slaves above the age of sixty and harsh penalties for anyone convicted of assisting fugitive slaves. The imperial army was given the demeaning mission of chasing runaway slaves.

After the enactment of the Saraiva-Cotegipe Law in 1885, parliament was dissolved and elections the following year returned one hundred three Conservative deputies, twenty-two Liberals, and no Republicans. Joaquim Nabuco, Rui Barbosa, and most of the other Liberal abolitionists lost their seats as the Conservative government evaded the safeguards of the Saraiva Law and resumed the time-honored practice of rigging elections. The Conservatives succeeded in divorcing imperial politics from Brazilian reality. The positivists' metaphysical assessments of the decadence of the existing order were confirmed. The military was outraged. Slavery was collapsing. The fall of the empire was not far off.

12

The Caribbean Vortex in the Nineteenth Century: Cuba and Central America

The liquidation of the Spanish Empire in the Caribbean began before the eighteenth century ended. Spain transferred Santo Domingo to France in 1795, and in 1795 Britain seized the island of Trinidad. Louisiana was ceded to France in 1802 and Florida to the United States in 1821. By mid-1821, revolutionary forces controlled most of Mexico, Venezuela, and New Granada, not including Panama. That left Spain with Cuba, Puerto Rico, Central America, and Santo Domingo—the last having been restored to Spanish sovereignty by the Congress of Vienna. Royal officials removed Santo Domingo and Central America from the Spanish Empire later in 1821 by declaring those colonies independent. Santo Domingo asked for admission to Bolívar's Republic of Colombia but was conquered by Haiti in 1822, while Central America joined the Empire of Mexico. Santo Domingo remained under Haitian domination until it recovered its independence in 1844; it rejoined the Spanish Empire for a brief period, 1861–65, and a few years later petitioned unsuccessfully for annexation by the United States. Central America, after the fall of the Mexican Empire in 1823, resumed its independence, except that most of its Caribbean coast remained under British hegemony until the second half of the nineteenth century. Cuba and Puerto Rico, the last remnants of Spain's American empire, were seized by the United States in 1898.

The old patterns of European colonialism—including colony swapping among the powers—persisted longer in Central America and the Spanish Caribbean islands than in the rest of Latin America. Prolonged colonialism and imperialist rivalries unavoidably affected the formation of the liberal order on the islands and mainlands of the strategic "American Mediterranean."[1] The disintegration of the Central American federation in the 1830s left Guatemala—with more than six hundred thousand people, more than the other four states combined—to assert Hispanic claims to British Honduras (Belize) and the minirepublics of Honduras, Nicaragua, and Costa Rica to contend with British aggression on the Mosquito Coast and Yankee demands for transit concessions across the isthmus. Nicaragua was the most affected of the Central American states by imperialist territorial claims and concessionary demands, while El Salvador, with no Caribbean coastline, was least affected. And Guatemala, despite problems with Britain over Belize and the Central American federation debt, experienced relatively autonomous development during most of the nineteenth century. In economic growth, however, Guatemala was far outstripped by the Spanish colony of Cuba, an area of comparable size and population at the beginning of the century.

Cuba: The Struggle for Autonomy, 1817–1878

In 1817, Great Britain pressured Spain into making a treaty outlawing the slave trade between Africa and the Spanish colonies in America within three years. Cuba was the Spanish Empire's principal importer of black slaves, who by 1817 comprised nearly thirty-nine percent of the island's population of about five hundred eighty thousand (whites were forty-two percent and free blacks and mulattos twenty percent). With Cuba's booming sugar and coffee industries dependent on slave labor, the prospect of losing their African source of supply greatly disturbed the island's planters and merchants. To console its faithful Cuban subjects, the Spanish crown issued a decree in the same year, 1817, permitting direct commerce between the island and the nations of the world. And the royal tobacco monopoly—long hated by native Cuban producers and consumers—was suppressed in 1817. The move toward a freer economy was accompanied by the introduction of steam power into Cuba, in 1819, to drive sugar mills and make up for some of the manpower loss expected after the activation of the slave-trade ban in 1820. The ban, however, like the one imposed on Brazil ten years later, proved less than effective: perhaps half a million African slaves were smuggled into Cuba in the forty-five years after 1820.

The slave-trade treaty did not slow the expansion of sugar and coffee production in Cuba in the 1820s. In coffee, Brazil had the advantage; Cuban production would peak early in the next decade and decline thereafter. Annual sugar exports from the island, however, surpassed those from Brazil by the end of the decade, making Cuba the world's leading exporter of that commodity. Cuba, like Brazil, was an underpopulated country with vast, unoccupied areas of fertile tropical soil, where commercial agriculture required, it was believed, the importation and coercion of labor. By 1827, the number of *ingenios* (plantations with sugar mills) in Cuba had reached one thousand, up from four hundred in 1800. The optimal ingenio output was thought to be one hundred tons of raw sugar, produced with one hundred slaves. The total number of slaves in Cuba, despite the slave-trade ban, had increased by sixty thousand in the decade after 1817, to two hundred eighty-seven thousand. While perhaps half of these were employed in sugar production, a substantial number worked on Cuba's 2,067 coffee plantations and lesser numbers on the 30,090 cattle ranches and 5,534 tobacco farms listed in the 1827 census.

Because of the abundance of vacant land, sugar plantations were slow to encroach on other agricultural properties. Cuban sugar production in the first three decades of the nineteenth century expanded through the proliferation of hundred-ton ingenios in virgin territory. Because sugarcane begins to spoil twenty-four hours after being cut, the supply radius of each mill was limited to the distance an oxcart would travel in less than a day, the time that remained after allowing for the collection, loading, and unloading of the cane. Also, sugar plantations required adjacent pasturage for the essential oxen and nearby woodlands to provide fuel for the mills. Larger plantations and mills would be economically justified only if means were available to bring cane and fuel to the mills over a greater distance and in a shorter time than oxcarts could manage. In the 1830s, railroads appeared in Cuba—the first anywhere in Latin America—and the island's ingenios began to grow in size and productivity.

Cuba experienced a liberal revolution of sorts in the 1830s. As the island remained a Spanish colony, the reforms it underwent were mostly transmitted from the mother country, where doddering and reactionary King Ferdinand VII finally died in 1833. Though the succession was contested by Ferdinand's even more reactionary younger brother, Don Carlos, the king had named his two-year-old daughter Isabel as his successor, and she was in fact proclaimed Queen Isabel II. The regency established to rule in her name displayed clear liberal tendencies, and the Carlists—followers of Don Carlos and professed guardians of ancient fueros—rose in armed revolt. The ultimately unsuccessful insurrection, the Carlist War of 1833–39, coincided with the enactment of important reforms by the government in power: it abolished press censorship, proclaimed individual rights, removed restrictions on foreign investment and other obstacles to economic enterprise, summoned a Cortes, confiscated the landed property of the church, made new commitments to end the slave trade, and, in 1837, adopted a constitution for the Spanish monarchy.

Spanish constitutionalism received a mixed reception in Cuba. Native property owners seemed eager to elect representatives to the Spanish Cortes, but the royal governor, a liberal army officer, informed them that they could not expect to participate in free government while they held others in bondage. As long as slavery existed in Cuba, Governor-General Miguel Tacón insisted, the island would be governed by "special laws"—that is, Tacón, who equated the Cubans with Carlists, would rule by military decree. Although the governor generally favored Spanish-born bureaucrats and businessmen—like the major shareholders of Cuba's first bank, established in Havana in 1833—he gave crucial support to at least one major creole-originated project: the construction of the Havana-Güines railroad. Proposed by a Cuban "Development Board," the project was adopted by the colonial government and financed by mostly British capital. The first tracks were laid in 1834, and in 1837 regular service was inaugurated between Havana and Bejucal, a distance of twenty-eight kilometers; the next year the railway reached Güines, completing an arc of eighty-two kilometers through the sugar country south and east of Havana. It was Latin America's first railroad, one of the first in the world. The government-owned line was enormously profitable and inspired Cubans and foreigners to organize private railroad companies and lay additional hundreds of kilometers of track in Cuba during the next two decades. Main lines connected ports and agricultural centers of western and central Cuba, while narrow-gauged tracks extended out from central sugar mills, creating ever larger production units.

Cuba experienced phenomenal economic growth in the years after 1837—by 1860, the island accounted for one-fourth of the world's sugar production—but little social or political progress. Under the Spanish constitution of 1837, Cuba was allotted four deputies to the Spanish Cortes. Tacón grudgingly permitted their election, but the Cortes refused them seats, on the same grounds cited earlier by the military governor: that they did not represent a free constituency. Slaveholders were constantly reminded of Spain's hostility toward Cuba's predominant labor system. Nevertheless, after the departure of Tacón in 1838, they found it easier to bribe Spanish officials to do their bidding—such as looking the other way as tens of thousands of African slaves were landed illegally on the island to satisfy the rising demand for labor on the expanding sugar plantations. In the 1850s, colonial officials further connived with planters to permit the importation of Indian slaves from Mexico, prisoners taken in the Yucatan Caste War. Coolies from China were imported in fairly large numbers as indentured servants under conditions little better than slavery. Several hundred Irish arrived to build the railroads, and some worked shoulder to shoulder with slaves and coolies in laying track, but few, if any, wound up as plantation laborers.

There was, in the view of most Cuban planters in the 1850s, no satisfactory alternative to black slavery in the sugar industry. With slave prices soaring in Cuba because of the increasing effectiveness of the British navy in intercepting shipments from Africa and the rising costs of bribing Spanish officials, planters could only envy their counterparts in the southern United States, who had access to a huge domestic market where seasoned field hands could be bought for ten to twenty percent less than what they sold for in Cuba. The prospect of U.S. annexation of Cuba was welcomed by many planters and businessmen. Before the end of the 1850s, the United States was buying more than half of the island's sugar exports, despite a U.S. tariff protecting Louisiana production, and, in overall terms, almost forty-two percent of Cuba's foreign trade was being conducted with its northern neighbor, compared to twenty-five percent with Britain and only twelve percent with Spain. Quite a few planters, merchants, investors, entrepreneurs, and public figures—on both sides of the Florida Straits—were convinced that Cuba's destiny lay with the United States. As a slave state in the North American union, Cuba, it was argued, would enjoy the autonomy it could never expect to achieve in the Spanish Empire. Even some Cuban critics of slavery supported annexation on the ground that the institution could be more effectively liquidated—in the long run—within the framework of a politically liberal society such as that of the United States.

Spain, backed by its European allies, resisted U.S. demands that it sell Cuba in the 1850s. Filibustering expeditions launched from U.S. territory attracted some support in Cuba but ultimately failed to deliver the island to the United States. The U.S. Civil War of the 1860s settled the matter for most slaveholders: annexation by a nation that prohibited slavery was out of the question. Their only hope for retaining their human property lay in pursuing autonomy within the Spanish Empire. For them, independence was not an option; it would require armed struggle that would weaken if not destroy the existing social order and lead to the abolition of Cuban slavery sooner rather than later. The idea of independence was more attractive to those Cubans who had little or no slave property; they could give freer rein to anger at being excluded from political power and disgust with the corruption of Spanish colonial officials and the vacillating rule of Isabel II, reigning queen of Spain from 1843 to 1868.

Autonomists were encouraged in 1865 when the Spanish colonial ministry invited Cuba's town and city councils to send representatives to Madrid to discuss the shape of future relations between the colony and the mother country. The colonial representatives formed a "Board of Information" which presented to the crown a plan for Cuban self-government that called for the establishment of an autonomous legislature on the island. The plan was similar to the one being worked out for British Canada at the time, 1866–67; in the case of Cuba, however, the hateful issue of slavery was involved, and the Cuban supplicants were constrained to commit the proposed autonomous regime to the gradual elimination of the island's peculiar institution. Despite the concession, the shaky Spanish government was unable to act on the proposal—although it did levy new taxes on Cuban property and incomes. As the empty-handed representatives returned to Cuba, autonomist hopes dimmed, and partisans of independence began preparing an armed uprising.

Independence sentiment was strongest in eastern Cuba, where coffee cultivation, ranching, and food agriculture still resisted the sugar culture that prevailed in the western region, which terminated with the district of Sancti Spíritus. In land area, the two regions of Cuba were about equal, but the west had more than four times the population of the east. The smaller population of the east had relatively fewer slaves and persons of Spanish birth than did the larger population of the west. Many small holders from the west had migrated to the east after selling out to the ingenios. In the east, land was plentiful and cheap, although much of it was rugged and irregular—forested mountains—and of low fertility. Communities of runaway slaves had found refuge in the Sierra Maestra since the early days of Spanish colonization; by 1861, free blacks and mulattos made up one-third of the eastern region's population. In the west, both black and white populations contained substantial numbers of nonnatives, that is, persons born in Africa or Europe. The African-born population, however, was dwindling with the effective ending of the slave trade by 1865, while the European-born element was increasing as more and more Spanish immigrants were attracted to Cuba by the prospects of becoming *colonos* (sharecroppers) on land provided by the expanding ingenios. By 1868, the total population of Cuba approached one and a half million, of whom about a quarter were slaves.

The Ten Years' War for Cuban independence began in eastern Cuba in October 1868 less than a month after a military coup in Spain ousted Queen Isabel II. Despite the confusion in the mother country, the rebels in Cuba made little headway. They offered freedom to any slave who would join their army, and the new government in Spain countered with a free-birth law, adopted by the Cortes in 1869 and put into effect in 1870. Slaves who deserted rebel masters were welcomed into the Spanish army in Cuba and promised full freedom at the end of their military service. With slavery definitely on the way out in Cuba, the government in Madrid declared in 1869 that the colony would become a full-fledged province of Spain, entitled to representation in the Spanish Cortes, once the revolt was over. In the meantime, the rebel government in eastern Cuba turned away from its stated goal of independence and appealed to Washington for annexation by the United States. The appeal eventually was rejected by U.S. President Grant, and the Cuban rebel president-in-arms who made it, Carlos Manuel de Céspedes, was removed in 1873 by officers of the insurgent army headed by Máximo Gómez, a white native of Santo Domingo and a veteran of Spanish service on the neighboring island. The struggle continued, now unequivocally under the banner of independence.

The rebel movement attracted some support from business and professional people in Havana, but Máximo Gómez's army was largely confined to the eastern countryside, which it dominated, to the detriment of the local economy, until peace was arranged in 1878. By the Pact of Zanjón, the rebels laid down their arms and were granted amnesty by the Spanish crown. Slaves who served in either army were given their freedom, and the free-birth law was reaffirmed; it provided for compulsory service to the age of twenty-two by the children of slave mothers but freed unconditionally all slaves above the age of sixty. The period of compulsory service was reduced by subsequent legislation, and slavery in Cuba was completely abolished in 1886. The 1878 Pact of Zanjón guaranteed Cuba representation in the Spanish Cortes but did not give Cubans the autonomy they desired. The struggle would continue.

The Central American Isthmus: In the Path of Empire, 1821–1885

In the 1820s, Central America was not of great importance to the world economy, and vice versa. The per capita value of Central

American exports in the peak year 1825 might have been as high as six dollars, about half that of Cuba at the time, but the volume was so small that most of it could be, and was, shipped through British-occupied Belize, a grubby little port with a population of around four thousand—about one-twentieth that of Havana. The principal export was cochineal, a red dye made from cactus bugs. Cochineal was one of three dyestuffs long associated with Central America, the other two being logwood and indigo. Belize was founded in the seventeenth century as an English logwood-cutting camp; it was retained by Britain—despite Spanish protests and armed attempts to dislodge the intruders—for strategic reasons and for the contraband trade in cochineal, which was legalized when Central America declared its independence from Spain. Independence initially gave a modest boost to the cochineal industry, but it spelled doom for Central American indigo, which had been protected under the Spanish imperial system; the British had much cheaper sources of indigo in India. After 1825, cochineal continued to increase as a percentage of Central American exports while indigo decreased, but in absolute terms cochineal shipments declined as the overall export economy of Central America contracted in the second quarter of the nineteenth century.

Most of the Central American cochineal was shipped from Belize and came from Guatemala. It was brought regularly to Belize on coastal vessels from Santo Tomás, near the mouth of the Río Dulce in Guatemala. Boats from the Caribbean ports of other Central American provinces, and from the kingdom of Mosquitia, sailed into Belize from time to time with such commodities as cowhides, crocodile skins, wild animal pelts, herbs, and mahogany logs, which were sold to resident British merchants who reshipped the goods to Europe or North America. Oceangoing vessels seldom called at Central American ports other than Belize, which, though occupied by the British, was claimed as national territory by the federal government of the United Provinces of Central America, which had separated from Mexico in 1823. At the Congress of Vienna, Britain had recognized Spain's sovereignty over Belize, in return for an indefinite lease on the port and its environs, an arrangement which the federation—as purported successor to Spanish rights in Central America—wanted to renegotiate. Spain, however, did not recognize the federation, and Britain perceived the split between Central America and its mother country as an opportunity to establish Belize as a formal British colony. A formalized and permanent British presence there would improve the security of Britain's puppet kingdom of Mosquitia, which controlled most of the Caribbean lowlands from the Río Sico in Honduras to the Matina Valley in Costa Rica.

George Frederick II, king of the Mosquitos—or Miskitos, in modern orthography—was crowned by the British superintendent in Belize in 1816. The first of the line had received the symbols of his royal office from the British governor of Jamaica in 1687. The subjects of His Mosquitian Majesty included indigenous Indians (mostly Miskitos), creole blacks (mostly descendants of slaves brought to the coast by English logwood cutters), and *zambos* (mixture of black and Indian). They were a fierce people, much given to pillaging Spanish settlements in Central America, who had been valuable allies of the British in the colonial wars of the eighteenth century. Their utility to Britain in the first half of the nineteenth century derived from their occupation of territory that lay astride the most likely transisthmian canal routes. As the world's premier maritime power and builder of ship canals—the Caledonian Canal across Scotland, nearly one hundred kilometers long with twenty-eight locks, was completed in 1822—and with growing interests in the Pacific, Great Britain was drawn to the idea of creating and exploiting an ocean passageway through Central America.

The kingdom of Mosquitia could be counted on to cede to the British whatever they needed along the Caribbean coast, but all the possible canal termini on the Pacific and much of the territory between the two coasts were effectively controlled by the provinces of the Central American federation, which claimed the Miskito lands and regarded the puppet kingdom with fear and loathing. While the British could not avoid dealing with Hispanic Central America for transit rights, their mastery of the Miskitos and their naval and economic power gave them considerable leverage in negotiation with the federation government in Guatemala City. Actually, the federation—a weak union under a constitution adopted in 1824 that resembled the Mexican charter of the same year—seemed to have little chance of surviving without British help. Aid came from England in the form of an eight-million-dollar loan, floated just before the London market crash of 1825–26.

Despite—or perhaps because of—the infusion of cash from England, the federation government faced armed revolt as it attempted to extend its authority over the provinces in 1826. Conservative centralists based in Guatemala City lost the civil war to liberals from the outlying provinces. The victorious liberals moved the federation capital to San Salvador and, under Francisco Morazán, a Honduran who became president in 1830, adopted centralizing policies similar to those that had brought down the conservatives. The British, who had supported the conservatives when they championed federal unity, now supported Morazán's liberal government. The British minister to Central America, Frederick Chatfield, became Morazán's chief financial adviser and drafted the president's tariff legislation. During the civil war, the provinces had taken over the federation's customs houses and the national tobacco monopoly. Morazán and Chatfield worked together to federalize these revenue sources; they would apply the proceeds from customs duties to the maintenance of the central government and earmark those from the tobacco monopoly for payments to British bondholders. Morazán managed to push the tariff and tobacco legislation through the federal Congress in San Salvador in 1838, but his legislative victory produced the immediate secession of Honduras, Nicaragua, and Costa Rica. A few months later, in 1839, Guatemala pulled out of the union, and Morazán resigned the federal presidency, hoping that his departure might clear the way for the reconstitution of the federation. It did not; Central America remained divided, and Morazán was executed in 1842 after a failed unionist revolt in Costa Rica.

The disintegration of the Central American union prompted British moves against the independent states, which London held responsible for proportionate shares of the federation debt. British troops from Belize seized the Bay Islands from Honduras in 1838, and London formalized the occupation in 1839. Two years later, British and Miskito forces seized the Nicaraguan customs house at San Juan del Norte; they soon withdrew from that Caribbean port, but in 1842, British warships blockaded both coasts of Nicaragua in another effort to force that country to make payments on its share of the federation debt. In 1843, Great Britain declared that its armed forces would repel any aggression against the kingdom of Mosquitia, thus formally establishing that entity as a protectorate of the British Empire. Chatfield, now roving British ambassador to the several Central American republics, completed a canal-route survey and recommended that Britain grab some territory along the Pacific coast of the isthmus.

Meanwhile, the United States had entered the picture with its occupation of California in 1846 and consequent need for transcontinental communications. As the United States negotiated with New Granada for the right to build a railroad across Panama, Great Britain took steps to extend its control over the most promising transisthmian canal route, across Nicaragua. In 1847, London declared that San Juan del Norte, Hispanic Nicaragua's only port on the Caribbean, by rights belonged to the kingdom of Mosquitia. On New Year's Day, 1848, British and Miskito troops occupied San Juan del Norte and renamed it Greytown. The United States joined Nicaragua in protesting the British action, and the Nicaraguans reciprocated by granting exclusive transit rights across their territory, including the right to build a canal, to a U.S. company headed by Cornelius Vanderbilt. The company, however, had no choice but to operate through Greytown and pay taxes to the Miskito kingdom, which it did under strong protest. Vanderbilt's Accessory Transit Company, which began regular service in 1851, operated a steamship line from the United States to Greytown, river steamboats from there up the Río San Juan and across Lake Nicaragua, a fifty-kilometer stagecoach and freight-wagon line from the lake to San Juan del Sur on the Pacific, and ocean steamers from there to California.

Meanwhile, the United States and Great Britain came to terms about Central America. By the Clayton-Bulwer Treaty of 1850, the two nations agreed that neither would station troops on the isthmus (Belize and the Bay Islands were excluded) and that no canal or other transportation system built or controlled by either would charge duties on goods in transit. The treaty required the removal of British soldiers from Mosquitian soil but did not prevent the British from supporting the native kingdom with warships standing offshore, nor did it prevent the Miskitos from levying exorbitant port charges on Vanderbilt's vessels. After a particularly nasty confrontation in 1851, in which the United States threatened armed action against the British and their native puppets, Vanderbilt reached a modus vivendi with the authorities in Greytown.

In Hispanic Nicaragua, Vanderbilt's interests were threatened by a Liberal revolt against the Conservatives who had granted him the transit concession. The Liberals had the support of a group of North American financiers who planned a hostile takeover of Vanderbilt's company. In California, they hired William Walker and a few dozen other filibusters and dispatched them to Nicaragua in 1855 to help the Liberals. More filibusters followed from the southern United States, and, within a year, Walker had collected and trained sufficient forces to defeat the Nicaraguan Conservatives. In 1856, after taking Managua, Walker pushed aside his Liberal allies, had himself elected president of the republic, canceled Vanderbilt's concession, legalized slavery in Nicaragua (it had been outlawed since 1824), and sent inquiries to Washington about the possibility of Nicaragua's joining the union as a slave state.

The U.S. legation in Managua recognized Walker as president of Nicaragua, but the United States did little to help him. The coalition that formed in Central America to fight the filibusters was formidable. The Conservatives of Nicaragua—beaten but not destroyed—had the support of the British Empire, Cornelius Vanderbilt, and the Conservative governments of the other four Central American republics. Guatemala contributed the largest contingent, three thousand men, to the allied army that was led by Costa Rican President Juan Rafael Mora. The Central American allies won the war in 1857, and Walker and his defeated filibusters were evacuated from Greytown by the U.S. Navy. William Walker died three years later before a firing squad in Honduras after a failed comeback attempt.

The identification of Liberals with Walker ensured Conservative control of every Central American republic for at least a decade and a half after 1856. In Nicaragua, where the Liberals' collaborationist burden was the heaviest, the Conservatives would retain power for thirty years. The common interest of Britain and the Central American republics in preventing Nicaragua's annexation by the United States produced a climate of conciliation that facilitated the settling of some long-standing disputes. In 1859, Britain withdrew from the Bay Islands, returning them to Honduras, and reached an agreement with Guatemala on Belize. Guatemala recognized Belize as a British colony in return for Britain's promise to build a wagon road from Guatemala City to the republic's Caribbean coast. This treaty, however, was later abrogated by Guatemala when the British welshed on the road deal. Another British treaty, with Nicaragua in 1860, recognized Nicaraguan sovereignty over the Mosquito Coast. Nicaragua, however, pledged not to occupy the former kingdom of Mosquitia; it was to be preserved as an autonomous Indian reservation. The treaty was broken by Nicaragua in 1894, when the government in Managua sent troops to occupy the Miskito territory. London protested and ordered the Royal Navy to blockade both Nicaraguan coasts, but the United States stood with the regime in Managua, the British backed down, and the Miskitos lost their freedom.

Cornelius Vanderbilt was on the winning side in the 1856–57 filibuster war, but his Accessory Transit Company lost the battle for transisthmian traffic to the Panama railroad, which went into operation in 1855. Passengers and shippers saved time as well as money by choosing the railway over the steamboat-wagon combination. A canal that allowed the passage of ships from one ocean to the other without unloading would have been even more efficient, but Vanderbilt gave up the idea of building one. In 1858, he sold his canal rights to a French company headed by Félix Belly, whose project had Nicaraguan approval but was obstructed by Costa Rica, which claimed jurisdiction over part of the San Juan River route. Unable to come to terms with Costa Rica, Belly sold his rights to a U.S. company that made a start digging the canal in 1889 but was ruined in the panic of 1893. The Nicaraguan ship canal, a dream since the sixteenth century, never materialized.

The Panama railroad had a tremendous impact on Central America. Within a few years of the railway's inauguration in 1855, almost all of Central America's overseas commerce had shifted from Caribbean to Pacific ports. In absolute terms, the trade did not amount to much in the 1850s—the heart of Central

America's withering export economy was still cochineal, which was being killed off by aniline dyes—but foreign commerce would revive in subsequent decades as coffee cultivation spread over the isthmus.

Tiny Costa Rica was the first Central American republic to export appreciable amounts of coffee. The beans were shipped from the Pacific port of Puntarenas, beginning in the 1830s, to Valparaíso, Chile. Some of the coffee was consumed in Chile, but this was one more example of the emergence of Valparaíso as an entrepôt linking Pacific ports of Latin America with the nations of Europe. Costa Rican producers, though, were at an obvious disadvantage as compared to the Brazilian, Cuban, and Venezuelan coffee growers with direct access to the Atlantic. Costa Rica's centers of population and agriculture were in the highlands near the Pacific, and the difficulty of communication between this area and the Caribbean coast limited the expansion of Costa Rican export production until the completion of the Panama railroad in 1855. At that time, Costa Rica was ruled by a Conservative oligarchy that promoted coffee cultivation with monopolistic concessions and subsidies. In 1871, the Liberals took over the government and offered more subsidies on a more egalitarian basis. The Liberal dictatorship of Tomás Guardia, 1871–82, pursued economic and social development with great energy. By the time of the dictator's death in 1882, Costa Rica's population of less than two hundred thousand was one of the most prosperous in Latin America. In 1885, Bernardo Soto came to power in Costa Rica and opened up the political system to such an extent that his Liberal party was voted out of office in the next election—the first time any such thing had happened in Central America. In 1885, Costa Rica was already on the road to democracy. The situation was different in Guatemala.

Guatemala: Rise, Fall, and Recreation of the Liberal Order, 1821–1885

With six or seven times more people than Costa Rica had in 1885, Guatemala was much closer to the Latin American norm in size of population. Also, Guatemala's ethnic diversity was more typically Latin American than Costa Rica's largely white creole population. Most of Guatemala's people were Maya Indians who spoke little or no Spanish, lived in ancient highland villages, and farmed communal lands in the manner of their ancestors. The next largest ethnic group consisted of mestizos—or *ladinos*, as they are called in Central America—people of mixed European-Indian ancestry who adopted the language, dress, and customs of the Spanish colonizers. Before independence, Guatemala's ladinos were mostly laborers, craftsmen, and petty merchants in the colony's cities and towns and small farmers in the Montaña region east of the capital; after independence, the ladino minority took control of the country from the smaller minority of native whites and Europeans. Blacks were fewer still in nineteenth-century Guatemala; like the whites whom they served, most blacks lived in the capital city, although some could be found in port towns on the Caribbean or the Pacific.

Guatemala's population was heavily rural and, at the beginning of the nineteenth century, mostly engaged in the production of food and fiber for local or regional consumption. The country's principal exports at the time of independence, cochineal and indigo, were produced mostly on small or medium-sized farms, although there were some large indigo plantations. Export production was financed by Guatemala City's monopolistic *Consulado*, or merchant guild, which legally controlled the overseas trade of Central America under the Spanish colonial system. As the Spanish Empire crumbled in 1821, the monopolists enlisted the aid of the colony's royal officials in implementing their plan to break Guatemala's formal ties with Spain and tie the country to the presumably conservative Mexican Empire, which they hoped would preserve their corporate privileges. Central America's union with Mexico, proclaimed in Guatemala in 1822, was resisted in other provinces and dissolved in 1823 after the fall of Iturbide's empire. One Central American province, Chiapas, elected to remain with the Mexican federal republic, while Guatemala and the other four joined in an isthmian federation.

In the capital of Central America, as in Mexico City, moderately liberal federalists prevailed in 1824. Attentive to the demands of provincial indigo producers, the framers of the Central American constitution of that year stripped the Consulado of its authority outside the province of Guatemala. Liberty was served—and a symbolic blow struck against the slaveholding intruders in Belize and Mosquitia—by the constitution's abolition of slavery in Central America. The indigenous peasantry was freed of discriminatory taxation with the abolition of the Indian tribute. Further liberal reforms were contemplated as the first national Congress under the constitution assembled in Guatemala City with liberals and provincial federalists together holding a majority of the seats. Legislation passed in 1826 was supposed to abolish the Consulado's mercantile court system, which had had jurisdiction in all commercial cases, but the federation president, Manuel José Arce, a Salvadoran, switched from the liberal to the conservative side, made common cause with the church hierarchy and the Guatemalan monopolists, purged the federal Congress, and allowed the Consulado courts to continue functioning. Arce's coup set off the bloody civil war, 1826–29, which has already been mentioned. The conservatives lost, despite their superior financial resources in the coffers of the Consulado, the archdiocese, and the federal treasury, repository of the proceeds from bonds sold in London in 1825.

The victorious liberals suppressed the Consulado in 1829 and launched a vindictive campaign against the church. The archbishop of Guatemala was expelled from the federal republic, along with other conservatives from the capital and from the provinces. The anticlerical laws that were enacted under federation president Morazán and provincial governor Mariano Gálvez and applied to Guatemala in the early 1830s exceeded in scope those of any other Latin American country at the time. (There seems to be no self-evident reason why Guatemala in particular should have attained this distinction.) The ecclesiastical fuero was abolished, regular orders were banished and their property confiscated, clergy were permitted to renounce their vows, religious freedom was proclaimed, tithes were made voluntary, civil marriage was authorized, and divorce was made legal. Governor Gálvez further alienated the clergy and other traditionalists by offering public lands to foreigners, including Protestants, and by importing a body of criminal law, the Livingston Codes, from the United States. Originally devised by Edward Livingston for the state of Louisiana, the codes provided for elected sheriffs and trial by jury, innovations that were seen by conservatives—especially in Guatemala City—as undermining the social order in the countryside.

Falling export demand for Guatemalan indigo and shrinking domestic markets for the province's raw cotton and textiles plagued Gálvez's liberal administration. The cochineal business, however, continued to thrive, and the provincial government sought to promote economic development with public investments in infrastructure and education. The funds for these projects were to come from a new head tax of two dollars cash per person. Unlike the old Indian tribute, Gálvez's head tax was to apply to all citizens alike, but the burden fell heaviest on the Indians, and they had difficulty distinguishing between this "liberal" tax and the hated colonial levy. Besides raising government revenue, the measure forced communal Indians into the wage-labor market to get the money with which to pay the tax. While trying to stimulate the creation of new jobs, Gálvez also sought to preserve old ones by raising tariffs on imported textiles, thus subsidizing the income of traditional weavers and the planters and farmers who supplied them with cotton.

Tariff protection for traditional industries was one of several concessions that Gálvez made to Guatemala City conservatives as Indian and ladino protests against the head tax and persecution of the church swept the countryside. Another concession was his suspension of the Livingston Codes, which greatly antagonized the main proponent of that reform, José Francisco Barrundia, and split the Liberal party. In 1837, Barrundia made an alliance with Rafael Carrera, proclerical caudillo of the Montaña district, a brilliant young guerrilla commander and idol of the ladino peasantry. Early in 1838, Carrera's peasant army occupied Guatemala City, ousted Gálvez's government, and installed Barrundia's Liberal faction in power. After getting the new government's promise to stop the persecution of the church and to recall the archbishop and the other clerical exiles, the caudillo pulled his troops out of Guatemala City and returned with them to the Montaña. (His departure from the capital might have been hastened by an eleven-thousand-dollar bribe.) Two months later, however, Carrera rose again in revolt, this time against the Barrundia regime, which then appealed to the federal government in San Salvador for help.

In 1838, President Morazán led federal troops into Guatemala to fight Carrera in the Montaña. On the other side of Guatemala City, in Quezaltenango, Liberals organized a government for a new province, Los Altos, which was promptly admitted to the federal union. Morazán's federation gained one province but soon lost three as Honduras, Nicaragua, and Costa Rica seceded from the union. It soon lost Guatemala, too, as white Conservatives of Guatemala City put aside their fear of the ladino hordes of the Montaña and made an alliance with Rafael Carrera. By early 1840, the ladino Carrera—an unlettered twenty-six-year-old ex-muleskinner and swineherd—had conquered the breakaway province of Los Altos, defeated Morazán, dismantled what was left of the Central American union, and made himself master of Guatemala.

Except for a few months in 1848–49, Carrera ruled Guatemala from 1840 until his premature death in 1865, probably from overindulgence in alcohol. The life of his regime—conservative, populist, and brutal—was extended to 1871 by his chosen successor, Vicente Cerna. Carrera and his white Conservative partners restored as much of the colonial corporatist order as they thought possible and desirable. Guatemala's Indian masses, who had rallied to Carrera's standard in the war with the Liberals and looked upon the ladino caudillo as their messiah, were encouraged to return to the peaceful life of the ejido. Indians who preferred the traditional life were better off than they had ever been, for not only did the Carrera regime guarantee the entailment of communal holdings, but it abolished Gálvez's head tax and did not revive the colonial tribute. Indians were made subject to compulsory tithing, which was reestablished by law, but that levy, which was paid in kind, was one the faithful villagers did not begrudge, and, in any case, it fell more heavily on the more productive elements in Guatemalan society.

The church was well pleased with Carrera's Conservative restoration. The ecclesiastical fuero was restored along with the tithes. The archbishop and the exiled clerics returned in triumph. Religious freedom was rescinded, and Roman Catholicism once again became the official religion of Guatemala. The regular orders, including the Jesuits, were invited back, and convents and monasteries were reestablished. Education was made the responsibility of the church, and the moribund University of San Carlos was revived under clerical control. Civil marriage and divorce were outlawed. In 1852, the privileges of the church in Guatemala were guaranteed by a concordat made by the Carrera government with the pope in Rome.

In the secular realm, corporatism was served by the resurrection of the Consulado in 1840. Jurisdiction in commercial cases was returned to the merchant guild's courts, which applied the Bilbao Ordinances from the colonial period. The Consulado was made responsible for the upkeep of the country's roads and bridges and was authorized to collect import and export duties for the government, monopolized foreign trade, and operated port facilities. In a country without banks, the merchant guild was, along with the church, a major source of investment capital. The government and the Consulado, while protecting vested interests, promoted economic development in the mercantilist manner. The merchant guild distributed a manual on coffee growing from Costa Rica in the 1840s, while the government provided public lands and other subsidies to favored individuals interested in cultivating the new crop. A few bags of coffee beans were exported in 1853.

Vestiges of postindependence liberalism disappeared with the reaction of the 1840s and 1850s. The press was censored, dissidents were jailed or exiled, and social and political peace was ruthlessly enforced by the predominantly ladino army and police. An authoritarian constitution, promulgated in 1851, created a national Congress based on corporate constituencies and assigned it a single duty: to elect the president of the republic. In 1854, Rafael Carrera was proclaimed president for life, and Congress was recessed indefinitely.

With the Indian majority outside the money economy, Guatemala's per capita exports declined to little more than a dollar in 1855—from the general Central American rate of about six dollars in 1825. The total value of Guatemala's exports in 1855 amounted to about 1.1 million dollars. Cochineal accounted for eighty-eight percent of the export total, which fell short of imports by about one hundred thousand dollars in 1855. The inauguration of the Panama railroad that year spurred Guatemalan cochineal production, which increased by more than four hundred thousand dollars the next year, to make up ninety-two percent of Guatemala's exports in 1856 and wipe out the trade deficit. By 1861, however, aniline dyes were driving cochineal out of world markets, and Guatemala's exports that year fell back to around 1.1 million dollars, of which seventy-one percent was represented by cochineal. As the prospects for cochineal dimmed, the Panama railroad and the U.S. Civil War offered Guatemalan export producers an alternative annual crop—cotton. Because of its low value-to-bulk ratio, cotton could not profitably be transported by the old means of mule train and riverboat from production areas in western Guatemala to the distant Caribbean, but with world prices high—as they were during the U.S. Civil War—it was economically feasible to ship cotton from the Pacific port of San José de Guatemala to Europe via the Panama railroad. By 1865, San José, which was linked to Guatemala City by a wagon road, had become the republic's main port, handling seventy-eight percent of Guatemalan exports.

President-for-life Carrera died in 1865 as the cotton boom was about to go bust. Congress convened and duly anointed Carrera's chosen successor, Vicente Cerna, but economic troubles and the liberal winds blowing from Mexico especially made it hard for him to govern. Coffee trees planted in the late 1850s were bearing increasing amounts of marketable fruit to replace some of the export earnings lost with the collapse of cotton, and a modern textile mill was established near the capital to use up some of the surplus fiber, but many educated Guatemalans believed that their country was not taking full advantage of the opportunities that the modern world offered them. Coffee orchards, unlike cotton fields, required long-term financing, which was difficult to arrange in a country with no banks and no modern commercial code, where the corporatist values of the Consulado and the established church clouded the environment for enterprise.

In 1871, President Cerna was overthrown in a Liberal revolution led principally by Justo Rufino Barrios, a Guatemala City lawyer-turned-soldier. Barrios ruled Guatemala as president or from behind the scenes from 1871 until his death in 1885. Upon seizing power in 1871, Barrios's Liberals abolished the Consulado for good and launched a campaign of repression against the church. The archbishop and most members of the hierarchy were expelled, along with the Jesuits and other orders. The Roman Catholic church was disestablished and most of its property confiscated. Civil marriage was made obligatory, and all education was made secular. Priests were forbidden to teach school or wear clerical garb in public. Religious processions were banned.

The religious reforms were not welcomed by Guatemala's devout Indian masses. Barrios, a heterodox positivist, ordered a public school for every communal village, with attendance made compulsory, to educate Indian children in the ways of the modern, secular world. But Barrios's order was too big to be filled, and many villages never saw a schoolmaster. The pedagogues who did appear among the Indians were treated coolly at best— certainly they were not accorded the respect due a revered padre. The Indian masses resisted Barrios's efforts to entice them to work for money on the new coffee plantations or in the modern textile mills that appeared in Los Altos in the 1870s. Where education and persuasion failed, Barrios—a dictator despite his Liberal label—resorted to coercion. In 1878, a vagrancy law was enacted requiring every adult Guatemalan male to work at least forty days a year for salary or wages; military commandants were ordered into the villages to round up all Indians deemed to be vagrants and deliver them to local coffee plantations at harvest time. The coerced workers were paid minimum wages and encouraged to buy goods on credit. The result was widespread debt peonage, which the Barrios regime legalized. Unpaid debts were passed from deceased father to his male heirs; creditors could demand that Indian debts be paid in labor at any time.

While Barrios practiced internal imperialism on Guatemala's conservative Indian majority, he pursued policies that created new opportunities for enterprising whites and ladinos, as well as for foreigners who would come to the country to plant coffee, build railroads, or establish textile mills. Legislation enacted in 1873 cleared the way for the founding of Guatemala's first bank in 1874, and a comprehensive commercial code was promulgated in 1877. Public lands suitable for coffee cultivation were plentiful and were granted to railroad concessionaires or sold cheaply to natives and foreigners, including quite a few Germans. Coffee seedlings were distributed free, or at nominal prices, by government nurseries. Coffee exports in the decade of the 1870s nearly tripled in volume; practically all the beans were handled by the port of San José, which in 1884 was connected by rail with Guatemala City. At the time of Barrios's death in 1885, another railroad was under construction from the capital to the Caribbean. This project was part of Barrios's plan to diversify Guatemala's economy by promoting the production and exportation of such commodities as sugar, cacao, and bananas.

A restless dictator, Barrios was killed in battle as he led Guatemalan troops into El Salvador in an attempt to recreate the Central American federation. His regime in Guatemala survived his death. He left the republic with a liberal constitution, adopted in 1879, which, if his successors had observed it, might have guided Guatemala toward democracy. They did not, and it did not. Brutal tyranny with constitutional wrappings continued to characterize the liberal order in Guatemala.

13

The Liberal Legacy and the Quest for Development

By the 1880s, the liberal order seemed more or less established in Latin America, and its creators had good reason—from their own perspective, anyway—to be satisfied with their handiwork. The closing years of the nineteenth century and the beginning of the twentieth were a period of marked quantitative growth for the Latin American economies and a relative consolidation of political order. Economic expansion was nowhere else as spectacular as in Argentina, but figures on production and trade, kilometers of railroads built, and other measurements of infrastructural development were almost everywhere rising more rapidly than before. As for the political settling down that accompanied economic advances, one scholar has calculated that the occurrence of coups in Latin America declined from an annual rate of three per year in the third quarter of the nineteenth century to a mere two by the first decade of the twentieth.[1] Obviously, the economic growth that increased the range of personal opportunities for members of the Latin American upper classes at the same time as it increased the resources at the disposal of Latin American governments was an aid to the cause of stability. Greater political stability, in turn, lessened the costs and uncertainties of doing business, so that the phenomena were mutually reinforcing.

The dominant ideology of Latin America—to the extent that there was one—continued to be liberal, although liberalism tended to become less doctrinaire and more pragmatic, with a distinct positivist tinge. With minor exceptions, the political constitutions were the same as those put in place during the immediately preceding period, or recognizably similar. Written constitutions were not always observed to the letter, which was not in itself anything new. But there was perhaps a greater willingness to recognize and to justify a degree of concentration of authority in the national executive that went substantially beyond what the legal texts called for. Rather common was the emergence of rulers who claimed to be liberal but governed in fact as military or civilian dictators and whose propagandists defended autocratic procedures as a necessary means to enter the promised land of "Order and Progress." Antonio Guzmán Blanco of Venezuela, Justo Rufino Barrios of Guatemala, and Porfirio Díaz of Mexico were three who helped establish the pattern, but other examples are not hard to find. The first two administrations under the Brazilian republic (established in 1889) more or less fit the pattern, and the regime of Julio A. Roca of Argentina (first elected president in 1880) and his successors, while no dictatorship in a strict sense, was notoriously arbitrary in its use of electoral fraud and in its misuse of the constitutional article permitting the president to "intervene" in the various provinces. Argentina was, at the same time, the one country where a correlation between order and progress was most obvious.

Progress and Development

Progress, in its economic dimension, was seen essentially in terms of net growth of total production (especially export commodities) and material infrastructure. Moreover, the growth that did occur took place within the institutional framework that Latin American liberals had erected in place of the vestiges of Hispanic colonial corporatism that had been cleared away in 1820–80. Gone were entailed estates, most communal landholdings, fueros, and all manner of legalized individual or group privileges. Slavery finally disappeared with the completion of abolition in Cuba and Brazil, in 1886 and 1888 respectively. The new order specified that advantages were to be gained through wealth, no longer by birth alone or membership in some functional group. Thus, while doctrinaire anticlericalism entered into decline, the institutional church—except, notably, in Colombia—never truly recouped the losses it had suffered. By the turn of the century, outright harassment of the church was usually at an end, but the privileged status it had enjoyed from the early colonial era until, say, the mid-nineteenth century was no more. In reality, the Latin American countries were beginning to approximate a regime of genuine church-state separation, which both represented a reaction against the excesses committed in earlier church-state conflict and reflected the feeling of a new generation of leaders that there were more important things to do than quarrel with the clergy.

More important was to create the conditions that would attract foreign investment and immigrants—the capital and labor that, in the view of most nineteenth-century liberals, were essential for the progress of Latin America. The governments that came to power after 1850 managed to remove much of the uncertainty of living and doing business in Latin America. Enterprise remained risky, but, after all, calculating and discounting risk were part of the investor's job. The enactment and more or less consistent application of civil legal codes in most Latin American countries in the third quarter of the nineteenth century made the assessment of risk easier and the enforcement of contractual obligations more certain—a matter of interest to prospective investors and immigrants alike. Of course, political uncertainties remained, and "revolutions" continued to occur, but with decreasing frequency and with scant economic consequences. In Mexico, Maximilian did not invalidate sales of church property under the Lerdo Law, and Juárez, though he repudiated most of the imperial government's debt, did not expropriate the bank or the railroad company chartered by Maximilian. While arbitrary or extortionate acts by government bureaucrats and judges or by insurgents could never be completely ruled out, private capital, both foreign and native, felt increasingly secure. Enterprise was encouraged, and economic growth fed on itself in the late nineteenth century. Greater exports made possible more imports, which brought more tariff revenue into the national treasuries.

Governments could afford to subsidize the construction of railroads, which hauled more outward-bound produce to ports or frontiers and distributed more imported goods inland.

Progress was evident, but "progress," as many scholars have pointed out, is not the same thing as "development." The essential characteristics of socioeconomic development, the professed goal of most Third World countries today, are (1) a highly monetarized economy (i.e., one with little subsistence farming or barter exchange), (2) a high per capita national income, measured in money, and (3) widespread distribution of education and health benefits (through market allocation, government command, or a combination of the two) to the general population. Wealthy nations—those with measurably high productivity—have these characteristics. In the nineteenth century, a high literacy rate was perhaps the most reliable indicator of development in education, while a low mortality rate would reflect favorable health conditions. By these measurements, no Latin American country in 1880 was as developed as the United States or any of several nations of northwestern Europe, although Argentina was on its way and in the first part of the twentieth century would take its place, for a time, among the ten wealthiest nations on earth. Other Latin American nations, while not attaining Argentina's results, at least made significant gains.

Since wealth does not occur spontaneously in nature, its presence, rather than its absence, requires explanation. The normal state of nature is poverty, or the lack of development. That some nations of the world achieved high levels of development in the nineteenth century is remarkable; that many others did not is not surprising. On average, the Latin American nations probably created more wealth than did their independent counterparts in Africa and Asia—such as Ethiopia and Siam—and also more than most colonies or imperial dependencies in eastern Europe and around the world. The eagerness of large numbers of people from other regions to migrate to Latin America in the late nineteenth century indicates a widespread perception, at least, that conditions of employment, health, and education were, on balance, better in Argentina, southern Brazil, Uruguay, Chile, and Cuba than in the lands whence the immigrants came.

The Export Economy

Exports were the key to development in the late nineteenth century, and in 1880 only Argentina, Uruguay, and Cuba in Latin America matched or exceeded the seventeen-dollar per capita exports of the United States that year (see Appendix 2). Shipments from North America, like those from Latin America, were then mainly food and raw materials, as manufactured goods were just beginning to figure significantly among U.S. exports. The foundations of U.S. industrialization, however, had been laid before 1820, before Latin America achieved its independence and the terms of trade turned in favor of producers of commodities. In the 1820s, world prices of manufactured goods began falling faster than the prices of raw materials, a trend that would continue for about a century. Countries with natural resources favorable for the production of commodities had little economic incentive to industrialize after 1820; it was usually cheaper to buy finished products with money they earned from raw material exports than to manufacture goods themselves. This applied not only to most Latin American nations but to some countries in northwestern Europe as well, such as Denmark.

A small country, much closer in population to the Latin American norm than was the mammoth United States, Denmark in the nineteenth century experienced political turmoil, multiple constitutions, secessionist movements, foreign wars, invasion, and dismemberment. Through it all, the Danish economy, based on agricultural exports, maintained its long-term growth. Long dependent on grain exports, Denmark lost most of its foreign wheat markets to the United States and Russia in the 1870s. Danish farmers responded by shifting from wheat growing to the production of butter and bacon for export. This advantageous switch was made in a highly monetarized, export-oriented economy, in a country with an ample financial infrastructure, small and flexible production units, and an educated population able to receive and respond efficiently to market information. Denmark, like Argentina, had achieved a high level of socioeconomic development by the beginning of the twentieth century without industrialization. Appreciable investments in manufacturing were made in both Denmark and Argentina after World War I, as the terms of trade for producers of commodities began to deteriorate. From the start, Danish manufacturers produced for export as well as for their domestic market, while Argentine industrial production was solely for national consumption. Thereafter, Denmark maintained its position as one of the world's wealthiest nations, while Argentina began its descent toward Third World status.

A striking example of industrialization in the late nineteenth century is that of Japan. The Japanese experience has no counterpart in Latin America or anywhere else. Japan's circumstances in 1868, at the onset of industrialization, were unique: a "feudal" tribute system imposed on a society and economy characterized by highly productive agriculture, a high degree of urbanization, little international trade, but a large and vigorous domestic market served by a well-developed financial infrastructure— including a grain futures exchange, an institution that did not appear in the Western world until a century after its 1759 debut in Japan. The monetary tribute that had supported a parasitic feudal class went, after 1868, to finance industrialization. Without valuable mineral resources or the land to expand agriculture, commodity exportation was not a Japanese option. Industrialization was, and it had the attraction of military utility. An industrialized Japan would be able to make the armaments it needed to defend itself against the white foreigners who violated its sovereignty and denigrated its culture in the second half of the nineteenth century.

No such racial-military threat preoccupied the ruling classes of late-nineteenth-century Latin America, who were little disposed to transfer assets from lucrative raw material production to less profitable manufacturing for reasons of national defense. They were prepared at times to subsidize manufacturing for reasons of social peace or internal political stability—for example, by giving the cotton planters of Brazil or Guatemala a market for their produce when it was priced out of world markets. Government subsidies like protective tariffs could also be justified on economic grounds—by all but dogmatic free traders—as temporary expedients to sustain infant industries during the learning process. Japan's infant industries, because of the "unequal treaties" imposed by foreign powers, could not receive effective tariff protection and went immediately into export production. Latin American industries remained in extended infancy in a protected home environment.

Dimensions of Dependence

Of today's Latin American republics, the most "dependent" in the nineteenth century was Cuba, which was a formal colony of Spain until 1898. Between 1820 and 1860, Cuba experienced more economic progress than any other Latin American country. Its exports per capita exceeded those of the United States in some years, and the island came to be considered the world's richest colony. In transportation infrastructure, the application of advanced technology, productivity, and general socioeconomic development, Cuba was comparable to the southern United States in 1860. The two areas, of course, shared the peculiar institution of black slavery, which limited the social, if not economic, growth of each. Slaves aside, Cubans were wealthy by Latin American standards throughout the nineteenth century, though not so rich as the Argentines at the century's end. A causal relationship between political dependence and socioeconomic underdevelopment is not evident from Cuba's experience.

More important than political dependence in questions of development and underdevelopment, according to some theorists, is economic concentration on the production of a limited number of export commodities, such as sugar (principally) and coffee and tobacco in Cuba and meat, wool, and grain in Argentina. Such commodity specialization is said to make the producing nation a "dependency" of consuming nations; industrial nations, on the other hand, are never (or almost never) at the mercy of their foreign customers or suppliers. However valid these concepts might be for the twentieth century—and there are doubters, among them both capitalists and socialists, to say nothing of oil sheiks—they are hardly relevant for most of the nineteenth century, when the terms of trade favored producers of primary materials.

The perceived "dependency" is a symptom of external demand, and it is demand, whether external or internal, that drives economies—even those tilted to the "supply side," where new or cheaper products are supposed to generate new demand. The subsistence farms, individually or communally owned, that predominated in much of Latin America at the beginning of the nineteenth century created little demand and could contribute only minimally to economic growth or socioeconomic development. Dependent on their own limited resources, the rural communities were self-sufficient in the best of times, but at all times they led a precarious existence, continually threatened by the vagaries of nature. When external demand arose for goods or services that they could provide, there were usually some members of the community willing to respond to the demand. Transition to an economy of markets and money expanded the options of peasant producers and could just as well enhance as diminish their security. At the same time, the appearance of new goods stimulated desires to possess them and created a new form of dependence that induced some individuals to abandon their villages altogether and seek remunerative employment elsewhere. The breakdown of traditional communities and the emergence of consumer-oriented societies, deplored by some modern scholars, were better understood in the nineteenth century. Karl Marx, for one, held no brief for "the idiocy of rural life."[2]

While the penetration of the world economy in some areas of Latin America increased individual opportunities and diminished personal dependence, in others it bolstered, at least temporarily, coercive labor systems. The expansion of sugar production in Cuba and coffee production in Brazil was accompanied by increased importation of slaves from Africa in the first half of the nineteenth century. In the second half of the century, with slavery in decline, Cuban and Brazilian producers began bidding seriously for free workers on the world labor market. Neither slaves nor free immigrants were available to cultivate coffee in Guatemala in the 1870s; when wage offers and inducement goods proved insufficient to lure indigenous workers onto the coffee plantations, the Guatemalan government resorted to forced-labor drafts.

Abuses of Latin America's indigenous populations were less characteristic of export operations than of large-scale production for the national markets that grew with the export economy. Widespread theft of Indian lands in Mexico occurred after 1880 as railroads linked remote areas with big-city markets and as haciendas expanded to supply Mexican factories and urban consumers with grain, sugar, pulque, and cotton. Landowners in Mexico and elsewhere also resorted to debt peonage to secure labor, though scholars disagree about the extent to which this form of bondage actually was practiced. It is known, however, that Mexican peasants seeking job security sometimes purposely borrowed excessively from hacendados, so that the lender would be compelled to continue the borrower's employment in order to collect the debt. The "dependency" relationship here is not unlike that between international bankers and some Latin American governments today.

As the world economy offered Latin Americans new options in the nineteenth century, it limited some others—like that of earning a decent living in traditional handicrafts, such as spinning and weaving. Artisans, as in Colombia in the 1850s, were sometimes militant in demanding the right to receive more for their products than these would fetch in market competition with machine-made equivalents, but in the end governments in Colombia and elsewhere chose not to artificially extend the life of costly preindustrial forms of production. Consumers, and liberal ideology, triumphed over special interest in this struggle but lost in many others. Sugar planters and refiners in Argentina and Mexico received tariff protection to tide them over while they modernized and expanded their mills and private rail lines, and textile manufacturers in several countries, as has been noted, were granted infant-industry protection—in theory. In fact, protection of these nineteenth-century industries was extended indefinitely, and the process was repeated as new manufacturing operations were established in the twentieth century. Until well into the second half of this century, Latin America pursued a program of national subsistence industrialization—or "import substitution," as its proponents preferred to call it. Latin American industrial growth was limited by dependence on national markets.

The Liberal Order: Demise and Rebirth

In the twentieth century, Latin America tended to drift away from the liberal model embraced by leaders of the previous period. State intervention in the economy came to be extensively practiced well before the world depression of the 1930s that seemed to finish off laissez-faire. It was practiced by regimes of widely varying political persuasion: by revolutionary Mexico, which led the retreat from absolute private property rights, and by the agro-exporting Brazilian oligarchy, which created the world's first commodity-producer cartel for its coffee in 1906 and subsidized faltering coffee exports with dual exchange rates. Politically, moreover, critics of both left and right began to question the liberal tenets to which nineteenth-century leaders had generally given at least lip service, regardless of how faithfully they practiced them. The social problems and tensions that were an inevitable by-product of economic growth helped convince the critics that authoritarian solutions were called for. Neither did the fact that Germany, Japan, and Russia—or, more recently, South Korea—industrialized under an authoritarian regime go unnoticed in Latin America, where such strongmen as Getúlio Vargas of Brazil and Juan Perón of Argentina correctly perceived that industrialization was the key to contemporary socioeconomic development and wielded the power of the state (Vargas rather more effectively than Perón) on its behalf.

A reason for intensified interest in industrialization, and a serious complication in its own right, was the fact that after the 1920s the terms of trade moved generally against the producers of commodities and in favor of their processors—and those who created value out of nothing. By the 1980s, a handful of worthless sand, when spun into optical fiber, could do the work of countless kilometers of copper wire made from tons of ore extracted from the mountains of Chile. As world populations leveled off or declined, except in areas too poor to exert much effective demand, prices of foodstuffs fell in relation to those of manufactured goods. Wealthy nations with market economies and high liquidity generally were able to shift assets from agriculture and mining to manufacturing and services as required. Consequently, most of the world's rich countries in 1900 also made the affluent list in 1980. Argentina was a notable dropout, and there were a few newcomers—but none from Latin America.

By 1980, in any case, the authoritarian model for development was also tarnished by disappointing performances in nations as far apart politically and geographically as Cuba and Argentina. And with the world's wealthiest nations all adhering to liberal democracy as a system, many Latin Americans came to think that it was not necessary, or even possible, to sacrifice freedom for development. It was becoming clearer that sustained economic growth was dependent on the free flow of information and that this was ultimately incompatible with authoritarian government. To be sure, in Latin America liberal political regimes had never disappeared entirely, and in the twentieth century, through suffrage extension and the creation of mass media and mass political parties, they developed a wider base of participation—in effect, became more democratic. Such regimes have not been limited to the well-known cases of Venezuela, Costa Rica, and Colombia, although in recent years they have been the most consistent practitioners. The much-heralded resurgence of Latin American democracy that has so far marked the 1980s is thus no more a historical aberration than the "bureaucratic authoritarianism" practiced by military dictatorships of the 1970s. It has roots in both the recent and the not-so-recent past—certainly going back to the experiments of liberal nation building in the nineteenth century.

Notes

Chapter 1

1. Arturo Ardao, *Génesis de la idea y el nombre de América Latina* (Caracas, 1980), p. 83 et passim.

2. John Lynch, *The Spanish-American Revolutions, 1808–1826* (New York, 1973), p. 7.

Chapter 2

1. Arturo Uslar Pietri, "Discurso de ingreso a la Academia Nacional de Historia de Venezuela," *Boletín de Historia y Antigüedades* (Bogotá) 48, nos. 557–558 (March–April 1961): 219–36.

2. Miguel Angel Asturias, *Bolívar: poema* (San Salvador, 1955).

3. The exceptions to the pattern mentioned were New Galicia in western Mexico and Cuzco in Peru, both of which had had their own audiencias but did not become separate countries, and Paraguay and Uruguay, which lacked audiencias but did separate. The present republics of Central America are cases comparable to the last two, but on first separating from Mexico Central America still conformed to the rule.

4. Simón Bolívar, *Selected Writings of Bolívar*, 2 vols., comp. by Vicente Lecuna and ed. by Harold A. Bierck, Jr. (New York, 1951), Vol. II, p. 738.

5. Ibid., Vol. II, p. 732.

6. Tulio Halperín-Donghi, *The Aftermath of Revolution in Latin America* (New York, 1973), p. 116.

7. Moisés González Navarro, *El pensamiento político de Lucas Alamán* (Mexico City, 1952), p. 63. Italics added.

Chapter 3

1. Neill Macaulay, *Dom Pedro: The Struggle for Liberty in Brazil and Portugal, 1798–1834* (Durham, 1986), pp. 13, 310.
2. John H. Coatsworth, "Obstacles to Economic Growth in Nineteenth-Century Mexico," *American Historical Review* 83, no. 1 (February 1978): 92.
3. Gorham D. Abbot, *Mexico and the United States: Their Mutual Relations and Common Interests* (New York, 1869), p. 93.
4. E. Bradford Burns, *The Poverty of Progress: Latin America in the Nineteenth Century* (Berkeley, 1980), p. 93.

Chapter 5

1. Francisco Frías Valenzuela, *Historia de Chile*, 4 vols. (Santiago, 1947–49), Vol. III, p. 8.
2. Diego Portales, *Diego Portales pintado por sí mismo* (Santiago, 1941), p. 70.

Chapter 6

1. See, e.g., Richard Alan White, *Paraguay's Autonomous Revolution, 1810–1840* (Albuquerque, 1978).

Chapter 7

1. Neill Macaulay, *Dom Pedro: The Struggle for Liberty in Brazil and Portugal, 1798–1834* (Durham, 1986), p. 147.
2. Ibid., p. 251.

Chapter 8

1. James D. Cockcroft, André Gunder Frank, and Dale L. Johnson, *Dependence and Underdevelopment: Latin America's Political Economy* (New York, 1972), pp. 34–35.
2. Claudio Véliz, *The Centralist Tradition in Latin America* (Princeton, 1980), pp. 9, 11, 279, et passim.

Chapter 10

1. A brilliant mishmash of cultural geography, memoir, history, and myth, *Facundo* was translated into English as *Life in the Argentine*

Republic in the Days of the Tyrants, or Civilization and Barbarism, with a biographical sketch by (appropriately) Mrs. Horace Mann, wife of the noted U.S. educator. The translation has gone through several editions since first appearing in 1868.

2. First published in Santiago in 1928.

Chapter 11

1. Eul-soo Pang and Ron L. Seckinger, "The Mandarins of Imperial Brazil," *Comparative Studies in Society and History* 14, no. 2 (March 1972): 215–44.

Chapter 12

1. Lester D. Langley, *The Struggle for the American Mediterranean: United States-European Rivalry in the Gulf-Caribbean, 1776–1904* (Athens, Ga., 1976).

Chapter 13

1. Warren Dean, "Latin American Golpes and Economic Fluctuation, 1823–1966," *Social Science Quarterly* 51, no. 1 (June 1970): 74.

2. Karl Marx and Friedrich Engels, "Manifesto of the Communist Party," in *The Marx Engels Reader,* ed. Robert C. Tucker (New York, 1972), p. 339.

APPENDIX 1

Latin American Population, 1820 and 1880

Country	1820 population	1880 population
Argentina	610,000	2,484,000
Bolivia	1,000,000	1,506,000
Brazil	4,494,000	11,748,000
Chile	890,000	2,066,000
Colombia	1,025,000	2,870,000
Costa Rica	63,000	170,000
Cuba	615,000	1,542,000
Dominican Republic	120,000	240,000
Ecuador	530,000	1,106,000
El Salvador	248,000	583,000
Guatemala	595,000	1,225,000
Haiti	647,000	1,238,000
Honduras	135,000	303,000
Mexico	6,204,000	10,488,000
Nicaragua	186,000	400,000
Paraguay	210,000	318,000
Peru	1,210,000	2,710,000
Uruguay	69,000	229,000
Venezuela	760,000	2,080,000
TOTALS	19,611,000	43,306,000

APPENDIX 2

Exports per Capita of Selected Latin American Countries, ca. 1830, 1855, 1880

Country	Year	Population	Exports[a]	Per capita exports[a]
Argentina	1829	745,000	$ 5,200,000	$ 6.98
	1855	1,106,600	15,240,986	13.77
	1880	2,484,000	78,720,000	31.69
Brazil	1830	5,343,000	16,032,000	3.00
	1855	7,050,000	50,993,827	7.23
	1880	11,748,000	100,180,800	8.53
Colombia	1836	1,733,000	3,261,600[b]	1.88
	1855	2,417,819	7,929,350	3.28
	1880	2,870,000	13,689,100[c]	4.77
Cuba	1830	764,000	14,200,000[d]	18.59
	1855	1,381,000	30,500,000[e]	23.81
	1884	1,593,000	73,130,000	45.91
Mexico	1830	6,365,000	13,022,000[f]	2.05
	1851	7,672,000	9,608,000[f]	1.25
	1873	9,172,000	31,691,000[f]	3.46
Peru	1831	1,363,000	4,973,550	3.65
	1855	2,266,697	16,880,303	7.45
	1878	2,680,000	25,208,435	9.41
Venezuela	1831	909,000	2,286,000	2.51
	1855	1,351,386	5,495,270	4.07
	1880	2,080,000	13,279,423	6.38

[a] In 1880 U.S. dollars.
[b] 1834–38 average, includes gold.
[c] 1878–80 average, includes gold.
[d] 1826–30 average.
[e] 1851–55 average.
[f] Includes gold and silver.

Chronology

1820   *Peru.* Expeditionary force commanded by José de San Martín lands on coast near Lima, to begin final stage of Peruvian liberation.

1821   *Argentina.* Bernardino Rivadavia, leader of liberal Unitario faction, becomes chief minister of Buenos Aires province and initiates comprehensive program of reform.
        Gran Colombia. Battle of Carabobo seals independence of Venezuela. Congress of Cúcuta issues formal constitution and adopts law of free birth.
        Mexico. Agustín de Iturbide assumes leadership of independence movement and forges coalition between exroyalists such as himself and old-time patriots. Spanish resistance crumbles, in Central America as well as Mexico itself.

1822   *Brazil.* Oldest son of King John VI of Portugal proclaims independence and becomes Emperor Pedro I of Brazil.
        Haiti. Occupies former Spanish colony of Santo Domingo, which had thrown off colonial rule the year before.
        Mexico. Iturbide crowned emperor.

1823   *Chile.* Bernardo O'Higgins, Chilean liberator, forced to resign as head of government and go into exile.
        Mexico. Iturbide overthrown.

1824   *Brazil.* Pedro I gives empire a liberal constitution, which among other things makes Brazil the second Latin American country (after Haiti) to establish religious toleration.
        Central America. Having formally separated from Mexico at fall of Iturbide, the five states of Guatemala, El Salvador, Honduras, Nicaragua, and Costa Rica join together under federal constitution.

Mexico. Mexican republic adopts liberal and federalist constitution.

Peru. Battle of Ayacucho won by patriots in southern highlands; last major engagement of independence struggle on American mainland.

1825   *Argentina/Brazil.* Revolt of Uruguay against Brazilian rule is assisted by Argentina, leading to war between Argentina and Brazil.

Bolivia. Declares itself independent country rather than continuing as part of either Peru or Argentina.

1826   Panama Congress convoked by Bolívar to implement Spanish American solidarity. Not much accomplished.

Argentina. National Congress adopts centralist constitution, with Rivadavia as president. Federalist backlash compels his resignation the following year.

1828   *Argentina/Brazil.* War peters out. With help of British mediation, both countries agree that Uruguay is to be independent country.

1829   *Argentina.* Juan Manuel de Rosas begins first period as governor of Buenos Aires province, with dictatorial powers.

Brazil. Liquidation of first Bank of Brazil (established 1808).

Chile. Conservative strongman Diego Portales takes power (to be exercised mainly from behind scenes).

Gran Colombia. Secession of Venezuela begins process of formal dissolution. (Ecuador will follow next year.)

1830   *Mexico.* Lucas Alamán founds Banco de Avío, government development bank which subsequently finances textile factories.

1831   *Brazil.* Abdication of Pedro I. Regency takes control of government in name of his young son Pedro II.

1832   *Colombia.* Back from exile, former Gran Colombian vice-president Francisco de Paula Santander becomes first constitutional president of New Granada.

1833   *Argentina.* British force seizes Falkland Islands (Islas Malvinas).

Chile. Conservative constitution issued, reflecting influence of Portales; will last until 1925.

Mexico. Antonio López de Santa Anna becomes president for first time.

1834   *Brazil.* Additional Act represents partial concession to federalist sentiment; does not prevent federalist rebels in Rio Grande do Sul from declaring independent republic two years later.

Venezuela. "Law of 10th of April," freeing interest rates, symbolizes liberal economic policy followed by Conservative Oligarchy of José Antonio Páez.

1835   *Argentina.* Rosas returns to power after three years' absence, with "sum of public power."

1836–39 *Bolivia/Peru.* Confederation formed between Bolivia and Peru under Andrés Santa Cruz; eventually broken up by Chilean invasion.

1836   *Mexico.* Texas declares and wins independence.

1837   *Mexico.* "Pastry War" with France; Santa Anna regains prestige that he had lost along with Texas.

1838–40 *Argentina.* French blockade.

1838   *Cuba.* Completion of Havana–Güines railroad, first in Latin America.

        Guatemala. With massive Indian support, future Conservative dictator Rafael Carrera takes power, ousting reformist Liberal regime.

1839–41 *Colombia.* "War of the Supremes," catalyst for emergence of long-lasting Liberal and Conservative parties.

1839   *Central America.* Guatemala secedes from collapsing federal union.

1840   *Brazil.* Pedro II, declared of age ahead of time, assumes throne in person.

1844   *Colombia.* Return of Jesuits, called by Conservatives to take part in educational reform.

        Dominican Republic. Santo Domingo throws off Haitian rule, becomes independent republic.

1845–48 *Argentina.* Blockade conducted jointly by France and Great Britain.

1846–48 *Mexico.* War with United States resulting in loss of northern territories.

1848   *Venezuela.* President José Tadeo Monagas throws off tutelage of Páez, replaces Conservative with Liberal Oligarchy.

1849   *Colombia.* Election of José Hilario López inaugurates period of frantic Liberal reformism.

1850   *Brazil.* Adopts legislation that will finally make effective abolition of slave trade.

        Colombia. Reexpulsion of Jesuits.

1852   *Argentina.* Overthrow of Rosas dictatorship.

1853   *Argentina.* Adopts first effective constitution, a liberal and federalist document that is again in force today.

        Brazil. Founding of second Bank of Brazil.

Colombia. Province of Vélez briefly offers vote to women for first time in America.

Mexico. Santa Anna becomes president for last time, with dictatorial powers. Makes agreement with United States for Gadsden Purchase.

1854   *Peru.* Final abolition of slavery and Indian tribute, both made possible by bonanza income from guano.

Venezuela. Also finally abolishes slavery.

1855–57 *Nicaragua.* Abortive regime of filibuster ostensibly in Liberal service, William Walker.

1855   *Colombia.* Completion of Panama Railroad, linking Atlantic and Pacific coasts of Isthmus.

Mexico. Overthrow of Santa Anna ushers in period of La Reforma.

1856   *Mexico.* Lerdo Law strikes at "corporate" property of church and Indian villages.

1857   *Mexico.* New constitution expresses Liberal Reforma ideology; remains formally in effect until 1917.

1858–61 *Mexico.* Civil war fought by Conservatives in unsuccessful effort to reverse reforms enacted by Liberals, now led by Benito Juárez.

1861–65 *Dominican Republic.* Rejoins Spanish Empire.

1862   *Argentina.* Bartolomé Mitre becomes first president of truly united Argentina, ending secession of his own Buenos Aires province.

1863   *Colombia.* Ultraliberal constitution takes federalism and other Liberal precepts to greater extremes than anywhere else in Latin America (lasts to 1885).

1864–66 *Peru.* Conflict with Spain degenerates briefly into open warfare, in which Peru is aided by Chile.

1864–67 *Mexico.* Maximilian von Hapsburg reigns as emperor at invitation of Conservatives and with French military backing.

1865–70 War of Triple Alliance, of Argentina, Brazil, and Colorado-dominated Uruguayan government against Paraguay.

1867   *Brazil.* Completion of Santos–Jundiaí railroad, linking city of São Paulo to sea and opening western part of province to coffee expansion.

1868–74 *Argentina.* Presidency of Domingo F. Sarmiento, dedicated to spread of public education and other forms of liberal modernization.

1868–78 *Cuba.* Ten Years' War fought for independence from Spain.

1870   *Brazil.* Republican party formed.

Cuba. Spain adopts free-birth law.

Venezuela. Antonio Guzmán Blanco seizes power and establishes Liberal autocracy. Among his first measures is one establishing free, compulsory primary education.

1871   *Brazil.* Rio Branco law establishes principle of free birth.

Guatemala. Justo Rufino Barrios takes power, establishes Liberal dictatorship of positivist tendency.

1872   *Peru.* Newly organized Civilista party elects Manuel Pardo president.

1876   *Argentina.* First transatlantic shipment of refrigerated meat, from France to Buenos Aires, to test technology.

Mexico. Porfirio Díaz becomes president for first time.

1878   *Guatemala.* Vagrancy law serves to compel labor on new coffee plantations.

1879–80 *Argentina.* "Conquest of the Desert" completes subjugation of Indians of pampa and Patagonia.

1879   Outbreak of War of the Pacific, of Chile against Bolivia and Peru, for control of nitrate territory (ends in 1883 with sweeping Chilean victory).

Brazil. Joaquim Nabuco and others launch abolition campaign.

1880   *Argentina.* Federalization of city of Buenos Aires.

Mexico. Manuel González becomes president, launches massive railroad-building campaign.

Further Reading

The listing of titles that follows does not pretend to be comprehensive but rather suggests sources in English from which the nonspecialist can quickly learn more about the topics covered in this history. For more complete coverage, including non-English works, the reader should consult Charles C. Griffin, ed., *Latin America: A Guide to the Historical Literature* (Austin: University of Texas Press, 1971), which lists the major works published to about 1967, and since then the *Handbook of Latin American Studies*, published yearly by the Library of Congress in collaboration with the University of Texas Press. History as a separate section appears in alternate numbers of the *Handbook*.

Chapter 1. Introduction

There are several excellent one-volume surveys of colonial Latin America, including Lyle N. McAlister, *Spain and Portugal in the New World 1492–1700* (Minneapolis: University of Minnesota Press, 1984); Charles Gibson, *Spain in America* (New York: Harper and Row, 1966); the classic institutional survey by C. H. Haring, *The Spanish Empire in America* (New York: Oxford University Press, 1947); and the recent interpretative synthesis by James Lockhart and Stuart Schwartz, *Early Latin America: A History of Colonial Spanish America and Brazil* (New York: Cambridge University Press, 1983). The first two volumes of the *Cambridge History of Latin America* (Cambridge: Cambridge University Press, 1984) offer monographic chapters by recognized scholars on all major aspects of colonial history.

Chapter 2. The Founding of a New Political System

The best survey of Spanish American independence in any language is John Lynch, *The Spanish-American Revolutions, 1808–1826* (New York: Norton, 1973). The independence of Brazil is covered by Neill Macaulay, *Dom Pedro: The Struggle for Liberty in Brazil and Portugal, 1798–1834* (Durham: Duke University Press, 1986). A comparative approach to the independence process in Spanish and Portuguese America is taken by Richard Graham, *Independence in Latin America* (New York: Alfred A. Knopf, 1972). Several of the major Spanish American liberators are the subjects of biographies in English, such as Gerhard Masur, *Simon Bolivar*, 2nd ed. (Albuquerque: University of New Mexico Press, 1969); Augusto Mijares, *The Liberator* (Caracas: North American Association of Venezuela, 1983); Hugh Hamill, *The Hidalgo Revolt* (Gainesville: University of Florida Press, 1966); and William S. Robertson, *Iturbide of Mexico* (Durham: Duke University Press, 1952). Unfortunately, there is nothing comparable for southern South America.

Both independence and most of the period covered by this volume are treated in the *Cambridge History of Latin America*, vol. 3, *From Independence to c. 1870* (Cambridge: Cambridge University Press, 1985). Few works, however, deal with the development of Latin America as a whole during the course of the nineteenth century. One exception is E. Bradford Burns, *The Poverty of Progress: Latin America in the Nineteenth Century* (Berkeley: University of California Press, 1980), a provocative essay emphasizing the clash between "elite" and "folk" cultures. Another referring to the period from independence to midcentury and, despite the title, to just Spanish America, is by Argentine scholar Tulio Halperín-Donghi, *The Aftermath of Independence in Latin America* (New York: Harper and Row, 1973). Leopoldo Zea, *The Latin-American Mind* (Norman: University of Oklahoma Press, 1963), is a study of Latin American thought that goes beyond, but still puts its chief emphasis on, the nineteenth century. Specifically political thought (again extending into the twentieth century) is reviewed by Miguel Jorrín and John D. Martz, *Latin-American Political Thought and Ideology* (Chapel Hill: University of North Carolina Press, 1970).

On the church question, the work by John L. Mecham, *Church and State in Latin America: A History of Politicoecclesiastical Relations*, rev. ed. (Chapel Hill: University of North Carolina Press, 1966), though somewhat legalistic in approach, is still useful. Studies of international relations include Harold Eugene Davis et al., *Latin American Diplomatic History: An Introduction* (Baton Rouge: Louisiana State University Press, 1977), not to mention the standard work by Dexter Perkins, *A History of the Monroe Doctrine*, rev. ed. (Boston: Little, Brown, 1963).

For an overview of political and related developments during the last century, it is often most convenient to consult the separate national histories that deal with that period among others. For most countries, such histories are available in English, and the following are all good to excellent except for the Colombian entry, which is badly outdated.

Argentina

Rock, David. *Argentina 1516-1982: From Spanish Colonization to the Falklands War*. Berkeley and Los Angeles: University of California Press, 1985.
Scobie, James R. *Argentina: A City and a Nation*, 2nd ed. New York: Oxford University Press, 1971.

Bolivia

Klein, Herbert S. *Bolivia: The Evolution of a Multi-Ethnic Society*. New York: Oxford University Press, 1982.

Brazil

Burns, E. Bradford. *A History of Brazil*, 2nd ed. New York: Columbia University Press, 1980.
Poppino, Rollie E. *Brazil: The Land and the People*, 2nd ed. New York: Oxford University Press, 1973.

Caribbean

Knight, Franklin W. *The Caribbean: The Genesis of a Fragmented Nationalism*. New York: Oxford University Press, 1978.

Central America

Woodward, Ralph L., Jr. *Central America: A Nation Divided*, 2nd ed. New York: Oxford University Press, 1985.

Chile

Loveman, Brian. *Chile: The Legacy of Hispanic Capitalism*. New York: Oxford University Press, 1979.

Colombia

Henao, Jesús María, and Gerardo Arrubla. *A History of Colombia*, trans. and ed. by J. Fred Rippy. Chapel Hill: University of North Carolina Press, 1938.

Mexico

Meyer, Michael C., and William L. Sherman, *The Course of Mexican History*, 2nd ed. New York: Oxford University Press, 1987.

Paraguay

Warren, Harris Gaylord. *Paraguay: An Informal History*. Norman: University of Oklahoma Press, 1949.

Peru

Dobyns, Henry E., and Paul L. Doughty. *Peru: A Cultural History*. New York: Oxford University Press, 1976.
Pike, Fredrick B. *The Modern History of Peru*. New York: Praeger, 1967.

Venezuela

Lombardi, John V. *Venezuela: The Search for Order, the Dream of Progress*. New York: Oxford University Press, 1982.

Chapter 3. The Social and Economic Dimensions

Social and economic conditions in the postindependence period receive major attention in the works of Burns and Halperín-Donghi mentioned above and in the more recent general national histories. The continuance of Latin America in a state of colonial dependence despite formal independence is argued by Stanley J. and Barbara H. Stein, *The Colonial Heritage of Latin America: Essays on Economic Dependence in Perspective* (New York: Oxford University Press, 1970). The case against "dependency" finds support in D. C. M. Platt, *Latin America and British Trade, 1806–1914* (New York: Barnes and Noble, 1973). Population studies include Eduardo E. Arriago, *New Life Tables for Latin American Populations in the Nineteenth and Twentieth Centuries*

(Berkeley: University of California Press, 1968), and Nicolás Sánchez-Albornoz, *The Population of Latin America: A History* (Berkeley: University of California Press, 1974). Comparative studies of slavery in the Americas are numerous; the trend began with Frank Tannenbaum, *Slave and Citizen: The Negro in the Americas* (New York: Alfred A. Knopf, 1946), and continues with Herbert S. Klein, *African Slavery in Latin America and the Caribbean* (New York: Oxford University Press, 1986).

Chapter 4. Mexico in Decline

The evolution of Mexican liberalism in the postindependence period is traced and analyzed in Charles A. Hale, *Mexican Liberalism in the Age of Mora, 1821–1853* (New Haven: Yale University Press, 1968). For the nationalistic implications of the early liberal-conservative struggle, see D. A. Brading, *The Origins of Mexican Nationalism*, reprint ed. (Cambridge: Cambridge University Press, 1986). A patron of the conservatives, the British minister to Mexico reports on economic and social conditions in the 1820s in H. G. Ward, *Mexico in 1827*, 2 vols. (London: H. Colburn, 1828). The Mexican scene in the 1840s is described in Frances Calderón de la Barca, *Life in Mexico* (Berkeley: University of California Press, 1982), a classic of travel literature. British enterprise in postindependence Mexico is studied in Robert W. Randall, *Real del Monte: A British Mining Venture in Mexico* (Austin: University of Texas Press, 1972). The hacienda system in central Mexico is the subject of D. A. Brading, *Haciendas and Ranchos in the Mexican Bajío* (Cambridge: Cambridge University Press, 1971); and a huge landed estate in the north gets the attention of Charles H. Harris III, *A Mexican Family Empire: The Latifundio of the Sánchez Navarros, 1765–1867* (Austin: University of Texas Press, 1975). Social pressures generated by the landholding system are viewed from a long-term, historical perspective in John Tutino, *From Insurrection to Revolution in Mexico: Social Bases of Agrarian Violence, 1750–1940* (Princeton: Princeton University Press, 1986). The problem of the church, its property and politics, is examined by Wilfrid H. Callcott, *Church and State in Mexico, 1822–1857*, reprint ed. (New York: Octagon Books, 1965), and more recently by Michael P. Costeloe, *Church Wealth in Mexico* (Cambridge: Cambridge University Press, 1967) and *Church and State in Independent Mexico: A Study of the Patronage Debate, 1821–1857* (London: Royal Historical Society, 1978).

The fall of Emperor Agustín I is related in Robertson's biography of Iturbide cited above and the expulsion of the Spaniards from Mexico in Romeo Flores Caballero, *Counterrevolution: The Role of the Spaniards*

in the Independence of Mexico, 1804–1838 (Lincoln: University of Nebraska Press, 1974). Mexico's troubles with the United States are sympa-
thetically treated in Gene M. Brack, *Mexico Views Manifest Destiny,
1821–1846: An Essay on the Origins of the Mexican War* (Albuquerque:
University of New Mexico Press, 1975). The flamboyant figure who
dominated Mexico during this time of troubles is brilliantly portrayed in
Callcott's *Santa Anna: The Story of an Enigma Who Once Was Mexico*
(Norman: University of Oklahoma Press, 1936); and the plodding
general who tried to reconstruct the nation from the wreckage left by
Santa Anna is the subject of a dull biography, Thomas E. Cotner, *The
Military and Political Career of José Joaquín Herrera, 1791–1854* (Aus-
tin: University of Texas Press, 1949). For an excellent account of the
Maya revolt in Yucatan, see Nelson Reed, *The Caste War of Yucatan*
(Stanford: Stanford University Press, 1964).

Chapter 5. Andean South America to Midcentury

The domestic history of Gran Colombia is studied in David Bushnell,
The Santander Regime in Gran Colombia (Newark, Del.: University of
Delaware Press, 1954; also Greenwood reprint). Developments in New
Granada after the breakup of Gran Colombia are the subject of both
Frank Safford, *The Ideal of the Practical: Colombia's Struggle to Form a
Technical Elite* (Austin: University of Texas Press, 1976), which throws
light on considerably more than its immediate topic, and William Paul
McGreevey, *An Economic History of Colombia, 1845–1930* (Cam-
bridge: Cambridge University Press, 1971), whose chronological cover-
age is broader than the title suggests. On Venezuela, John Lombardi's
The Decline and Abolition of Negro Slavery in Venezuela, 1820–1854
(Westport, Conn.: Greenwood Press, 1971), is still another work that
offers more than the title page suggests. And for Ecuador, the theme of
Linda Alexander Rodriguez, *The Search for Public Policy: Regional
Politics and Government Finances in Ecuador, 1830–1940* (Berkeley:
University of California Press, 1985), inevitably impinges on most other
principal developments of the period.

The political history of early independent Chile is authoritatively
discussed by Simon Collier, *Ideas and Politics of Chilean Independence,
1808–1833* (Cambridge: Cambridge University Press, 1967), which takes
the story up to the time of Portales. Portales himself is the subject of the
brief monograph by Jay Kinsbruner, *Diego Portales* (The Hague: Marti-
nus Nijhoff, 1967); the military are treated by Frederick M. Nunn, *The
Military in Chilean History: Essays on Civil-Military Relations, 1830–
1973* (Albuquerque: University of New Mexico Press, 1976); and tradi-

tional rural society receives both authoritative and remarkably readable treatment in Arnold J. Bauer, *Chilean Rural Society from the Spanish Conquest to 1930* (Cambridge: Cambridge University Press, 1975), a work that focuses above all on the nineteenth century. Robert Burr, *By Reason or by Force: Chile and the Balancing of Power in South America, 1830–1905* (Berkeley: University of California Press, 1965), discusses, among other things, the successful Chilean effort to disrupt the Peru-Bolivian Confederation. On Peru and Bolivia themselves in the early national period, the best course is to consult the general national histories mentioned above.

Chapter 6. The Road to Dictatorship in the Platine Area

The historical literature on Argentina in the period covered by this chapter includes the masterly study of political economy by Miron Burgin, *The Economic Aspects of Argentine Federalism, 1820–1852* (Cambridge, Mass.: Harvard University Press, 1946), and the excellent study of Rosas by John Lynch, *Argentine Dictator: Juan Manuel de Rosas, 1829–1852* (Oxford: Clarendon Press, 1981). Valuable, too, for the early years is Tulio Halperín-Donghi, *Politics, Economics and Society in Argentina in the Revolutionary Period* (Cambridge: Cambridge University Press, 1975); for British economic and other relations, Henry S. Ferns, *Britain and Argentina in the Nineteenth Century* (Oxford: Oxford University Press, 1960); and for general economic history, Jonathan C. Brown, *A Socio-Economic History of Argentina, 1776–1860* (Cambridge: Cambridge University Press, 1979). Neither should one overlook the Argentine classic by Domingo F. Sarmiento, *Life in the Argentine Republic in the Days of the Tyrants, or Civilization and Barbarism* (New York: Hafner, 1960), or the numerous excellent accounts by foreign visitors. Several of the latter have been recently reprinted, including Francis B. Head, *Rough Notes Taken during Some Rapid Journeys across the Pampas and among the Andes* (Carbondale: Southern Illinois University Press, 1979), and William MacCann, *Two Thousand Miles' Ride through the Argentine Provinces*, 2 vols. (New York: AMS Press, 1971).

The work of John F. Cady, *Foreign Intervention in the Rio de la Plata 1838–50: A Study of French, British, and American Policy in Relation to the Dictator Juan Manuel de Rosas* (Philadelphia: University of Pennsylvania Press, 1929), is still a standard treatment of its subject. For Paraguay, a balanced overview of the period is John Hoyt Williams, *The Rise and Fall of the Paraguayan Republic, 1800–1870* (Austin: University of

Texas Press, 1979). A rather polemical but well-researched study focusing on the Francia regime is Richard Alan White, *Paraguay's Autonomous Revolution, 1810–1840* (Albuquerque: University of New Mexico Press, 1978).

Chapter 7. The Rise of the Brazilian Monarchy (1822–1850)

The economic foundations of imperial Brazil are masterfully analyzed in Nathaniel H. Leff, *Underdevelopment and Development in Brazil*, 2 vols. (London: Allen and Unwin, 1983). Social and demographic consequences of economic change are discussed in Thomas Merrick and Douglas Graham, *Population and Economic Development in Brazil, 1800 to the Present* (Baltimore: Johns Hopkins University Press, 1979). There is only one history in English that attempts to deal systematically with the entire empire period, C. H. Haring, *Empire in Brazil: A New World Experiment with Monarchy* (New York: Norton, 1968), a thin volume, superficial and misleading. Much better, though idiosyncratic in its coverage, is Emília Viotti da Costa, *The Brazilian Empire: Myths and Histories* (Chicago: University of Chicago Press, 1985). The myths challenged by Costa include some allegedly propagated by Brazil's most celebrated social historian, Gilberto Freyre, in *The Masters and the Slaves: A Study in the Development of Brazilian Civilization* (New York: Alfred A. Knopf, 1964) and *The Mansions and the Shanties: The Making of Modern Brazil* (New York: Alfred A. Knopf, 1966), the latter more specifically concerned with the empire period. Freyre's work focuses on slavery, family, and race relations in northeastern Brazil; for Rio de Janeiro, see Mary C. Karasch, *Slave Life in Rio de Janeiro, 1808–1850* (Princeton: Princeton University Press, 1986). The economic factors that undermined slavery in the northeast are discussed in Peter L. Eisenberg, *The Sugar Industry in Pernambuco, 1840–1910: Modernization without Change* (Berkeley: University of California Press, 1974). Slavery as practiced in Brazil is compared with the servile institution of the southern United States in Carl N. Degler, *Neither Black nor White: Slavery and Race Relations in Brazil and the United States* (New York: Macmillan, 1971). Robert E. Conrad examines the Brazilian slave trade in *World of Sorrow: The African Slave Trade to Brazil* (Baton Rouge: Louisiana State University Press, 1986); the story of abolition of the trade is told by Leslie Bethell, *The Abolition of the Brazilian Slave Trade: Britain, Brazil, and the Slave Trade Question, 1807–1869* (Cambridge: Cambridge University Press, 1970). The big picture of British-Brazilian relations through the middle of the nineteenth century is painted by Alan K. Manchester,

British Preeminence in Brazil, Its Rise and Decline: A Study in European Expansion (Chapel Hill: University of North Carolina Press, 1933). The reign of Dom Pedro I is examined in Macaulay, *Dom Pedro*, already cited, and early Brazilian foreign policy in Ron Seckinger, *The Brazilian Monarchy and the South American Republics, 1822-1831* (Baton Rouge: Louisiana State University Press, 1984). The emergence of a purely Brazilian sociopolitical establishment following the departure of the Portuguese-born emperor is discussed in Fernando Uricoechea, *The Patrimonial Foundations of the Brazilian Bureaucratic State* (Berkeley: University of California Press, 1980); and the role of the judiciary is analyzed in Thomas Flory, *Judge and Jury in Imperial Brazil, 1808-1871: Social Control and Political Stability in the New State* (Austin: University of Texas Press, 1981).

Chapter 8. Latin America at Midcentury: A Quickening Pace of Change

For additional general readings on the themes discussed in this chapter, there are few works apart from those already included among the references given for chapters 2 and 3. One further title is J. Fred Rippy, *Latin America and the Industrial Age* (New York: Putnam's, 1944; reprint ed. 1971), a slightly dated but still useful study of the beginnings of technological modernization.

Chapter 9. The Heyday of Liberal Reform in Spanish America (1850-1880) I: Mexico and Colombia

Most of the books on specific countries that are noted in the sections of this bibliography corresponding to chapters 4, 5, and 6 are also pertinent for the period of chapters 9 and 10. For Mexico, additional sources worth consulting on the Reforma and beginnings of the Porfiriato include Charles R. Berry's case study of Oaxaca, native state of both Benito Juárez and Porfirio Díaz, *The Reform in Oaxaca, 1856-1876: A Micro-History of the Liberal Revolution* (Lincoln: University of Nebraska Press, 1981). A northern border state is studied in Mark Wasserman, *Capitalists, Caciques, and Revolution: The Native Elite and Foreign Enterprise in Chihuahua, Mexico, 1854-1911* (Chapel Hill: University of North Carolina Press, 1984). Mexico's midcentury economy and the transformations it underwent as a result of railroad building are analyzed in John H. Coatsworth, *Growth against Development: The*

Economic Impact of Railroads in Porfirian Mexico (DeKalb: University of Northern Illinois Press, 1981). Jan Bazant focuses on the effects of expropriation of church property in *Alienation of Church Wealth in Mexico: Social and Economic Aspects of the Liberal Revolution, 1856–1875* (Cambridge: Cambridge University Press, 1971). Useful political and diplomatic studies of the period include Walter V. Scholes, *Mexican Politics during the Juárez Regime, 1855–1872* (Columbia: University of Missouri Press, 1957); Donathon C. Olliff, *Reforma Mexico and the United States: A Search for Alternatives to Annexation, 1854–1861* (University: University of Alabama Press, 1981); Alfred Jackson Hanna and Kathryn Abbey Hanna, *Napoleon III and Mexico: American Triumph over Monarchy* (Chapel Hill: University of North Carolina Press, 1971); and Thomas D. Schoonover, *Dollars over Dominion: The Triumph of Liberalism in Mexican-United States Relations, 1861–1867* (Baton Rouge: Louisiana State University Press, 1978). Among biographies of Juárez are Ralph Roeder, *Juárez and His Mexico*, 2 vols. (New York: Viking Press, 1947), and Ivie E. Cadenhead, Jr., *Benito Juárez* (New York: Twayne Publishers, 1973). Other major figures of the period are portrayed in Frank A. Knapp, *The Life of Sebastián Lerdo de Tejada, 1823–1899* (Austin: University of Texas Press, 1951); Ivie E. Cadenhead, Jr., *Jesús González Ortega and Mexican National Politics* (Fort Worth: Texas Christian University Press, 1972); Carleton Beals, *Porfirio Díaz: Dictator of Mexico* (Philadelphia: Lippincott, 1932); and Joan Haslip, *The Crown of Mexico: Maximilian and His Empress Carlota* (New York: Holt, Rinehart and Winston, 1971). Most importantly, the main currents of the Mexican Reforma are identified and skillfully analyzed in Richard N. Sinkin, *The Mexican Reform, 1855–1876: A Study in Liberal Nation Building* (Austin: University of Texas Press, 1979).

There is no counterpart to Sinkin's work dealing with the Colombian reform process, but the general political history of the period is expertly set forth in Helen Delpar, *Red against Blue: The Liberal Party in Colombian Politics, 1863–1899* (University: University of Alabama Press, 1981). Much of the same story is presented again, with particular attention to the role of Rafael Núñez, in James William Park, *Rafael Núñez and the Politics of Colombian Regionalism, 1863–1886* (Baton Rouge: Louisiana State University Press, 1985). For the beginnings of the coffee industry, see Marco Palacios, *Coffee in Colombia 1850–1970: An Economic, Social, and Political History* (Cambridge: Cambridge University Press, 1980). Settlement patterns and agrarian conflicts are the subject of Catherine LeGrand, *Frontier Expansion and Peasant Protest in Colombia, 1850–1930* (Albuquerque: University of New Mexico Press, 1986).

One important travel account of the 1850s has been reprinted in abridged version: Isaac F. Holton, *New Granada: Twenty Months in the Andes* (Carbondale: Southern Illinois University Press, 1967).

Chapter 10. The Heyday of Liberal Reform in Spanish America (1850–1880) II: Argentina, Chile, and Some Other Cases

Argentina after Rosas is dealt with in older studies of two of its key figures: Alison Bunkley, *The Life of Sarmiento* (Princeton: Princeton University Press, 1952); and William H. Jeffrey, *Mitre and Argentina* (New York: Library Publishers, 1952). The growth of Buenos Aires as political and commercial center is analyzed by James R. Scobie in *Buenos Aires: Plaza to Suburb, 1870–1910* (New York: Oxford University Press, 1974). Scobie also contributed *Revolution on the Pampas: A Social History of Argentine Wheat, 1860–1910* (Austin: University of Texas Press, 1964), while still another dimension of the nation's economic and social transformation is studied in Richard W. Slatta, *Gauchos and the Vanishing Frontier* (Lincoln: University of Nebraska Press, 1983).

Less has been written in English on Chile during the liberal era. John J. Johnson, *Pioneer Telegraphy in Chile, 1852–1876* (Stanford: Stanford University Press, 1948), covers one aspect of technological modernization, and the more recent work by sociologist Maurice Zeitlin, *The Civil Wars in Chile (or the Bourgeois Revolutions That Never Were)* (Princeton: Princeton University Press, 1984), gives a provocative and slightly controversial treatment of the socioeconomic roots of political conflicts. The work of Allen Woll, *A Functional Past: The Uses of History in Nineteenth-Century Chile* (Baton Rouge: Louisiana State University Press, 1982), examines the golden age of Chilean historical writing in the larger context of intellectual and political trends. On the war of 1879–83, see the recent study by William F. Sater, *Chile and the War of the Pacific* (Lincoln: University of Nebraska Press, 1986).

On Venezuela in the period of this chapter, there is disappointingly little even in Spanish. For want of much else, still useful is George S. Wise, *Caudillo: A Portrait of Antonio Guzmán Blanco* (New York: Columbia University Press, 1951). For Peru, the case study of guano in Jonathan V. Levin, *The Export Economies: Their Pattern of Development in Historical Perspective* (Cambridge, Mass.: Harvard University Press, 1960), remains a basic point of departure for discussion of that industry and its repercussions, even though not all scholars agree that guano was in a strict sense an "enclave economy" as Levin contends. On a related aspect of socioeconomic development, one can read Watt Stewart, *Chinese Bondage in Peru: A History of the Chinese Coolies in Peru, 1849–1874* (Durham: Duke University Press, 1951). Highland Indian society is studied in the notable recent work of Florencia E. Mallon, *The Defense of Community in Peru's Central Highlands: Peasant Struggle and Capitalist Transition, 1860–1940* (Princeton: Princeton University Press, 1983). Finally, while for the War of the Pacific there is only Sater's study from a Chilean perspective, the curious conflict between Peru and Spain in the 1860s is studied in William Columbus Davis, *The Last Conquistadores: The Spanish Intervention in Peru and Chile 1863–1866* (Athens: University of Georgia Press, 1950).

Chapter 11. The Flowering and Decline of the Brazilian Empire (1850–1885)

Most of the works mentioned in the bibliography for chapter 7 are also pertinent for chapter 11. Suggested additional readings for the period after 1850 include two excellent socioeconomic studies by Stanley J. Stein, *Vassouras: A Brazilian Coffee County, 1850–1900* (Cambridge, Mass.: Harvard University Press, 1957) and *The Brazilian Cotton Manufacture: Textile Enterprise in an Underdeveloped Area, 1850–1950* (Cambridge, Mass.: Harvard University Press, 1957), and Richard Graham's insightful *Britain and the Onset of Modernization in Brazil, 1850–1914* (Cambridge: Cambridge University Press, 1968). Also recommended is Warren Dean's case study, *Rio Claro: A Brazilian Plantation System, 1820–1920* (Stanford: Stanford University Press, 1976). Not so good are the biographies available in English, which tend to the hagiographic: Mary Wilhelmine Williams, *Dom Pedro the Magnanimous, Second Emperor of Brazil* (Chapel Hill: University of North Carolina Press, 1937); Anyda Marchant, *Viscount Mauá and the Empire of Brazil* (Berkeley: University of California Press, 1965); and Carolina Nabuco, *The Life of Joaquim Nabuco* (Stanford: Stanford University Press, 1950). The story of the struggle to abolish slavery is best told in Robert Conrad, *The Destruction of Brazilian Slavery, 1850–1888* (Berkeley: University of California Press, 1972), although Robert B. Toplin, *The Abolition of Slavery in Brazil* (New York: Atheneum, 1972), is also useful. The "bishops question" of the 1870s is examined in Mary C. Thornton, *The Church and Freemasonry in Brazil, 1872–1875: A Study in Regalism* (Washington: Catholic University of America Press, 1948). A good introduction to Brazilian positivism and the ideological ferment of the post-Paraguayan War period can be found in João Cruz Costa, *A History of Ideas in Brazil* (Berkeley: University of California Press, 1964). The causes of the War of the Triple Alliance are dispassionately set forth in Pelham H. Box, *The Origins of the Paraguayan War* (Urbana: University of Illinois Press, 1930), and the war itself is the subject of Charles J. Kolinski, *Independence or Death! The Story of the Paraguayan War* (Gainesville: University of Florida Press, 1965), and Gilbert Phelps, *Tragedy of Paraguay* (New York: St. Martin's Press, 1975).

Chapter 12. The Caribbean Vortex in the Nineteenth Century: Cuba and Central America

Lester D. Langley provides a valuable overview of great-power rivalry in the Caribbean Basin in his *Struggle for the American Mediterranean: United States-European Rivalry in the Gulf-Caribbean, 1776–1904* (Athens: University of Georgia Press, 1976). U.S. designs on Cuba are discussed in Basil Rauch, *American Interests in Cuba, 1848–1855* (New York: Columbia University Press, 1948). The objectives and motivations of the filibusters in Cuba and Central America are scrutinized in Charles H. Brown, *Agents of Manifest Destiny: The Lives and Times of the Filibusters* (Chapel Hill: University of North Carolina Press, 1980), and Robert E. May, *The Southern Dream of a Caribbean Empire, 1854–1861* (Baton Rouge: Louisiana State University Press, 1973). Specifically on William Walker, the best account remains William O. Scroggs, *Filibusters and Financiers: The Story of William Walker and His Associates* (New York: Macmillan, 1916). U.S.-British rivalry figures prominently in Mario Rodríguez, *A Palmerstonian Diplomat in Central America: Frederick Chatfield, Esq.* (Tucson: University of Arizona Press, 1964), and Craig L. Dozier, *Nicaragua's Mosquito Shore: The Years of British and American Presence* (University: University of Alabama Press, 1985). The attraction of a Central American canal for promoters from various outside countries is discussed in Cyril Allen, *France in Central America* (New York: Pageant Press, 1966), and David I. Folkman, Jr., *The Nicaragua Route* (Salt Lake City: University of Utah Press, 1972). The decline of Britain's last Central American colony is the subject of Wayne L. Clegern, *British Honduras: Colonial Dead End, 1859–1900* (Baton Rouge: Louisiana State University Press, 1967).

The transition of Central America from Spanish colonial rule to independence and its existence as a federal republic are covered in Miles L.

320   *Further Reading*

Wortman, *Government and Society in Central America, 1680–1840* (New York: Columbia University Press, 1982). The Spanish roots of Central American liberalism are discussed in Mario Rodríguez, *The Cádiz Experiment in Central America, 1808–1826* (Berkeley: University of California Press, 1978); and a prominent conservative of the federation period is portrayed in Louis Bumgartner, *José del Valle of Central America* (Durham: Duke University Press, 1963). The collapse of the federation and the various attempts to restore it are dealt with in Thomas L. Karnes, *The Failure of Union: Central America, 1824–1975* (Tempe: Arizona State University Press, 1976). There are many fine travel accounts of Central America; a good sampling for the federation period is in Franklin D. Parker, *Travels in Central America, 1821–1840* (Gainesville: University of Florida Press, 1970). Modern research on Central America by outsiders has focused on Costa Rica and Guatemala. Noteworthy for Costa Rica is Lowell Gudmundson, *Costa Rica before Coffee: Society and Economy on the Eve of the Export Boom* (Baton Rouge: Louisiana State University Press, 1986). For Guatemala before the liberal reform of the 1870s, there are William J. Griffith, *Empires in the Wilderness: Foreign Colonization and Development in Guatemala, 1834–1844* (Chapel Hill: University of North Carolina Press, 1965), and Ralph Lee Woodward, Jr., *Class Privilege and Economic Development: The Consulado de Comercio of Guatemala, 1793–1871* (Chapel Hill: University of North Carolina Press, 1966). The early impact of the liberal reform on Guatemalan society is graphically displayed in E. Bradford Burns, *Eadweard Muybridge in Guatemala, 1875: The Photographer as Social Recorder* (Berkeley: University of California Press, 1986), a superb collection of photographs enhanced by the author's lucid commentary. More conventional in technique but equally thoughtful is David J. McCreery, *Development and the State in Reforma Guatemala* (Athens: Ohio University Press, 1983).

Hugh Thomas gives extensive coverage to the liberal reform in Cuba and the nineteenth-century struggle for autonomy in *Cuba, or the Pursuit of Freedom* (London: Eyre and Spottiswoode, 1971). Some of the works of Cuba's best social and economic historians have been translated into English, including Ramiro Guerra y Sánchez, *Sugar and Society in the Caribbean: An Economic History of Cuban Agriculture* (New Haven: Yale University Press, 1964); Fernando Ortiz, *Cuban Counterpoint: Tobacco and Sugar* (New York: Alfred A. Knopf, 1947); and Manuel Moreno Fraginals, *The Sugarmill: The Socioeconomic Complex of Sugar in Cuba, 1760–1860* (New York: Monthly Review Press, 1976). Slavery and the slave trade to Cuba have attracted the attention of numerous scholars; noteworthy are Arthur F. Corwin, *Spain and the Abolition of Slavery in Cuba, 1817–1886* (Austin: University of Texas Press, 1967); David Murray, *Odious Commerce: Britain, Spain, and the Abolition of the Cuban Slave Trade* (Cambridge: Cambridge University Press, 1980); Kenneth F. Kiple, *Blacks in Colonial Cuba, 1774–1899* (Gainesville: University of Florida Press, 1976); Franklin W. Knight, *Slave Society in Cuba during the Nineteenth Century* (Madison: University of Wisconsin Press, 1970); and Verena Martínez-Alier, *Marriage, Class and Colour in Nineteenth-century Cuba: A Study of Racial Attitudes and Sexual Values in a Slave Society* (Cambridge: Cambridge University Press, 1974). Comparative studies of slavery involving Cuba include Herbert S. Klein, *Slavery in the Americas: A Comparative Study of Virginia and Cuba* (Chicago: Quadrangle, 1967); Gwendolyn Hall, *Social Control in Slave Plantation Societies: A Comparison of Saint Domingue and Cuba* (Baltimore: Johns Hopkins University Press, 1971); and Kenneth F. Kiple, *The Caribbean Slave: A Biological History* (Cambridge: Cambridge University Press, 1984). The last adds new dimensions in focusing on diet and disease.

Chapter 13. The Liberal Legacy and the Quest for Development

Thomas E. Skidmore and Peter H. Smith use a "modified 'dependency' approach" in analyzing the main trends of Latin American history since 1880 in their compact and readable *Modern Latin America* (New York: Oxford University Press, 1984). Full-blown dependency theory is propounded in André Gunder Frank, *Latin America: Underdevelopment or Revolution* (New York: Monthly Review Press, 1969), and Fernando Henrique Cardoso and Enzo Faletto, *Dependency and Development in Latin America* (Berkeley: University of California Press, 1979). The "structuralist" approach—which provides the main theoretical support for import-substitution industrialization—gained currency with the appearance of Raúl Prebisch, *The Economic Development of Latin America and Its Principal Problems* (Lake Success, N.Y.: United Nations, 1950), and attained its fullest expression in Celso Furtado, *Economic Development of Latin America: Historical Background and Contemporary Problems*, 2nd ed. (Cambridge: Cambridge University Press, 1976). A contrasting view of the making of the world economy and Latin America's role in it can be found in Arthur Lewis, *The Evolution of the International Economic Order* (Princeton: Princeton University Press, 1978), which stresses the operation of market forces. From a similar perspective, the problems of Third World underdevelopment are addressed in Peter T. Bauer and Basil S. Yamey, *The Economics of Under-*

Developed Countries (Chicago: University of Chicago Press, 1963), and more recently in Peter T. Bauer, *Reality and Rhetoric: Studies in the Economics of Development* (Cambridge, Mass.: Harvard University Press, 1984). The history of the revival of Latin American liberalism in the 1980s is still to be written.

Index

332